Stage Two
Riding & Stable Management

with

The Riding and Road Safety Test

by

Hazel Reed BHSAI (Reg'd)

No**v**a Publications

Copyright © Hazel Reed 1996

Stage Two - Riding & Stable Management with The Riding and Road Safety Test.

First published in Great Britain by Nova Publications, 1996.
Reprinted 1996
Reprinted 1997
Reprinted 1998
Reprinted 2000
Reprinted 2001

Nova Publications,
Olive House, 22, Frys Lane, Yateley, Hampshire, GU46 7TJ.

Hazel Reed has asserted her right to be identified as the author of this work in accordance with the Copyright, Designs and Patents Act 1988.

ISBN 0 9525859 2 8
British Library Cataloguing in Publication Data.
A Catalogue record for this book is available from the British Library.

Typeset in Yateley by Dreke.
Printed and bound by Intype, Input Typesetting Ltd., Wimbledon.

Illustrations by Hazel Reed and Tracey Humphreys.
Computer Graphics by Hazel Reed.

Contents

Part I The Riding and Road Safety Test

Part II The BHS Stage Two Examination

Foreword

The Stage One book in this series is proving to be a very popular text for trainers and students and I have no doubts that the Stage II book will be even more successful.

To have the whole syllabus for the BHS Stage II Examination covered in one volume, together with the Riding & Road Safety Test information is very unusual but the author has achieved this. The clear, friendly way in which the book has been written ensures the text can be understood easily. The systematic layout will also enable the reader to use the book as a quick reference guide.

I am sure it will be of immense benefit not only to students working towards their Examinations but also to the one horse owner who wishes to learn more about caring for his horse.

I recommend this book to all trainers, students, horse owners and, indeed, anyone interested in learning more about horsemastership.

Valerie Lee. B.H.S.I

Valerie Lee, BHSI

Cheif Examiner.

Acknowledgements

Once more we would like to express our gratitude to all those who aided and abetted us in this project. Jody Redhead, BHSAI, Caroline Lycett BHSII BHS Stable Manager (Reg'd), Dr. Jamie Whitehorn, Diane Salt BHSAI, Margaret Heritage, Andrea Hinks, Bronia Hill BHSII (Reg'd), Ian Spalding, Robert Dibben BHSII, BHS Stable Manager, Jean Gill HND (HS), BHSII, BHS Stable Manager. Thanks also to Sophie Reed, Robert Kennedy and Susie Evans for modelling. Derek Reed and Jamie Whitehorn for back up on computer. To Sophie, Martyn and Helena for being the most patient children in the world!

This book is dedicated to the 'Caroliners', a great group of people and steadfast friends and to all those horses and ponies who through the years have taught us all so much. Thank you Oscar, Irishman, Roley, Quinn, Red and Pip.

Thanks to;

Sharon Sayers, an angel of mercy in need, at Perrybridge Farm, Sandhurst, Berkshire and to Mr. & Mrs. J. Sayers.

Mark Sayers, dip WCF, the 'model' Farrier.

Mr. & Mrs. W. Hundley of Rycroft School of Equitation, Eversley, Hampshire.

Mr. & Mrs. J. Goodman, Robert Pickles and Linda Sawyer of Wellington Riding Ltd., Heckfield, Basingstoke, Hampshire.

Gawthorpe Saddlers for supplying the 'props'.

Note: We do apologise once more to all fillies and mares for the use throughout this book of the male gender. We avoided using 'it' as this sounds impersonal, so 'he', 'his' or 'him' with great respect refers to all horses and ponies everywhere.

Cover photograph by David Hart, taken at Rycroft School of Equitation.

Introduction

This book is a continuation to the Stage I, taking candidates onto and through the BHS Stage II examination. It includes the Riding and Road Safety Test which must be taken and passed before the Stage II.

The Riding and Road Safety Test

When the Riding and Road Safety Test is taken as part of the Preliminary or Assistant Instructors course, the focus is often on the 'Stage Examinations'. The Test then tends to be dismissed as insignificant. Yet to be successful in this Test the student will need to study and practise. The information necessary for the Test is covered in this book, including where to train, the Test format, and descriptions of the Simulated and Road Tests.

The Stage II Examination

Riding

Equitation information and techniques are described to help the rider progress to the Stage II standard.

Horse Knowledge and Care

This guide introduces the new subjects covered by the Stage II syllabus and expands upon the relevant subjects already covered at Stage I. To avoid constant repetition, the Stage II guide has been written as a continuation from the Stage I and students may revise from the previous book to obtain the background knowledge necessary.

Purpose of this Guide

When read in conjunction with the Stage I book, this Guide will take the student through their BHS Stage II Examination.

This book is written in such a way as to expand the student's *understanding*. Being able to understand a subject makes it much easier to remember. The text includes aids for learning, together with exam tips gained from personal experiences.

We hope this book will be enjoyed as much as the Stage I and we have again used humour as a learning aid to emphasise relevant points. Our increase in knowledge will take us nearer to our ultimate goal, the better care and well-being of horses and ponies.

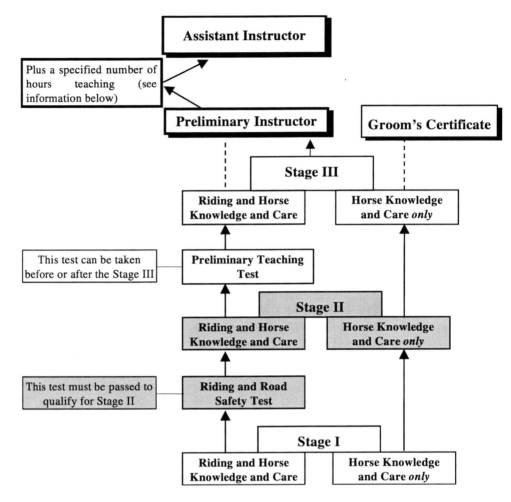

Figure 1: Table of BHS qualifications to Assistant Instructor level from July 1998.

BHS Examination Structure

To gain an Assistant Instructor qualification students must pass the Stages I, II, III Riding and Care, the Riding & Road Safety Test and the Preliminary Teaching Test. They must also complete a BHS Log Book to show that they have a specific number of hours of practical teaching experience. Those who teach at BHS 'Where to train' centres (listed in the 'Where to train' book) need 250 hours, those teaching in any other BHS Approved Riding School need 350 hours, whilst those who teach at other establishments need 500 hours. Some of the hours required may be offset by attending teaching courses given by the British Horse Society. A Groom's Certificate will be awarded to those candidates who pass the Care Sections in the BHS Stages I, II and III.

Part I

The Riding
and
Road Safety Test

CHAPTER 1
General Information

There are approximately 3000 *reported* road accidents involving horses every year, according to statistics from the British Horse Society. On average that is eight a day. The BHS Riding and Road Safety Test is designed to increase the knowledge and safety of riders on the Public Highway.

This Test is an important part of the BHS training scheme benefiting all riders, their horses and ponies however infrequently they encounter roads and traffic.

Aims of the Test

The aims of the Test are to *prevent accidents and reduce suffering* by giving recognition to those who ride responsibly and competently on the road. Riders are taught the rules of the Highway Code, courtesy for all road users and an awareness of the dangers of riding on the Public Highway.

Eligibility

The Riding and Road Safety Test is open to all riders between the ages of 12 and 70 who can ride independently at walk, trot and canter. Persons over 70 years can take the Test provided they take out their own insurance.

The Syllabus

There are four parts to the Test:

Assessment The rider's clothing and horse's tack are inspected for safety. Each candidate's riding ability and control will be assessed at walk, trot and canter.

Theory Each candidate is required to complete a theory paper.

Simulated Test This involves individual candidates riding around a planned route marked out in a field or paddock.

Road Test Each candidate will ride individually around a specific route on the road adjacent to the Test Centre.

Format

Candidates should arrive at the Centre at least 30 minutes before the Test begins. The starting time should be confirmed before the day for any alterations to schedule.

On arrival candidates will be checked in at Reception and issued with numbers and name tags. The Examiners will be introduced and the group escorted to the Test Area.

There will be two or three Examiners; a BHS Road Safety Examiner and a County Council Road Safety Officer or a Police Officer. Riders may ride their own horse or pony or one provided by the Test Centre. Horses and ponies ridden in the Test must be at least four years old.

Preparation for the Test

The information given in this book should be studied in conjunction with the **Highway Code and the BHS Manual of Riding and Roadcraft**. Candidates can also attend the courses offered at various riding establishments.

Where to Train

Most Riding and Road Safety Centres offer a course of lessons prior to the Test. These provide valuable training and help the candidate to become accustomed to the Centre and the horses used in the Test.

Test Information

An important point is that this Test is not held frequently. Not all BHS Examination Centres or Approved Riding Schools offer the Riding and Road Safety Test and those that do, may only hold a few Tests a year.

If the Riding and Road Safety Test is being taken to qualify for the Stage II, then the Test should be applied for in plenty of time. There may not be a Test within the area for months, which will then mean either travelling great distances or postponing the Stage II. Also, for the unsuccessful candidate, the Test will have to be retaken.

Application

Prospective candidates may contact the British Horse Society for an application form and for the telephone number of their local Area Road Safety Officer. This Officer will be able to give information on the dates and venues of the Test within the area. Many Pony and Riding Clubs organise BHS Riding and Road Safety Tests for their own members.

The BHS is always very helpful and supportive. They will be able to advise prospective candidates on the necessary documentation and details.

CHAPTER 2
The Assessment

During the Assessment the Examiner will be inspecting the rider's hat and clothing, the horse's tack and shoes. Candidates will then be required to ride a horse or pony within an enclosed area.

Clothes and Tack

- All candidates will need a riding hat, boots, gloves, jodhpurs, hacking jacket or a light coloured jacket. Shirt and tie are advisable but not compulsory.

- Every rider must carry a short whip to help control the horse. A long whip may become caught up or frighten the horse.

- Numbered, fluorescent tabards should be supplied by the Centre but on some occasions candidates may be required to take their own. This should be checked at the Centre before the Test day.

Hat

Hats should conform to the standard laid down by the British Standards Institute (BSI) and, because this is changing, candidates are advised to check before the Test that their hat is acceptable. At the present time the hats that meet the requirements are those with a kite mark - the 4472, the 6473 and the PAS 015.

The rider's hat should fasten securely with a three-point harness and fit snugly.

Boots

Boots should be strong to protect the foot and ankle. They should also be heeled to prevent the foot sliding into the stirrup and becoming stuck. The soles should be smooth to allow the rider's foot to slip out of the stirrup easily when dismounting or in the case of a fall.

Gloves

White or light coloured gloves make hand signals more visible. The gloves should be non-slip, particularly in wet weather when the reins can become damp and slippery.

Tack

The tack will be inspected carefully during the Assessment, so riders on their own horses should make certain that this is up to the requirements. Any incorrect tack must be repaired or replaced before the Test day. Check for loose stitching, splits in the leather and worn or weak areas in the bridle, the saddle and the girth. The girth must also be the correct size and fastened properly. For those candidates riding the school's own horses, the tack is the school's responsibility and any incorrectly fitting or worn tack will be changed by them. All candidates should, however, make a check of the tack before mounting.

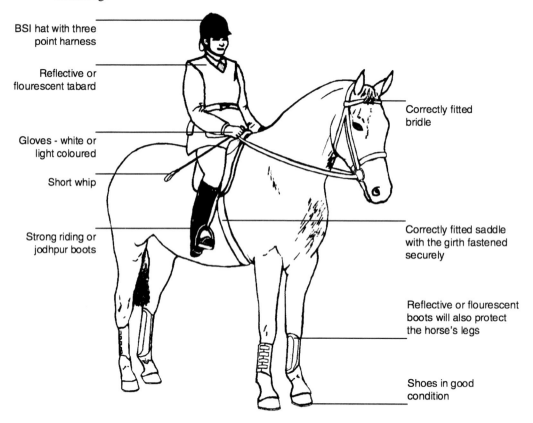

BSI hat with three point harness

Reflective or flourescent tabard

Gloves - white or light coloured

Short whip

Strong riding or jodhpur boots

Correctly fitted bridle

Correctly fitted saddle with the girth fastened securely

Reflective or flourescent boots will also protect the horse's legs

Shoes in good condition

Figure 2: The clothes and tack

The **stirrups should be a suitable size for the rider's foot,** ideally about a 6-12 mm (¼ to ½ an inch) wider than the width at the ball of the foot. If the stirrup is too small, the foot could become stuck in the iron; too large a stirrup and the foot could easily slip out making the rider insecure.

The horse's shoes must be in a good condition. A horse should not go onto the road if he has lost a shoe or if the shoes are worn or loose.

Fluorescent or reflective brushing boots will offer greater protection and visibility.

In practical terms all these safety checks should be made not just for the Test but every time a horse and rider ventures out onto the Public Highway. Taking risks with a horse and rider on the road can cost lives.

The Riding Test

The Examiners need to determine that each rider is competent in all three basic paces, capable of riding the horse in a straight line, bringing the horse to halt and keep him still when standing. Each rider should also be capable of controlling the horse whilst riding with the reins in one hand.

The group of candidates will be taken to an indoor or outdoor school and each candidate asked to mount their own horse or the horse chosen for them. The group, as a ride, will perform some simple school figures in walk and trot. Each candidate should be capable of controlling the horse's speed and pace when working with others.

The format may vary according to the Examiners but usually each candidate will be requested to show some trot and canter work individually. With the rest of the ride in walk, each leading file in succession may be asked to go forward to trot and into canter at the next corner. They may then have to canter a circle somewhere within the school or canter past the inside of the ride. Each rider should come forwards to trot and walk in plenty of time to join the rear of the ride.

The Examiners are not looking for a beautiful position; *they are checking for control and safety.*

Control

This is one of the most important aspect of the Riding and Road Safety Test. Learning to ride competently and developing an awareness of horses and their behaviour is all part of control.

Reins

Keep the reins short. The rider should be able to feel the horse's mouth through the reins and bit. When on the road, horses should never be ridden with a loose rein; riders should always be able to use the reins for control instantly. Having to gather up loose reins wastes precious seconds in a dangerous situation.

Transitions

All changes of pace should be smooth and prompt. Transitions that are jerky or too fast may cause the rider to lose balance and control. If the transition takes time and considerable effort by the rider, then the horse is not sufficiently obedient. A horse who is not listening and acting upon the rider's instructions could be a danger on the road.

Halt and stand still

This is an important manoeuvre and not as easy as it sounds. Horses who fidget or become excited when waiting at junctions are a hazard. The rider needs to learn to keep the horse quiet and still at halt.

Pace

The rider needs to control the speed whilst maintaining a constant, active pace. If the horse is allowed to dawdle along or dash off at his own pace, it will appear that the rider is not in control.

The Whip

The whip is held so that it lies diagonally across the thigh pointing towards the horse's hind leg. In the school the whip is carried in the inside hand and passed to the other hand when changing rein.

On the road the whip is carried in the right hand between the horse and traffic *except when signalling with the right hand*. At these times the top of the whip is held in the left hand, and returned to the right hand when the signal has been completed.

Turns and Circles

Riders will be asked to ride 20 or 15 metre circles. The Examiners will be watching for rider control over the horse's direction and pace. The turns at each corner of the school should also be correct with the horse being ridden into the corners and not allowed to cut in and take his own track.

Safety

The main aim of the Test is safety; on the road, in traffic and when riding with others. In the Assessment, riders should keep a safe distance from the other horses. There should be one horse's length from the horse in front and a similar distance when riding past the ride.

C H A P T E R   3
Theory

The Theory section, although consisting of only ten questions on a Theory Paper, covers every aspect of riding on the Public Highway. The Examiners may also query candidates on various topics of Theory after the Simulated or Road Tests.

Format

The group is taken into a room or separate area and each candidate given a sheet of ten questions. **An example of a Theory paper is given at the end of this chapter.**

The questions are multiple choice having a number of possible answers from which the candidate chooses the correct one, sometimes two or more. Occasionally this section is conducted orally, in which case candidates are tested individually.

At least eight out of the ten questions must be answered correctly. Any candidate with more than two questions wrong will fail the whole Test.

Rules for riding on the roads

Before going out onto the road there are certain rules of which every rider should be aware.

- Always wear the correct clothes. (Riders under the age of 14 must **by law** wear an approved safety helmet.) Always check the horse's tack and shoes before riding on the road.

- Ride on the left-hand side of the road. Ride straight, look ahead, keep the legs in contact with the horse's sides and maintain a good rein contact.

- Look, listen and think ahead at all times.

- Be alert for possible hazards. Keep looking behind, in front and to the sides to check the road situation.

- Avoid placing the horse in a dangerous situation. Do not upset the horse in traffic. The road is not the place to teach the horse discipline.

- Horse riders are **NOT** allowed to ride on motorways.

- Horses should not be ridden on footpaths or pedestrian areas.

- When manoeuvring, have both hands on the reins to keep control.

- Avoid obstructing other road users.

- Be aware of surrounding areas particularly on narrow roads with high hedges. Busy main roads are hazardous enough but accidents also occur on narrow, winding country lanes. Stock in fields or even a farmer using his tractor can cause the horse to jump unexpectedly.

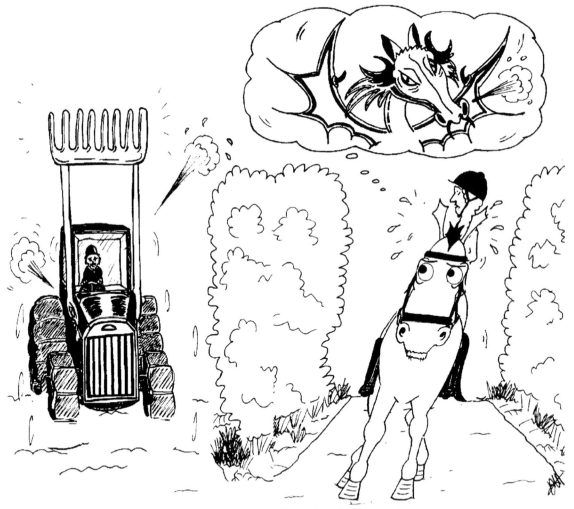

Where there be dragons!

Traffic Signs

There are a variety of traffic signs on the roads that signify orders, warnings or instructions. A few examples are given here but **there are a number of others within the Highway Code, and all these should be learnt.**

Signs giving orders - most are circular - red circles are mostly prohibitive

No horses

No entry for vehicular traffic

No pedestrians

No motor vehicles

Warning signs - most are triangular with a red border

Crossroads

Accompanied horses or ponies

Road works

Road narrows on both sides

Positive instruction - blue circles no red border

Mini-roundabout

Buses and cycles only

Keep left

Ahead only

Information signs - all rectangular

One way street

Parking

Police Signals

Occasionally riders will encounter police or officials on the Public Highway and their hand signals must be obeyed.

This signal means stop for traffic approaching from the front.

This signal means stop for those approaching from behind.

This signal instructs all traffic to stop.

The Police Officer will instruct the traffic to move off by waving his right hand for traffic to the front and right, his left hand for traffic behind or to his left.

Traffic Lights

Some instructions are given by lights; regulating the traffic at junctions, at school crossings and to warn of danger at level crossings. The lights at junctions and cross-roads have a specific sequence that informs road users when to stop and when to proceed.

RED alone - means stop.

RED and **AMBER** together also means **stop**. (Prepare to move.)

GREEN alone - means **go**, *but only if it is safe to do so.*

AMBER alone - means **stop**.

Filter Arrow - a green filter arrow allows the traffic to continue in the direction indicated by the arrow.

Warning lights at level crossings are usually yellow and red flashing lights. Riders must stop when these lights show.

Warning lights at pedestrian crossings must be obeyed. Flashing amber lights indicate **that the rider may proceed if there are no pedestrians on the crossing.**

By law riders must stop at zebra crossings or those without lights, **when a pedestrian has at least one foot on the crossing** and **may only continue when the pedestrian has reached the opposite kerb or a traffic island.**

Road Markings

Riders need to be aware of the markings painted on the road.

1. Stop at the white line

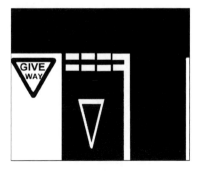

2. Give way at major road

3. Give way at roundabout

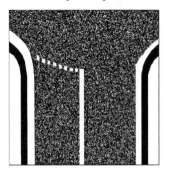

4. Give way at mini roundabout

Stopping Distances

Vehicles on the roads are not capable of stopping immediately and, depending on various factors, take some distance to come to a halt.

The 'stopping distance' of a vehicle is calculated by working out the probable 'thinking distance' plus a 'braking distance'. The thinking distance is the distance a car would travel at certain speeds before the driver has the time to think of applying the brake. The braking distance is the distance a car would travel once the brake is applied and before the car comes to a stop. These depend on various factors:

- The size of the vehicle.
- How good the brakes are.
- How quickly the driver can think.
- If the driver is tired or talking to someone else.
- Weather conditions.
- Road conditions.

Lorries or heavy vehicles will need more space to stop.

To give the rider an idea of just how far a car travels at speeds before it stops here is a table of the **SHORTEST STOPPING DISTANCES**.

Shortest Stopping Distances

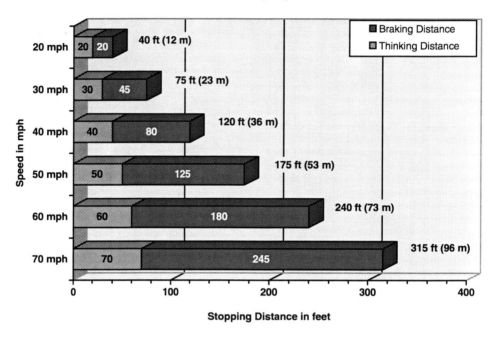

Stopping Distance in feet

These distances are for cars braking in good conditions; dry roads, driver alert. When the ground is wet or slippery, the stopping distance will be as much as three times longer. Also the vehicle may skid if the brakes are applied very quickly.

Motorists' signals

Drivers *normally* warn of their intentions by signalling with their lights. If turning right or left, they will signal with the appropriate indicator light. Always be aware though, that drivers do sometimes inadvertently forget to switch off the indicator light. This is particularly hazardous at junctions; riders should always wait until the vehicle actually begins to turn before riding onwards.

If a vehicle is slowing down or coming to a stop the red brake lights will show at the rear. When reversing, two white lights will appear at the rear. Sometimes, particularly on large lorries or vans, a bleeping noise can be heard, (which can often spook horses).

At junctions cars coming towards the rider from the opposite direction may flash their headlights. **According to the Highway Code this means 'I am here', and nothing else.** Though it is often translated as meaning please go ahead and cross my path, *riders should never assume that it is a signal to proceed.* Even if the vehicle actually stops and the driver starts waving the rider on, the rider should be wary of other traffic in the vicinity.

Leading horses on the road

- When leading a horse in hand on the road, the **horse should be wearing a bridle**.
- The **handler leads on the horse's offside (right), between the horse and the traffic**.
- The **handler** should wear a **riding hat, gloves and boots**.
- **Never lead more than one horse when on foot**.
- For **one-way streets ride or lead in the direction of the traffic** and **keep to the left**.
- A horse **should not be led on footpaths, pavements, pedestrian areas or cycle paths**.
- When leading a horse whilst riding another, the **horse being led** should be on the **inside (left) of the ridden horse**. Only one horse should be led at a time.
- If a rider has to lead a horse who is wearing a bridle, the **reins should be passed through the right bit ring** and the rider leads the horse as normal.
- When the horse is wearing a martingale, the rider should **take the reins out of the martingale** and **tie the martingale up safely out of the way**. The reins are then passed through the right bit ring.

Riding in Groups

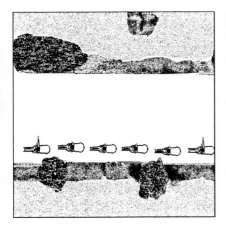

For groups of riders a few precautions will increase their safety on the Public Highway.

- Experienced horses and riders should be at the front and the back of the ride.
- Young, inexperienced or novice horses and riders should be in the middle of the ride. A young or nervous horse should not be ridden out alone on the road but accompanied by an experienced horse and rider.
- Each rider should keep the **distance of half a horse's length behind the horse in front**. This, whilst giving a safe distance between horses, also keeps the ride together.

- The whole group should ride a little way in from the kerb or verge to prevent dangerous overtaking by vehicles. If the horse is a little way from the kerb, motorists tend to slow down and look before passing. If the horse is ridden in close to the kerb, motorists tend to think they have room to squeeze past; they may not always reduce their speed.

- The pace should be regular, at a speed that can be followed by the whole group.

- Signals are given by the front and back riders.

- Groups should ideally never be more than eight.

- A large ride is safer split into separate groups with a maximum of eight riders in each group. There should be at least 30 m (100 feet) between each group. Motorists can then pass the ride in stages instead of being stuck for long periods behind a long line of riders.

Riding in Pairs

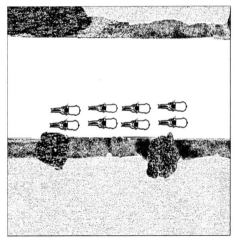

- Riders should never ride more than two abreast.

- Groups of riders may ride in pairs on wide roads **except** when approaching a hazard such as a corner, a brow of a hill or a narrow bridge.

- In heavy traffic, narrow lanes or where the road has bends, riders should form a single file.

- Two horses who clearly do not like each other should not be paired.

- A group of eight can further divide into two groups of four leaving a space of 9 - 15 metres (about 30 to 50 feet) between each group. Overtaking traffic can then negotiate the groups separately.

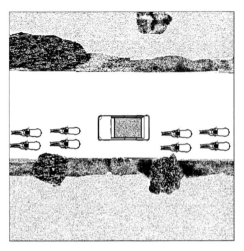

Crossing roads in a group

- The group should cross all roads and junctions together. A group should NEVER separate when crossing a road or junction, the horses being left behind can become anxious and restless.

- Occasionally the leader may deem it necessary to stop the traffic; there may be a steady stream of vehicles where the gaps are not large enough for the whole ride to pass in safety. If the leader has to stop the traffic by standing in the middle of the road while the group crosses, there should be an experienced horse and rider who can take the lead.

- A horse who will nap or shy when in the lead should not be expected to go in front when crossing a road.

Junctions

- Always prepare well in advance before junctions.

- Keep the pace at a steady walk. Never rush a junction.

- Look behind, signal. At the junction look right, left, right again, behind over the right shoulder once more (the life-saver look) and cross when the road is clear.

- The looking behind and signalling should be repeated if the rider has to wait at a junction. The traffic situation will have changed.

- Keep to the left *even when turning right*. Riders keep to the left of the road at junctions to prevent being sandwiched between vehicles.

- Position the horse so that there is maximum visibility without the horse being in danger.

- When turning right at traffic lights, keep to the left of the road. Wait for the green light; do not anticipate and rush across on amber. Look behind again, signal right and walk straight ahead.

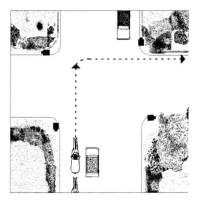

- To turn right at junctions walk straight ahead to the opposite kerb and then turn right.

- When turning right at cross-roads, *keep to the left* and turn when level with left hand kerb.

Roundabouts

Be aware before the roundabout of the traffic situation.

- Look behind, halt if necessary.

- When the road is clear, look behind again and signal. With both hands on the rein take a life-saver look behind to the right and a quick glance to the left for bicycles and then move.

- Keep the pace to a steady walk. The road surface can become slippery on roundabouts and the horse may slip if in trot.

- Keep to the left of the road. The horse may become trapped in the middle of two lanes of traffic if ridden in the centre of the road.

- Look behind and signal **right** every time an exit is passed. Watch for cars trying to rush in front and turn left.

- Go all the way round on the left. Once the required exit is reached, look behind and signal to the left.

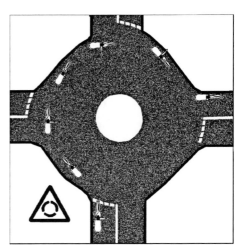

Hazards

Stationary vehicles, road works or other hazards

When overtaking an obstacle, the rider should give way to oncoming traffic, stopping if necessary, and allowing the traffic through.

When the road is clear, the rider looks behind, signals and moves out, giving the hazard plenty of room. The rider keeps a slightly stronger contact on the right rein to keep the horse's head slightly to the right and the right leg on the horse's side. This will prevent the horse from swinging his hindquarters out into the traffic should he spook at the hazard.

It is wiser to avoid hazards where possible, particularly when the horse is likely to react. For instance, if there are diggers and noisy machines at road works ahead, it would be safer to turn back or take an alternative route. Avoid busy times; rush hours, demonstrations or parades; plan to ride at a quieter time.

Dismounting

There are occasions when it may be necessary to dismount and physically lead the horse past a hazard. The rider should dismount quickly, place both stirrups across the horse's withers and lead from the off-side.

Remounting

This is a particularly dangerous period when, for a few seconds, the rider has less control over the horse's actions. The rider should choose a safe place; preferably with a raised verge to make mounting easier. The horse is positioned in the same direction as the traffic and, with short reins to keep the horse still, the rider mounts quickly and safely.

Riding on Verges

Riders should **never** ride on lawns, ornamental verges or ground belonging to private houses. In some rural districts riders are allowed to use the grass verges, in other areas it is an offence to do so. If in doubt, the bylaws relating to the area can be checked at the Public Library or the local Council Offices.

The rider should take care when using grass verges. Litter is frequently dumped here, often there is broken glass, plastic bags, bottles, open cans and other rubbish that may be hidden by the grass. Ditches, holes or stones can also be concealed. Riders should keep a steady pace at walk or, if safe, trot. Horses should never be cantered along a verge. It is more difficult to stop and, should the horse spook at something in the hedge, he will quickly be on the road before the rider can control him.

Pedestrians

Riders should give way to pedestrians especially at crossings. As most pedestrians can be wary of horses, riders should pass at a walk and keep the horse under control at a safe distance.

Transitions on the road

Before performing any transition, the rider should look behind, check the traffic situation and when clear make the transition. A horse or pony should never be cantered on the road as the surface is too hard and slippery.

Trotting

The rider should choose a straight piece of road. It is unsafe to trot around corners, at junctions, roundabouts or downhill. A horse can so easily slip, even on the best road surfaces.

Downward transition

To return to walk the rider should prepare well in advance, look behind to check the traffic, and make the transition smoothly. Downward transitions should never be made directly in front of traffic without warning from the rider.

Holding the right arm out straight, steadily raise it up and down to give the slowing down signal. Look behind and make sure the driver has given enough space for the transition.

Riding in the dark

It is safer to avoid riding at dusk or at night time particularly on busy main roads, but if this is absolutely necessary there is one main rule and that is **BE SEEN**. This also applies when riding in rainy or murky conditions when the motorist's view is obscured by wet windscreens, wipers and steamy windows.

1. View from a car window on a wet night with the windscreen wipers blurring the view. The rider and horse are almost invisible.

2. Same view with rider and horse wearing reflective clothing. Here they are clearly visible and therefore safer.

Wear fluorescent or reflective clothing. Fluorescent clothing should be worn during the day as the colours show up well in daylight. Reflective clothing should be worn during murky or dark conditions as this reflects car headlights.

Rider

Reflective tabard, white gloves, arm bands. Reflective silk or band on the hat. Lights on boots (particularly the right boot) with a white light showing to the front and a red light to the rear.

Horse

Reflective brushing boots or bands above the fetlocks, *especially on the offside fore and hind legs*. Bright coloured or reflective tail bandage. Reflective pads on the bridle or a reflective cavesson.

If there is no reflective or fluorescent clothing available, light coloured or white clothes should be worn. A white handkerchief or some similar material can be tied round the right arm of the rider. White brushing boots on the horse will also help.

In a group the riders at the front and the back, at least, should have reflective clothing. Grey or light coloured horses are also useful if positioned at the front and rear of a ride.

Road Studs

If the horse is frequently ridden in wet, slippery conditions the farrier can fit road studs to the horse's shoes. This will improve grip and stability.

Snow and Ice

Road studs are also useful when riding in snow and ice. Even if the road appears dry, there may still be icy patches under the trees or in shady areas. Studs may give the horse a better foothold but will not totally guard against slipping. It is safer to avoid riding on roads in really bad conditions.

In snowy conditions, snow can accumulate under the horse's feet making it difficult for the horse to walk. To prevent this a layer of grease can be applied to the horse's soles.

If the horse keeps slipping on an icy road, it is safer for the rider to quit the stirrups. Then, if the horse does slip and fall, the rider can dismount quickly. If safe, the horse can be ridden closer to the verge or kerb where the grit will give him a better foothold.

Courtesy

Horses and riders have the same rights and responsibilities as other road users. There are still drivers though who think that horses should not be on the roads at all and will drive aggressively to prove their point.

Any driver who shows courtesy to riders and horses should be thanked in appreciation. The three points of the courtesy code are **consideration** from both rider and driver, **good manners** and **acknowledgement**.

Aggressiveness and rudeness do not help anyone.

Thankfully the majority of drivers are considerate. They should be thanked for their patience. It will encourage them to be considerate to other riders in future.

Insurance

As riders can be held legally responsible if their horse damages other people's property, riders should be covered by a valid third party legal liability insurance, particularly when riding on the Public Highway.

It is also advisable to be covered by Personal Accident Insurance.

All full members of the BHS are automatically covered by a Personal Liability Insurance and a Personal Accident Insurance.

Example of a Theory Paper test

Name: ....   **Age** ....
                                                                        (If under 18)

Please indicate your answer by circling the letter of your choice.

1. Are you allowed to ride or lead on a footpath or pavement?
   - a) Yes.
   - b) No.
   - c) Sometimes.

2. What should a rider do at a road junction where there is a continuous thick white line across the carriageway?
   - a) Stop only if there is traffic approaching.
   - b) Give way to traffic on the main road.
   - c) Stop at the white line.

3. At traffic lights, which colour follows green?
   - a) Red.
   - b) Red and Amber.
   - c) Amber.

4. If you are leading a horse on foot, are you advised to;
   - a) Place the led horse between you and the traffic?
   - b) Keeping to the left, place yourself between the horse and the traffic?
   - c) Walk ahead of your horse?

5. What is the general meaning of road signs in blue circles?
   - a) Warnings.
   - b) Prohibitions.
   - c) Positive instructions.

6. Which is the most important reason for walking your horse around a corner?
   - a) In case you meet something.
   - b) To give your horse a chance to see where he is going.
   - c) The road surface is often slippery and a horse might easily slip and lose his balance.

7. Why are you advised not to ride too near the edge of the road?
   - a) Because of overhanging bushes and brambles.
   - b) In case the road surface is bad.
   - c) Because it invites drivers to overtake when it may be unsafe to do so.

8. What is the first thing you should do before overtaking a parked vehicle or other obstruction?
   - a) Signal.
   - b) Move to the middle of the road.
   - c) Look behind.

9. Which three items are important for the rider to wear?
   - a) Jodhpurs.
   - b) Shirt.
   - c) Riding hat to BSI Standard.
   - d) Smooth soled boots with heel.
   - e) Fluorescent/reflective tabard.

10. In a group out riding, how would you cross a main road?
    - a) Each rider crosses individually.
    - b) Cross in pairs, leading rider to make the decision when to cross.
    - c) Wait until all the riders can cross together without getting separated.

CHAPTER 4
The Simulated Test

During the Simulated Test the Examiners assess, in a safe environment, each rider's ability to cope with various hazards, their awareness of traffic situations and their road knowledge.

Format

A route is prepared in a field or paddock with poles, shavings, tapes or painted lines to mark the edges of the 'roads'. There are a variety of designs for the Simulated Test but all will include a T junction, right and left hand turns, at least one U-turn and space for a short trot.

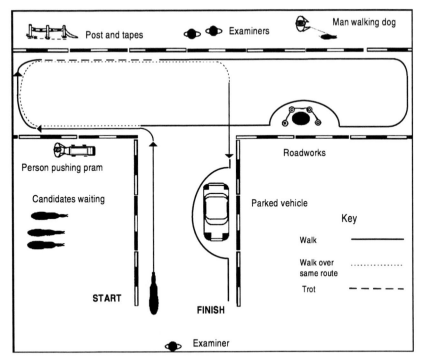

Figure 3: Example of possible Simulated Test

There will also be 'obstacles' along the road, such as some red and white road work tapes fluttering in the breeze, anything that could be a hazard whilst riding on the Public Highway.

This is possibly the hardest part of the Test because it is difficult to act realistically in simulated surroundings. In this chapter the phrases in italics are imaginary situations to help students understand how 'real' the Simulated Test needs to be handled.

General Rules

Look

Before doing anything; signalling, moving off or overtaking an obstacle - ALWAYS look behind, over the right shoulder. This look behind is an essential action of the Simulated and Road Tests.

Make this a good look to a count of four, not a quick glimpse.

Then, after signalling and before any manoeuvre, take another quick 'life-saver' look over the right shoulder.

Throughout the test the candidate should continue to look around and behind periodically. The rider must show an awareness of obstacles or situations in the surrounding areas.

Periodically, and especially at junctions, take a quick look over the left shoulder as well, to watch for *bicycles sneaking up behind on the inside.*

Signal

Hand signals should be clearly visible and correct.

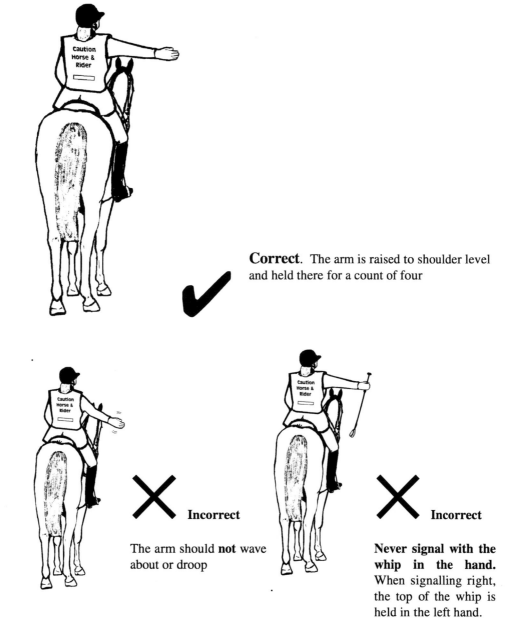

Correct. The arm is raised to shoulder level and held there for a count of four

Incorrect

The arm should **not** wave about or droop

Incorrect

Never signal with the whip in the hand. When signalling right, the top of the whip is held in the left hand.

Ride

Keep the pace steady and regular. Too slow and the *cars behind may start sounding their horns or revving their engines.*

Ride on the left **a little way in from the** *kerb.* The rider has the right to be on the road so no need to cower into the side. This space will also give you room for manoeuvre.

The Test

Three or four riders at a time, or possibly the whole group, will be taken to the field where the Simulated Test is prepared. Riders will be asked to ride the Test individually and shown where to begin.

Start

At the starting position make the horse stand quietly. Check that the reins are sufficiently short and that the whip is held in the right hand.

Before moving, **look behind.** Be observant; an Examiner will often stand behind to check that the 'look' is sufficient. Check what she is wearing and where she is standing. Otherwise check the scenery behind, how many trees are there, what type of fence? This will encourage **observation**. *There may be a bus coming to a stop behind; it is possible a car may overtake.*

Start - look behind, signal, both hands on the reins, 'life-saver' look over right shoulder and quick one to the left. Move off at walk and proceed a little way in from the *kerb.*

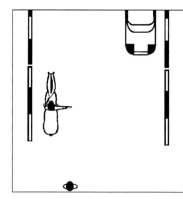 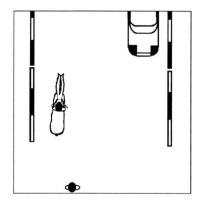

Junctions

Prepare in plenty of time when approaching junctions.

- Look behind over the right shoulder.

- Signal to inform the traffic which way you intend to turn.

- If required, halt at the junction. Look to the right, to the left and right again.

- Check behind to the right once more, (life-saver look) and quick glance to the left.

- Put both hands back on the reins before moving.

Left turn at junction

Look and then signal.

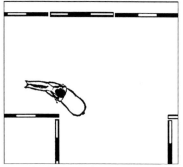

Keep looking and turn when clear.

Right turn at junction

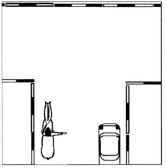

Walk straight ahead; turn on reaching the opposite kerb. Do not cut the corner or wander across the junction.

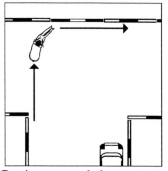

Continue around the route at a steady but active walk.

U-turn

The next manoeuvre may be the U-turn and again, the rider needs to prepare in advance.

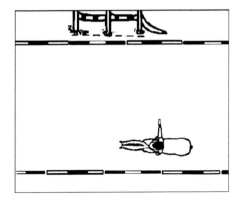 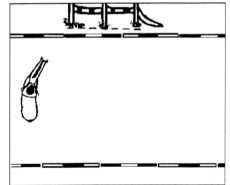

Look behind, to the right and in front. Signal in plenty of time and when the road is clear begin the U-turn. **Continue to look around until the turn is completed.**

Trotting

On a straight section the rider will be asked to trot.

Shorten the reins slightly, **look behind** to check the traffic and if all is clear go forwards to trot.

- The trot should be at a good pace, not too slow and certainly not too fast - rhythmical, balanced and in a straight line. The horse should never be allowed to wander across the *road*.

- **Always look behind just before the transition to walk.** The horse must be returned to walk some distance before junctions or hazards. The rider needs to allow sufficient time to prepare and carry out the transition.

Hazards

There will be hazards along the route. The rider will have to pass parked vehicles and road works.

- Look ahead to check for *oncoming traffic*. Slow down on approach and **look behind**.

- If all is clear, signal to the right and keep checking for oncoming traffic. Then with both hands on the reins move around the vehicle.

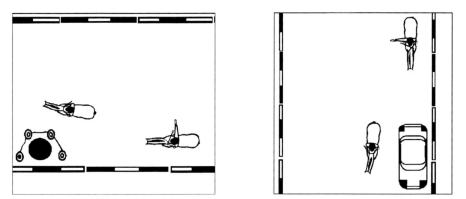

- Keep the horse's head slightly to the right and the right leg on to prevent the horse looking to the left and swinging his hindquarters to the right if he shies. (Do this also when passing other hazards such as children playing, a person walking with an umbrella, anything that may cause the horse to shy.)

- **Talk to the horse as this will help to keep him calm.**

- **At anytime the rider can request that people stop making a noise.** Always thank them afterwards.

Dismounting

The Examiners may ask the rider to dismount and lead the horse past an obstacle. The rider should first check behind, then dismount and place the stirrups over in front of the saddle. The reins are taken over the horse's head (unless he is wearing a martingale when the reins should remain on the horse's neck) and he is led from his **offside.** The whip should be carried in the right hand ready to control the horse's hindquarters.

Remounting

Keep the horse well into the verge, the reins short and mount quickly.

To resume the course, repeat the procedure for the start - look behind again, signal and move.

Emergency dismount

Use the imagination here to think of a situation such as a *car crash.* The emergency dismount needs to be performed very quickly.

- *Check behind first in case there is a car directly at the back of the horse.*

- Stop the horse and **at the same time** take both feet out of the stirrups.

- Quickly place the right stirrup over the front of the saddle.

- Dismount; place the left stirrup over the front of the saddle.

- Take the reins over the horse's head and walk quickly around the front of the horse. Keep hold of the reins whilst moving to his offside. Do not let the horse stand unrestrained even for a second.

- Stand on the offside holding the reins by the horse's chin in the left hand and the buckle end in the right with the whip.

Finish

At the end of the Simulated Test the rider should walk their horse quietly back to the group. Continue to look around and act as though this is still the Public Highway until out of the simulated road area.

C H A P T E R   5
The Road Test

All the points covered in the Simulated Test will be tested on the road and, in addition, the Examiners will be assessing how each rider deals practically with traffic.

The Route

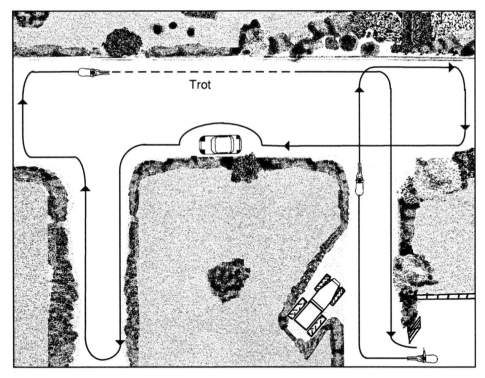

Figure 4: Example of possible Road Test

The route for the Road Test will be marked with special warning signs but, apart from these, the traffic will move normally. The Examiners and Stewards will be positioned at strategic points around the route.

Format

Riders may proceed directly to the Road Test after the Simulated Test or may have a short break first. The group will be gathered together and the route explained. There may be a map of the route available. The Examiners will ask the riders to proceed around the route individually.

General Rules

Look, Signal, Ride

Remember the basic rules, **look before any manoeuvre**, **signal clearly in plenty of time and ride at a steady pace. Keep the reins short and control the horse at all times.**

The Traffic

Riders should not become anxious or flustered in traffic, try to rush the horse or step onto the pavement to let vehicles pass.

The Test

Start

Each rider will be instructed to commence either by exiting from the yard gate, a lane or by starting from the side of the road.

Keeping the horse still and quiet, prepare to start by assessing the traffic situation.

If exiting from a gate or lane, look behind then to the right, left and right again.

Do not move until the road is clear. There is no need to rush, move only when the traffic allows. Signal right or left and then, with both hands on the reins, walk forwards.

If turning right, walk straight ahead to the opposite verge before turning.

When moving from a stationary position on the road, look behind over the right shoulder and signal. Glance once more over the right shoulder (life-saver) quickly over the left, and when safe with both hands on the reins, walk forward.

Ride on the left, a little way into the road from the verge. Do not ride on the verge. Keep listening as well as looking for traffic.

Junctions

Assess the traffic by looking and listening **before** arriving at the junction.

Look behind and observe the traffic situation.

Signal clearly before reaching the junction.

Halt at the junction. The horse should be halted in such a position that there is maximum visibility without placing the horse in danger. Even if turning right, **keep to the left**.

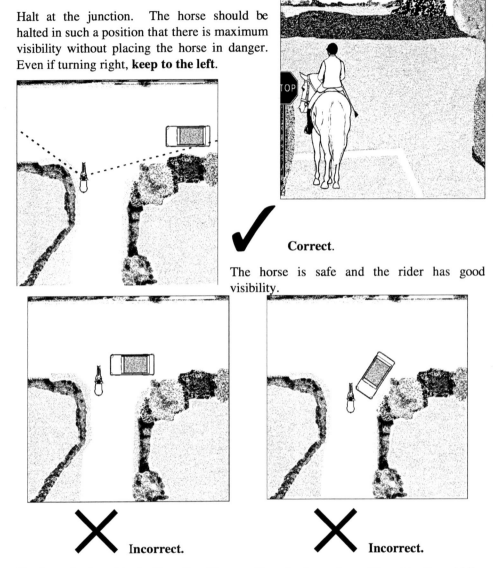

Correct.

The horse is safe and the rider has good visibility.

Incorrect.

The horse is placed in the line of traffic.

Incorrect.

Here the horse is positioned in the middle of the road. Not only can traffic sneak up on the inside, but the horse will be in danger if a car should turn into the road.

If the road is not clear, wait. Never try and rush out, or squeeze into a space.

Look behind and signal once more. Take a quick glance behind to the left, then if all is clear, with both hands on the reins, move.

The U-turn

Choose the spot carefully. A U-turn should be done where there is a good clear view of the road in front and behind. A U-turn should **NEVER** be made near a corner, a hill, a hump back bridge, a junction or indeed anywhere that is not straight and clear. Cars move at a tremendous speed in relation to a walking horse doing a U-turn on a road.

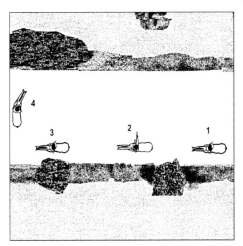

1. When there is an appropriate place, look in front, behind and to the front again.

2. If the road is clear, look behind and signal right.

3. Keep looking and listening for traffic.

4. With both hands on the reins perform the U-turn quickly and smoothly.

Never attempt a U-turn if the traffic situation is not clear, even if it takes miles before it can be executed safely. The Examiners would prefer it to be done in the next county rather than the rider make a mess of it!

Continue walking until all the traffic has passed safely. Never stop by the side of the road, or try to halt the traffic and attempt the turn. There may be some idiot three cars back who decides he is going to overtake the lot. If the traffic is heavy, then carry on until the turn can be made safely.

Parked vehicles

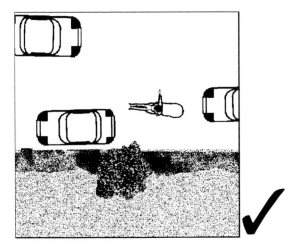

Negotiate stationary vehicles as in the Simulated Test, give way to traffic travelling in the opposite direction by halting if necessary. Look behind, signal and pass the parked vehicle keeping the horse's head slightly to the right.

The rider should position the horse slightly out from the kerb to avoid being 'boxed in' by other traffic.

Here the rider has positioned the horse so that the cars behind respect his position and give room.

Here the rider has stayed into the kerb and has consequently become 'boxed in'. A situation where the rider may have to wait some time before being able to move and overtake the parked vehicle.

Whilst passing the vehicle, be alert and prepared for any sudden noise or movement - a barking dog in the car, children winding down the windows, car doors slamming or car boots being opened. People who do not ride horses have very little idea of the problems that may be caused by sudden movement or noise. If, for instance, someone is unloading the boot of the car and the horse begins to shy, the rider may ask that person to stop and keep still for a minute. Always remember to thank them afterwards by smiling and nodding. Keep both hands on the reins.

Incorrect.

Turning into a minor road

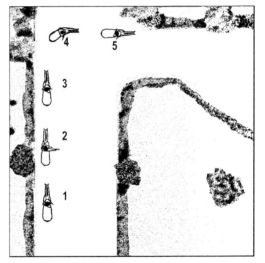

1. Look behind and check the traffic.

2. Signal well in advance.

3. Check the traffic situation again behind and in front. If the traffic is busy, halt at position 3 until clear. (If the traffic continues to be heavy, ride straight along the main road until it is safe to cross. Do a U-turn and then turn left into the minor road.)

4. When the road is clear, turn just as the horse is level with the left hand kerb of the minor road.

5. Ride in a straight line across the main road into the minor road. Do not cut the corner or ride across at an angle. Keep checking for traffic.

Trotting

Candidates will be required to trot on a straight part of the course. **Look behind** before making the transition and keep the trot straight and active but steady.

Trot to Walk

Prepare to slow down from trot to walk in plenty of time. **Always look behind before the transition.** There could be a car stuck right behind which, because of the trotting sound on the road, has not been heard. It may be travelling at trotting speed so, to suddenly bring the horse to walk, would have disastrous results.

Stopping the Traffic

If, for some reason, the rider has to ask the traffic to stop, the signal should be made clearly with hand and palm outstretched. Try to make eye contact; this is important even with drivers in cars.

Finish

When the Road Test is complete the rider should ride correctly into the yard, or back to the spot where the rest of the group are waiting. The look behind, signalling and riding with short reins must be maintained. The Examiners may still be watching; the traffic will still be a potential danger.

Test Tips

Theory

As part of the preparation, learn the relevant sections of the Highway Code thoroughly, and be observant whenever you are being driven, or driving yourself. Watch the sequence of traffic lights, look at road signs and markings; it is amazing how many of us drive around, automatically obeying the Highway signals, but when asked questions about them suddenly go blank.

Read the questions on the Theory Paper carefully and slowly. It is so easy for a question to be read incorrectly and answered incorrectly. It would be a pity to fail the Theory and consequently the whole Test because one question was misread.

Think about each question and answer; some of the answers are not immediately clear. This tests the candidate's comprehension, which is necessary in reading and understanding road signs and signals.

For candidates who have difficulty reading and comprehending the written word, for instance those with dyslexia, this should be mentioned when applying for the Riding and Road Safety Test. The Theory section may then be taken orally.

Simulated Test

For the Simulated Test the important point is to imagine a real life situation. Candidates may feel silly acting this way in the middle of a field, with all the other candidates watching (giving signals for non-existent traffic) but it does not matter what the others think. If acted realistically, they will probably be impressed! A failure in the Simulated Test means a failure in the whole Test.

The important point in both the Simulated and Road Tests is **always look behind before doing anything.** If a candidate signals, moves off, overtakes an obstacle or trots *before looking behind*, they will immediately fail. This must be an automatic reaction; practise it constantly when out hacking. The look behind must be a long, observant look. In the real world, riders have to look and notice all the traffic behind them.

However, this look should be balanced with observations to the side and front. One candidate failed his test the first time because he did not look behind. The second time he failed because he was constantly looking behind and did not observe in front or to the side.

At any time, and particularly during a potentially difficult situation, **talk to the horse** - this will help and reassure him. Riders are permitted to talk to the horse.

The Road Test

Ride the Road Test **steadily but not too slowly**. Many candidates fail because they dawdle along the road; the pace should be active but not fast. If there is a situation which may trouble you, do not panic, take everything carefully and above all remember SAFETY.

Keep both hands on the reins when thanking motorists for their consideration, nod, smile and shout 'Thank you'.

Do not worry if you cannot perform the U-turn because of the amount of traffic, continue along the road until it is sufficiently clear to make the manoeuvre safely.

Do not panic either if you ride the route incorrectly, as long as your Roadcraft is good you will not fail for taking the wrong route. The Examiners may request that you ride part of the Road Test again.

General

This Test should not be considered **easy**, especially by those who drive themselves. It is a totally different concept of using the road whilst riding a live animal. Motorists, although benefiting by experience on the road, will discover there is still a lot to learn about Roadcraft when horses are involved.

It is essential that all prospective candidates have training before taking the Riding and Road Safety Test. The pass mark is 80% and if at any time during the test the candidate makes a move that is dangerous to themselves, the horse or other road users, they will fail instantly. Each candidate must be well taught by a knowledgeable and experienced instructor. They also need to gain experience of the Simulated Test and, more importantly, they need to build up an awareness and ability to ride in traffic.

With more riders taking the Riding and Road Safety Test, this should hopefully reduce the number of those horses and riders killed on the roads every year.

Part II

The BHS Stage Two Examination

CHAPTER 6
General Information

The successful candidate of the Stage II will gain a greater competence and a wider experience through the various subjects covered in this Exam. It also takes the candidate one step closer to the British Horse Society Assistant Instructor qualification.

Eligibility

All applicants must;

1. Be a member of the British Horse Society at the time of application and on the day of the examination

2. Be 16 years or over

3. Have passed their Stage One Riding and Horse Knowledge and the BHS Riding and Road Safety Test.

The certificate for the Riding and Road Safety Test must either be sent with the Stage II application, or presented at the Test Centre on the day of the examination. If this certificate is not presented, the candidate may not be allowed to proceed with the Stage II.

The Riding and Care can be taken separately if required, providing the appropriate section has been passed at Stage I level.

The Syllabus

This examination is divided into two sections - Riding which includes flatwork and jumping and the Horse Knowledge & Care which includes lungeing.

Riding

General   Assess the horse's tack for fitting and condition and alter if necessary.

Equitation   Maintain a balanced and independent seat at walk, trot and canter - to ask for and canter on a named leg. To perform correct school figures at walk, trot and canter - and to ride at all three paces without stirrups.

Ride transitions smoothly and in balance. Ride with the reins in one hand at walk and trot. Knowledge of riding up and down hills and over small ditches. Understand how the horse adjusts his balance to carry the rider.

Jumping   a short course of fences up to 2 foot 6 inches or .76 metres which may include small ditches.

Opening and shutting gates   open and/or shut a gate. Knowledge of procedures for opening and shutting gates when in company and how to secure the fastening.

Safety   Knowledge of school etiquette, rules and commands. Knowledge of rules when riding in the countryside.

Horse Knowledge and Care

Candidates must show a greater practical experience and efficiency in handling and caring for horses than in Stage I.

General   Candidates should be capable of looking after horses and ponies stabled and at grass at all times of the year, and sufficiently competent to be left in charge for short periods without supervision. They should have the ability to cope with minor problems when these arise and know when a problem needs experienced or professional help.

Candidates should be quietly confident and show co-operation and good manners to fellow workers.

Anatomy & Physiology   The points of the horse and main external areas. Skeleton of the horse, names and position of the bones. Descriptions of certain bones and their functions; how these relate to the horse's movement.

Basic description and function of the digestive system and how this affects the horse's lifestyle. Structure and functions of the horse's foot. Position of the main internal organs in the horse's body.

Health   How to recognise when a horse is ill or unsound. Different types of minor wounds and their relative treatment. Basic nursing and when to call the Vet. Worming; when to worm and the importance of a regular worming programme. The inspection and care of the horse's teeth. Health records.

Watering   Importance of water to the horse. Methods of watering in the stable and the field.

Feeding   Types of feed and their respective values. Preparation of food including cooked foods. Feeding horses and ponies in medium work, at grass and for special cases. Reasons for feeding soaked hay.

Shoeing   Reasons for shoeing. The farrier's tools. Shoeing procedures and the method of removing a shoe.

Saddlery   The principles of bitting. Cleaning and care of saddlery. Fitting boots, breast plates, martingales and lungeing equipment. How to recognise ill fitting tack and how this causes injuries.

Grooming   Procedures for strapping and quartering. Method of wisping. Care of the horse after exercise.

Fittening   The **theory** of bringing a horse back to work after a rest at grass. Timetable for getting a horse fit; relating feeding to exercise. Injuries caused by roadwork, hard ground or heavy going. Roughing off a horse.

Lungeing   Lungeing a quiet horse for exercise. Safety precautions.

Clothing   Rugs and blankets; their uses, care and maintenance. Bandages; stable bandages for warmth, protection and medical reasons. Method of putting on and taking off a stable bandage.

Travelling   Preparing a horse for travelling. Fitting and putting on protective clothing, when to use and reasons. **Theory** of loading and unloading, precautions and awareness of possible difficulties.

Clipping and Trimming   Different types of clip, clippers and clipping machines. Reasons for clipping and trimming. Preparation of site and horse - care afterwards. How to handle a horse during clipping - how to give assistance. Trimming.

Plaiting   Pulling and plaiting manes and tails; reasons for and practical knowledge of plaiting.

Stable Design Size, condition and position of stables and boxes. Construction - materials their advantages and disadvantages. Fixtures and fittings in the stable.

Grassland Management   Recognising good pasture - its maintenance. Importance and reasons for daily inspections. Poisonous plants.

General Knowledge The rules of the Country code. Safety precautions and procedures when riding on the Public Highway. Accident procedures and the prevention of further incidents. Knowledge of the aims and structure of the British Horse Society.

PLEASE NOTE; to avoid repeating information already covered in Stage I, included at the beginning of the relevant chapters is a short description of the subjects that were described in the previous book.

Where to Train

Many British Horse Examination Centres will offer Stage II training for students. Some establishments take groups of working pupils for a few months, whilst others offer courses specifically designed for clients. Many BHS Approved Riding Schools, whilst not being Examination Centres, offer training towards the Stage II. A useful publication to purchase if any student or prospective candidate has difficulty, is the BHS 'Where to Train' booklet. This lists Approved Schools together with their standards of training.

Certain Agricultural Colleges offer courses for the BHS Stage Examinations. The student can combine these with training for other qualifications such as business, secretarial and 'A' levels. A number of these colleges are included in the 'Where to Train' book or can be found in the advertisement section of equestrian magazines. These courses are excellent for students wishing to gain a comprehensive range of qualifications.

Preparation for the Exam

Because the Stage II is quite a step up from the Stage I it is wise to obtain an assessment from a knowledgeable instructor before application. Training is essential, ideally at a BHS Examination Centre, or at a BHS Approved Riding School.

For the riding section, students should aim to reach the standard required well before the Exam Day. They will need to practise the school figures required with other riders in a menage.

Much of the Horse Knowledge and Care syllabus is based on practical experience. Examiners are not just looking for 'book learning' but will also assess candidates on their experience of working with and handling horses.

Subjects will need studying thoroughly (from this book) and this should be combined with practical experience derived through handling or working with horses.

For those who do not work with horses, or who are not fortunate enough to have their own horse, this experience can be gained from *practical lectures* and by *spending time helping out at the stables.*

CHAPTER 7

Equitation

Having mastered the basic techniques at Stage I the rider training for Stage II will advance by improving the suppleness and balance of the seat, and effectiveness of the aids.

The following chapters describe the standard required for the Stage II, in both flatwork and jumping. The Examination format for the riding sections are outlined including examples of school figures, exercises, a short course for the jumping section, and the opening and shutting of gates.

General Preparation

An important part in the foundation of the good rider is the *good instructor*. Whilst advice on technique can be described in books there is no substitute, in practical terms, for a knowledgeable, qualified instructor.

Training should be taken at a Riding School or Establishment that has the facilities and standard of horses relevant for the Stage II. Students will certainly benefit from having lessons at a BHS Examination Centre under the auspices of an instructor who actively deals with the Stage II Examination.

It is important that the student rides a variety of horses to increase his or her adaptability, learning to assess the different action of each horse, their good points and their problems.

Preparation for flatwork

The student should practise riding as much as possible in a school with others, particularly in open order. Performing school figures and exercises in the company of other riders takes planning and this ability needs to be developed before the Exam day.

The rider's position and feel can also be improved by having lessons on the lunge. This is an excellent method of developing physical ability and of deepening the seat because the rider can concentrate on his or her own position in a relaxed way. Being lunged can also increase the rider's awareness of the horse's paces, balance and rhythm.

Another method that helps the rider to improve, is to actually *see* himself or herself riding. Sometimes it is difficult to understand exactly what an instructor is trying to explain. Working in a school that has wall mirrors can be useful as a teaching aid, clarifying the instructor's points and directing the rider towards self improvement.

If the rider can arrange to have a video of the lessons this will be an advantage. Videos are a tremendous bonus and are becoming popular as a teaching aid. Being able to watch the lesson at home, slowing down and replaying the video at relevant parts, helps the rider to understand what is happening. Through this teaching aid the rider can also learn positive self criticism, an essential part of advancement. The first step to improvement is recognising faults and then learning to correct them.

Revision

The following points were covered in the Stage I book and the student can revise these if necessary.

Basic position, the natural aids, artificial aids. Mounting and dismounting, checking girths and stirrup lengths. The horse's three basic paces and their footfall sequences. Transitions, basic information on turns and circles. School rules and commands.

Flatwork at Stage II

The rider at this level should be capable of maintaining a balanced, independent position at walk, trot and canter, when riding with and without stirrups. He or she should demonstrate control over the horse in all three basic paces, ride the horse forward actively from the leg and know the correct aids for transitions and school figures.

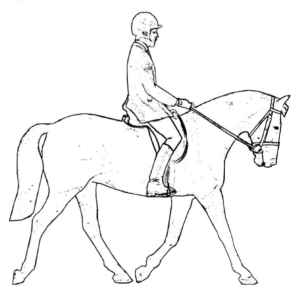

The rider's position

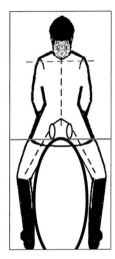

The rider sits with the seat level in the saddle and with equal weight on both seat bones. To check this, with the horse at halt either being held or while the rider is being lunged, place one hand on each hip bone and feel if they are level.

The thighs and knees lie relaxed against the saddle. The lower leg from below the knee should be in constant contact with the horse's sides. The legs should remain still unless giving an aid. When the lower legs are kept close to the horse's sides, the leg aids are more subtle, the rider can use the legs with less movement but with more effect.

The heel should be lower than the toe. Gently stretch the back of the calf and heel down without pushing the lower leg forward.

The toe should be pointing to the front. If the toe is pointing out this is a problem with the hip and leg rather than the toe itself. Take hold of the back of the thigh and **gently** pull it back and out to rotate the hip and bring the leg into position.

The upper body is maintained upright with the shoulders level and relaxed. Slightly shrug the shoulders raising them towards the ears, then back and down.

Take a deep breath and then slowly exhaling maintain the expansion of the ribcage.

There should be a 'lightness' in the upper body. Try and imagine the weight dropping down into the seat, the legs and heels without losing the height of the upper body.

The head should be level and looking forward. When riding think about looking at the area in front where the horse should be in three paces, focusing between the horse's ears.

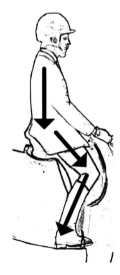

The upper arms are kept close to rider's sides with the elbows bent. The shoulders again should feel 'light', feel the 'weight' drop down into the elbows.

The rider can make the mental check on the imaginary 'lines'.

- The vertical line through the ear, the shoulder, the hip and the heel.
- Line from the elbow, through the lower arm, hand and reins to the bit, both as seen from the side and from above.

When the rider is able to maintain this position, the natural aids of seat and body, legs and hands can be used with more effect. The rider sits quietly in the saddle asking for movement with the leg aids and containing this energy with quiet hands.

The Seat and body

The rider should now be learning to 'feel' with the seat, creating the energy with the legs and allowing this to flow through the horse. The rider will develop an awareness of the horse's movements and an ability to stay in balance with him.

If the rider tries to use the seat too actively at this level the body will become stiff and rigid, working against the horse rather than with him.

The Legs

The leg aid should be applied using the inside of the calf. The rider should not raise the heel to kick the horse as this alters the balance pushing the rider's weight forwards and the lower leg backwards.

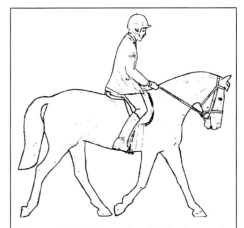

Figure 5: Raising the heel alters the rider's position

The Hands

The hands should develop 'feel'. With the reins kept sufficiently short the rider is able to feel the horse's mouth. The fingers should be closed around the reins firmly but gently. An analogy often used is to imagine holding one small bird in each hand. The birds need to held firmly enough to stop them escaping but not too tight to squash them.

By maintaining an even, light contact with the bit, signals can be passed to the horse by squeezing and releasing with the fingers.

The rider should allow slight 'give and take' movements from the shoulders. Think of the shoulders, arms and hands rather like elasticated side reins, fairly still and constant but with slight yielding to the horse's mouth.

Straight, outstretched arms with locked elbows can be rigid and restrictive.

Co-ordination of Aids

Once the basic use of the natural aids is learnt, the rider is then taught to use the aids in combination with each other.

This co-ordination of the aids will become progressively important as the rider advances. It is by the use of all the aids in conjunction with each other that informs the horse of the rider's requirements. The position of the seat and body, the area where the leg aid is applied and the feel on the reins conveys the message that the rider wants a particular movement or a change of pace.

It is important to learn this co-ordination of aids, rather like learning a new language, starting with the basic alphabet and single words then progressing onto phrases and sentences. We are learning to communicate with the horse in the language in which he has been taught to respond.

The inside leg applied in the region of the girth creates impulsion and, on circles and turns, asks for bend. The outside hand remains in contact, receiving the energy and controlling the pace and the amount of bend. The inside hand controls the direction. The outside leg controls the hindquarters, prevents them from swinging out and, when used behind the girth, asks for canter and lateral movements.

The Half-halt

One of the most important co-ordination of aids that the rider learns is the half-halt. This is an essential part of equitation and one that should be taught from the beginning. It is the vital 'aid' helping both rider and horse to understand each other and to work in harmony.

In effect the half-halt is a momentary slowing of the horse by the rider, followed by increased impulsion. The result should be that the horse softens and engages his quarters more effectively.

The basic half-halt is performed by combining the seat (and body), legs and hands. The rider sits up a little straighter and at the same time applies the leg aid. The hands momentarily squeeze and release the reins. It will help if the rider thinks of asking the horse for a downward transition **just for a second** and then encourages the horse to go forwards.

When practising think of applying the half-halt just before and after every corner, at every quarter marker in the school or on a circle. Prepare for every transition with a half-halt. Learn to feel how the horse responds; he should slow slightly, balance his body, bring his hocks underneath and then go forwards more energetically.

The half-halt should become an automatic preparatory action, just like calling a person's name to receive their attention before speaking to them. It should also be applied subtly as an imperceptible signal between rider and horse.

School figures

The aids are used in co-ordination for all school figures, that is the manoeuvres performed around the school.

Circles and turns

Riding circles and turns accurately and correctly helps the rider's co-ordination and the horse's balance, rhythm, suppleness and obedience.

The rider effectively 'moulds' the horse around the circle or turn using the natural aids. With the seat remaining level in the saddle, the inside aids are applied asking for bend and direction whilst the outside aids control the amount of bend. In this way the rider encourages the horse to curve around the circle whilst maintaining his 'straightness'.

Straightness

The term 'straightness' refers to the horse's 'line' from poll to tail. When the horse is straight this line is constant through his body. The horse's hind foot follows on the same track as the corresponding fore foot.

As the rider progresses to more advanced work, the straightness of the horse becomes very important. At this level the rider should begin to recognise straightness and to ask for it during simple school figures and exercises.

If the horse is to be in balance and working correctly, he must be straight. Practise this around circles, first by asking the horse to turn using the inside aids only. Watch how the horse 'breaks' the line at the withers. He may also feel as though he is 'falling into' the circle.

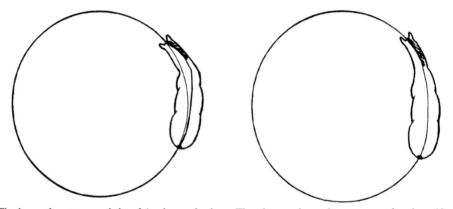

The horse has too much bend in the neck, the 'line' is broken at the withers and the horse is falling out through his outside shoulder.

The horse has the correct bend uniform throughout the body.

Then practise keeping the horse straight by using the outside aids in conjunction with the inside leg and hand; the horse should feel more balanced and work with a better rhythm.

Straight lines

Where the horse really shows if he is straight or not is on straight lines. Watch a lesson in the school, particularly when horses are ridden down the side of the school. Observe how many horses swing their hindquarters in from the wall.

Practise keeping the horse straight down the centre line of the school or on the inner tracks on the long sides.

Transitions

During the riding session, riders will be asked to show upward and downward transitions and to come forward to halt smoothly and in balance.

To achieve this, preparation is vital. The rider should first decide where to make the transition and apply the half-halt a few steps before this point.

The original pace should be active. This is particularly important for downward transitions, where using the hands only to slow the horse will result in a poor transition. The aids should be applied in the sequence, seat, legs and then hands as if the rider is *pushing* the horse forwards into a slower pace rather than *pulling* back.

The rider asks for halt with the same aids, sitting upright, applying the leg aids and allowing the horse to come forwards to halt into the hands. Effectively the rider is asking the horse to halt from behind.

The rider who asks for halt by restraining strongly with the hands only, will cause the horse to resist, lose his balance and make a bad transition.

School rules and commands

Riders at Stage II level should be familiar with the school rules and commands. Here are some examples.

Rules

- When working on different reins, pass left to left.

- Riders at a faster pace are given priority on the outside track.

- A safe distance should always be kept between horses, a minimum of 1-1½ of a horse's length.

- When entering or leaving the school ask permission of those inside.

- Riders should at all times be aware of others in the school.

Commands

- Proceed in open order, that is more than 4 horses' lengths between horses or evenly spaced around the school.

- Work as a ride.

- Each leading or rear file in succession.

- Go large or work on the outer track.

- Work on an inner track.

The Examination

This outline of the Exam format includes hints on techniques to help students practise and then perform the equitation skills needed at this level.

Flatwork

The flatwork lasts 45 minutes to an hour and consists of riding two or three different horses. Almost three-quarters is performed in open order with riders working as individuals on the same rein, unless instructed otherwise. The candidates may also be required to ride for part of the session in a field or paddock to assess how they control the horse outside the confines of a school.

Each group, numbering four or five candidates, will be escorted to the school and will be allocated or ask to choose a horse. The Instructor in charge may allocate horses according to the height and weight of the riders. On some occasions, when the riders are similar in size, the Instructor will ask each rider to choose a horse themselves. Those who have taken lessons at the Examination Centre will now have an advantage. They will know the horses and should be able to pick the horse they feel they ride the best. Having a good first ride is a tremendous boost to the confidence and will give the candidate a good start to the riding session.

Checking the tack

All candidates should check their tack before mounting. This may seem an obvious point but it is not always an automatic action.

The girth should be checked on both sides first and then tightened, ideally, to the same number hole on all girth straps. This is to ensure that the girth is level.

The stirrup lengths can be assessed and changed if necessary by placing the knuckles of one hand on the stirrup-bar and raising the stirrup so that the iron just reaches the armpit. The stirrup should be pulled gently down the stirrup leather, snapping the iron down eventually ruins the leather. The girth and stirrup lengths can be checked again once the rider has mounted.

Make an appraisal of the horse at the same time; colour, height, gender and possible breed or type. The Examiners may query the candidates at some point about the horse they are riding.

Mounting

The riders will normally be expected to mount from the ground and some Examiners may insist on this. In the case where a small rider has a large horse, the Instructor may be requested to give a leg up or supply a mounting block.

Position check

The rider can now take a few seconds to quietly think about their position. Check that the seat is level in the deepest part of the saddle; thighs and knees relaxed allowing the lower legs to come into contact with the horse's sides.

Shrug the shoulders a few times, straighten the head and look forwards. Take a deep breath and, whilst maintaining the raised ribcage, slowly exhale.

Moving off

The Instructor will give the command for the whole ride to proceed onto the left or right rein with riders working in open order as individuals or as a ride. Change the whip hand if necessary and ask the horse to walk on actively, *straight* to the track.

The School

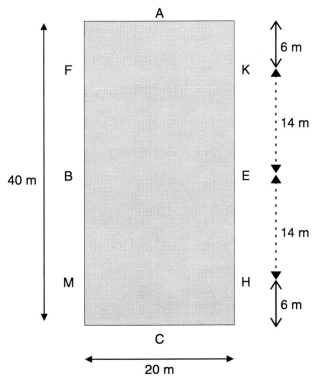

The rider needs to learn how to 'use the school'. Use the corners to make the horse bend around the inside leg, ride accurate school figures to ask the horse for obedience. The rider can use different school figures down the long sides to encourage the horse to be more supple. Riding shallow loops or taking the horse onto an inner track will all help to improve the horse's bend and straightness.

Riders at the Stage II level should avoid riding continuously around the outside track.

If working in open order, riders will be requested to work in walk until satisfied with the horse, then to proceed into trot.

Whilst candidates will need a little time to assess their horse in walk, this must not take too long. The trot work should start fairly quickly. Each candidate will only have a limited time on each horse and the Examiners will want to see all three basic paces as well as school figures.

The walk

The walk should be active, forward going but not too fast or rushed. Include some school figures as soon as possible, for example a 20 metre circle at A or C and a shallow loop down the long side.

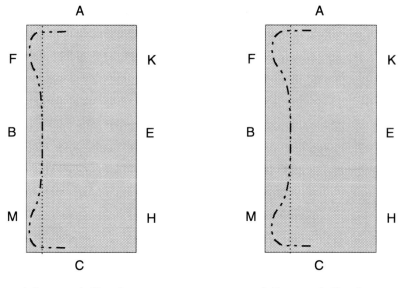

A 3 metre shallow loop   A 5 metre shallow loop

When the rider is ready the horse should be prepared for trot. The rider should choose the marker or spot where the trot is to begin and prepare the horse with a half-halt a few strides beforehand.

Trot work

As in walk, the work in trot should be varied and include 20 or 15 metre circles at the A, C, E or B markers, shallow 3 or 5 metre loops down the long sides, half twenty metre circles across the school.

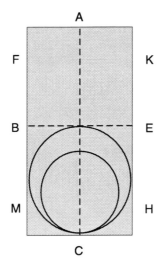

Figure 6: 20 and 15 metre circle at C

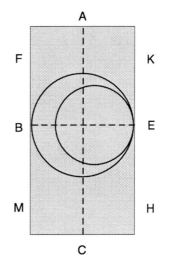

Figure 7: 20 and 15 metre circle at E

Transitions

Working in a open order as individuals, the riders may now be requested to include transitions from trot to walk and then to halt. When making the downward transition to walk whilst others are in trot, the rider must come onto an inner track to make the transition.

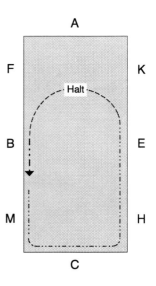

One of the exercises used is for the rider to leave the track on one of the long sides and make the transition to walk. The transition to halt is asked for on the centre line. The rider then walks on and trots when reaching the opposite long side.

Change of rein

At some point the Instructor will command that all riders come forward to walk and change the rein. Change the rein via a short diagonal or a half 10 metre circle (demi-volte) and incline back to the track if possible. Riders who change the rein via the long diagonal or down the centre line will almost always find themselves in the path of, or being blocked by, another rider.

Canter work

The canter work may be performed by individual riders in open order or with the group as a ride. The exercises in canter will vary depending on the wishes of the Examiners.

Examples of canter exercises

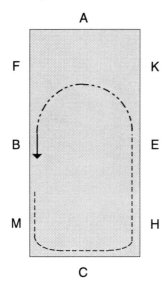

1. **In open order** work in trot on the outer track. Come across the school from a long side on a half 20 metre circle. On leaving the track ask for canter and, on reaching the opposite side, return to trot.

2. In open order, individual riders to ask for canter in one corner and, on the long side, to come across the school in a half 20 metre circle. Return to trot when ready and safe to do so.

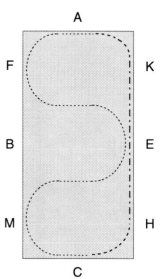

3. In open order whole ride to ride a continuous 3 loop serpentine in trot from A to C or vice versa. Use the long side for canter coming forwards to trot at A or C.

4. **Working as a ride,** leading file in succession, canter large around the school returning to trot before joining the rest of the ride as rear file.

5. Rear file to come forwards to halt. From halt go forwards to trot. Ride onto a 20 metre circle and when ready canter. Canter a circle. Go large and make a downward transition to trot before reaching the rest of the ride. Pass the ride and take leading file.

When working in open order it can be quite difficult to find a suitable space. The rider does need to plan, prepare and be adaptable. The rider may chose a point, canter across the school to where moments ago there was space, only to find the whole group trotting into that spot! Turn the canter half circle into a 15 metre whole circle and return to the original point. The Examiners would prefer this, rather than have a rider trying desperately to slot into a small space between two other horses.

The horse should be prepared in advance, by a half-halt, a few strides before the chosen transition point. If the horse is rushed into the transition he may strike off on the wrong leading leg.

Riding with the reins in one hand

The candidates will be instructed to form a ride. Then each leading file in succession will be requested to take the reins and whip in one hand and perform some walk and trot before returning to the ride.

The reins are held in the outside hand. The inside hand is allowed to hang by the rider's side.

There are various ways of holding the reins but the best method is to have one rein passing between the thumb and first finger and the other rein passing outside the little finger. The reins should be kept sufficiently short to maintain a contact and control.

The hand can be held 'flatter' than normal to give an even contact on both reins.

Riding without stirrups

The riders will usually be asked to ride without stirrups on their second horse. Work will be requested at walk, trot and canter. The group will normally form a ride and each individual asked to trot and canter individually by the Instructor. This may include cantering a large circle at some point in the school away from the ride.

Riding outside

The whole group may be taken to a field, paddock or outside arena to work at walk, trot and canter on both reins (unless bad weather conditions make this impossible).

Horses can often work differently outside in an open space; some are freer in their paces whilst others decide to spook at anything. The rider needs to keep the horse under control, working on circles and turns, and using the half-halt.

The Thinking Rider

From Stage II upwards, as riders progress, they will be expected to *think* more for themselves. When working in open order, riders have to judge their space and plan ahead to perform school figures.

They will also begin to realise that each horse is different, is an individual; that an aid applied to one horse works perfectly well but when applied to another is totally ignored or causes confusion. Riders should begin to judge what aids are applicable on each horse. This is developed only by riding different horses of different ages and stages of development and training.

Opening and Shutting Gates

In practice dealing with gates is necessary when hacking in the countryside or whilst hunting. Control of the horse is important when opening and shutting gates and it is this, together with the safety factor, that the Examiners will be assessing.

The school movements used for opening and shutting gates are *the turn on the forehand* and *the rein back*. These need to be practised first so that the co-ordination of aids required is almost automatic even with the reins in one hand.

The aim is to open the gate wide enough to allow riders through without causing danger to the horses and to shut the gate afterwards, making sure that the fastening is properly secured.

Normally in the Examination the first rider will be asked to open the gate and the next rider to shut it. The whole group will take this in turns.

Gates vary in design, some open towards the rider, some open away, some have springs attached and others have weights so that they close automatically.

Opening a gate towards the rider

Walk the horse directly to the gate and position him side on (parallel) to it, with his head towards the catch.

If necessary, walk the horse forwards a step or two so that the catch is within reach. Stand the horse quietly. Lean forwards and sideways, whilst keeping a contact with the reins to prevent the horse from moving, and reach for the catch with one hand.

Undo the catch and open the gate carefully and slowly. Rein the horse back a few paces by applying the leg aids and resisting with the hands as the horse moves forward.

When the gate is opened, turn the horse on the forehand in the other direction, so that his hindquarters move away from the gate. This is done by applying the leg slightly behind the girth to ask the horse to move his quarters away.

When it is safe, swing the gate open, making sure that it is wide enough to allow the horse through.

Do not try to walk through a small gap. Be aware of gates that close automatically, these can swing back and catch the horse on his hindquarters.

Opening a gate away from the rider

Ride towards the gate and position the horse parallel to it, with his head towards the catch. Open the catch carefully and push the gate open wide. Walk through, watching the gate to make sure that it does not swing back and hit the horse.

Shutting the gate towards the rider

Position the horse next to the gate with his head towards the catch. Lean over and hold the gate.

Slowly close the gate whilst simultaneously reining the horse back. The gate must not touch the horse.

Shutting the gate away from the rider

Position the horse parallel to the gate as normal; lean over and push the gate. Repeat as necessary until the gate is shut. Check that the gate is fastened properly.

In both cases make sure the catch is properly closed and secured. **If necessary, turn the horse around and approach the gate again to shut it correctly.**

Safety

Gates must be opened and shut carefully. At no point should the gate touch the horse, swing back into him or hit him on the way through. This is not a speed test; it is better to be slow and careful than to rush and cause an accident.

Consideration for other riders

In practice, if other riders are going to pass through the gate, open it as wide as possible to allow their passage without hindrance. Always shut the gate afterwards and ensure that the fastening is secure, especially on farmland where there may be stock in the field.

If another rider is shutting the gate, give him or her plenty of room and wait until the gate is shut properly before moving on. Never ride off, especially at canter, before the rider has shut the gate.

Exam Tips

For the Stage II the rider needs to be more positive and look more efficient than at Stage I. Checking the tack, altering the girth and stirrup lengths needs to be done fairly quickly and without fuss. If you do need help, ask for assistance. This is preferable to a rider struggling with the tack.

Whilst checking the tack, quickly assess the horse. Practise this before the day so that you are accustomed to recognising colour, gender and height. Start assessing horses' heights against your own height; eventually you will be able to judge this just by looking. For example, a person of 5 feet 5 inches measures 16.1 hh.

Throughout the riding session keep the horse's pace active but not too fast. Speed is as much an evasion as laziness. Keep varying the exercises, avoid becoming 'trapped' on the outside track.

Think and plan ahead all the time so that you appear and ride efficiently in the school with others, particularly important when performing transitions. Though at this level, you should be starting to feel for the correct diagonal at trot, on a strange horse in this situation it is not always easy. So take a quick glance if necessary to check. Check too by taking a quick glance that the horse is leading with the correct leg at canter. The Examiners may not penalise a rider if the horse keeps striking off with the incorrect leg, but it will influence them if the rider does nothing about it and allows the horse to continue on the wrong leg.

When the horse is obedient and going well, remember to reward him with the voice and a pat. As well as making a good impression, it will also give the horse the reward he deserves and encourage him to try even harder!

Relax and remember to breath! Try and assess how the horse is working, how you could improve his pace or ride that circle better next time. Concentrating on the horse sometimes takes the pressure off the rider and gives the appearance that the rider is at least trying to improve the horse.

C H A P T E R   8
Jumping

Jumping is 90 % flatwork, so all the principles and techniques learnt on the flat are just as important in the jumping arena. It is so easy to focus on the fence itself, whereas the essential basis of a good jump is actually on the approach to each fence.

Once the flatwork is established, that is when the rider can control and direct the horse on circles, turns and straight lines in canter, the jumping position can be taught.

With a good instructor from the start, the rider will learn the correct technique and gradually his or her suppleness and security will increase. The rider can then progress onto different types of fences, over varying terrain, practising and building up on experience so that jumping becomes almost an instinctive action.

Basic position

The jumping position varies from the flatwork position so that the rider can maintain balance without interfering with the horse's own action and balance. The rider needs to move with the horse at take off, in the air and on landing.

To allow this greater range of movement, the stirrup lengths are shorter closing the angles at the hip, knee and ankle. The rider needs flexibility at hip and knee so that the body can fold at the appropriate times.

The knee and thigh come into closer contact with the saddle to give stability. The heel is stretched down to give the rider balance through the knee, leg and heel. The ankle joint acts as a shock absorber and so should be flexible and supple.

Figure 1 showing the position for flatwork.

Figure 2 showing the jumping position on the flat, closed angles of hip, knee and ankle.

Figure 3 showing position over a jump. The flexibility at the hip allows the body to move with the horse.

Preparation

The rider starts training by practising the jumping position to supple the hip, knee and ankle joint. The muscles in the thigh, back of the calf and the lower back need time to become accustomed to the new 'style'. The rider needs to learn the 'new' balance, which is totally different from riding on the flat.

The stirrups are usually taken up two holes, but this can vary from one to four holes depending on the rider's physique, security, comfort and the cut of the saddle. The rider can primarily practise the jumping position during flat work in walk, trot and canter. Hacking out with shorter stirrups (providing the stirrup length is not too short and the horse is quiet and well-behaved) can improve and strengthen the rider's jumping position. Stirrups will normally be at least one hole shorter for hacking, so try riding another hole shorter.

The rider should feel that the position can be maintained without struggling or losing balance. The ankle joint should feel 'bouncy' as though it is moving with the movement of the horse. If the ankle joint feels stiff or hard, it must be made supple with exercises.

Exercises

One exercise to help the rider improve the balance can be practised with the stirrups at flat work length. With the horse in walk, the rider stands up in the stirrups and, holding onto the neck strap or the horse's mane, stretches the legs and lowers the heels. This should be practised on a quiet horse in an enclosed area.

There are exercises that can be practised at home to help supple the joints, stretch and strengthen the muscles.

1. To supple the ankle joints, stand on a piece of wood or thick book about 7 cm (3 ins) high and lower the heels to the ground. Then, holding onto a chair or something stable, raise the body until the heels are a little higher than the toes. Then lower the body until the heels touch the ground again.

2. To strengthen the thighs; place the heels, with legs slightly apart, on a block of wood or book again about 7 cm high. Slowly lower the body by bending at the knees. Keep the back straight and head looking up and forward.

3. To strengthen and supple the hip joints, place the feet flat on the ground, legs apart, and slowly lower the body into the jumping position. Keep the back straight and the head looking forward. Hold onto a chair if this helps.

4. To stretch the thigh and calf muscles, place the heel of the foot on a step with the toe pointing upwards. Place the hands on the *thigh* of the leg and slowly bend the other leg at the knee.

Practise all these exercises slowly and with care. It is better to improve the muscles, tendons and ligaments gently over a period of time than cause any strains by jerky, fast movements.

These exercises together with practice, practice and more practice on a horse will improve the rider's suppleness and security. The rider can also learn in more detail exactly when, how and why the position changes relative to the horse.

The Phases Of The Jump

When thinking about a single fence, there are five phases to consider - the approach, the take off, in flight, the landing and the getaway or recovery. For a course there is also the 'track' between the fences. This is just as important as the other phases. Often if the track is ridden badly this can influence the approach and take off.

The Track

The track is the line from the beginning of the course to the first fence, between the fences and from the last fence to the finish. Between fences the rider needs to keep control of the horse's direction and pace. The horse should be forward going, but steady in a regular, constant rhythm.

The track includes the turns before and after the fences. The turn before a fence is a vital part of jumping. The turn must be judged so that the horse is ridden onto a straight line of approach.

To achieve this the rider first assesses how the horse manoeuvres around turns. Some large, long-backed horses, take time and space to turn corners. Others, particularly small, agile horses, turn on a proverbial sixpence. The rider learns to allow more space for turning the larger horse and to control the smaller agile animal around the turn with the inside leg and outside hand.

The rider should look at the fence before the turn and mentally calculate the size of the turn to make a good line of approach.

If the turn is not ridden correctly and is too shallow or too large, the rider may have to 'wiggle' the horse into a straight line. This can take up precious space and the horse may not be truly straight at the take off point.

The rider

The rider adopts a light, slightly forward seat (the rider is sitting up but with the shoulders slightly forward in front of the hip line). This allows the horse freedom of movement whilst at the same time the rider is able to control the speed of pace.

The rider maintains this position with the weight down the legs into the ankles and heels *without the leg and knee gripping tightly*. The rider can then use the lower legs on the horse, which is almost impossible if the knees are rigidly holding on with a vice-like grip.

The five stages of a single fence

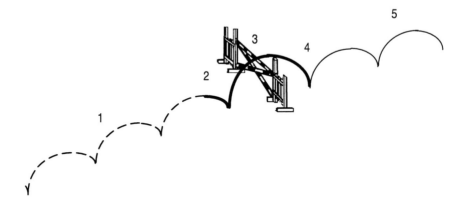

(1) The Approach

The line of approach starts after the turn, about three to six strides away from the fence. If the turn has been ridden well the horse will be positioned straight and at the centre of the fence.

The horse

As the horse approaches the jump he balances his body to lighten the forehand, building up the energy in the hindquarters.

The rider's position

The rider sits quietly for the last few strides maintaining the impulsion with the legs in contact with the horse's sides, without disturbing the horse's concentration on the fence. The rider should remain relaxed and be thinking forwards and over the fence. If the rider 'freezes' the last few strides, this will convey fear to the horse and stifle his enthusiasm. The rider needs to think positively, smile, relax and enjoy.

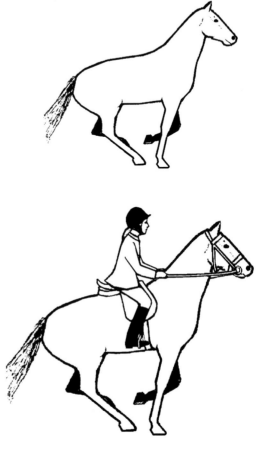

The slightly forward seat is maintained with the hands inviting the stretch forward by a relaxing of the shoulders and arms.

The rider who sits bolt upright has a tendency to be left behind over the fence. The rider who sits too far forward will be insecure should the horse stop.

(2) The Take Off

Many riders worry about the striding before a fence and become anxious about the correct take off point. **It is much more important to position the horse on the straight line and to ask him for a correct pace.** If the rider has ridden the approach correctly, in most cases the horse will sort the jump out himself. The rider should sit quietly and let the fence 'come to the horse'.

The horse

The front legs take off first. The horse stretches his frame and pushes off with the hind legs to propel himself and the rider over the fence.

The rider's position

The rider folds from the hips, bringing the shoulders forward whilst keeping the weight down and into the lower legs and heels. The back and shoulders are straight, the head looking forwards and over the fence. The hands begin to move forwards allowing the horse to stretch his neck.

(3) In flight

The horse

In flight the horse **bascules**, that is he raises his shoulders and stretches his neck to give the feeling of arching his back.

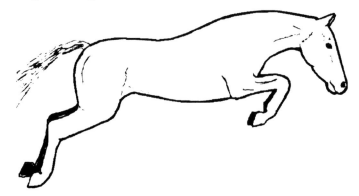

The rider's position

The rider maintains the fold keeping in balance with the horse. The lower legs with the heel down, remain steady and firm to give security.

The shoulders should remain straight and level. The back should be straight or even very slightly hollowed. Think about keeping the head up looking forward; this will help the shoulders and back. Rounded shoulders unbalance the rider and impede the movement.

The elbows should be kept in; they should never shoot out at right angles to the body. The arms with elbows bent should be free to move, allowing the horse to stretch and lower his head and neck. Keeping the elbows into the body also helps to keep the back straight.

The hands should follow the horse's movement. There are various schools of thought on exactly where the hands should go. In practical terms it really does depend on the horse. Horses are all different and riders have to be adaptable.

- On most horses with a medium head carriage the hands can travel forward halfway down the neck.

- When a horse carries his head high the hands can move a little lower.

- With a horse who jumps with his head and neck low, the hands can move a little higher towards his ears encouraging the horse to carry himself more correctly over the jump.

The important point is that the position is sufficiently strong, established and balanced so that the hands are free to allow the horse his movement and *to keep a contact*. A rider who has to balance by laying the hands on the horse's neck will not be able to allow or keep a controlled contact on the horse's mouth.

(4) The Landing

The horse

The horse lands with one front leg taking the weight. The concussion of landing is absorbed by the horse's foot, pastern and fetlock joint with the energy travelling up through the leg and into the shoulder.

The rider's position

The rider begins to return to the normal position with the shoulders coming back into balance. The concussion is absorbed by the rider's ankle and knee joints. The legs should remain in contact with the horse's sides ready to encourage the horse to balance himself and pick up his stride. The hands come back reflecting the shortening of the horse's neck enabling the rider to keep contact and control.

The rider really needs to maintain the balance at this point. Landing with a thump on the saddle is not doing the horse any favours. The rider's legs should stay in the same position.

(5) The Getaway or Recovery

The horse

The other front leg (usually the leading leg) touches the ground followed by the hind legs. The horse's body swings over the front legs and the hind legs push the horse forwards.

The rider's position

The rider should now return to the slightly forward seat.

The getaway or recovery is often the line to another fence. (The rider should be *thinking* of the next fence before landing at the first one.) Once the horse has landed and has collected himself, the rider steers the course, controlling the pace ready for the next jump.

The approach

The take off

In flight

The landing

The recovery

Pace

The rider needs to ask for, and maintain, an active but steady pace. This is where the flatwork schooling is put into effect; *improved flatwork helps the jumping*. The rider should learn *to use the ability and knowledge gained on the flat to improve the jumping*.

So many riders on entering a jumping arena seem to forget their flatwork expertise. The rider should learn to use the half-halt to control the horse's pace; use their legs, seat and body to direct the horse and to ride correct turns and straight lines.

Training for the Stage II

By the time the student is considering applying for the Stage II, the basic jumping position should be well established. Training needs to include jumping as many varied courses as possible. Negotiating a course of fences is very different to jumping single jumps. The skill of course jumping needs to be learnt. Courses of six to eight jumps, with various types of fences and different fillers, should be included in the training.

In most Stage II Examinations the course will be set out and the fences numbered. Occasionally though, the Examiners will request that the candidates jump a course of their own choosing over the fences. Training should therefore include a course of fences that can be approached and jumped from either direction so that the student can make up their own route.

Jumping at Stage II

Depending on the timetable, the jumping session is either taken immediately after the flatwork, later before the lunch break or in the afternoon. At the appointed time the riders will be taken to the outside arena for the jumping. Only in severe weather conditions will the course be inside. The fences will be no higher than 0.76 metres or 2 feet 6 inches. A change of rein will be required at some point.

All the riders will need a short whip. Body protectors are not compulsory but if any rider wishes to wear one this should be mentioned to the Examiners.

Each rider will normally jump two of the school horses, allocated by the Instructor in charge, over the same course. Before jumping the riders are asked to warm up the horse in the arena and requested to jump a practice fence two or three times.

Inspecting the Course

It is essential that all candidates walk the course before their jumping session. If possible, candidates should do this before the actual Exam starts. Plan to arrive at the Centre early, in time to inspect the course two or three times.

Look for the line of approach to the centre of each fence. Try sighting along this line taking an obstacle outside the course as a point of reference.

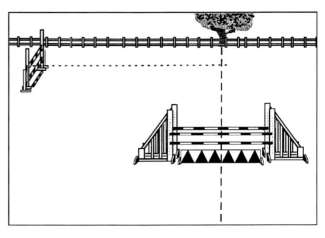

Look at the centre of the jump and a point of reference, the tree; this will indicate the approach line. It will also help the rider, when riding, to think over and beyond the fence. Walk along the line from

the first fence until a line for the second fence is reached.

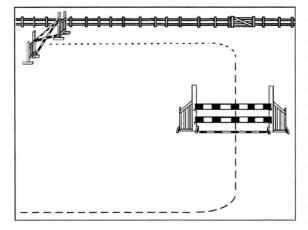

The line of approach to fences is one of the most important points that the Examiners will be assessing. The line must be straight towards the centre of each jump. The rider can then use the space to judge the turns accurately so that each line of approach can be straight towards the centre of each fence.

Here the focal point is the left hand post of the gate.

The jump must be taken in the centre. No angled jumps, fancy turns or twists.

This line of approach is at an angle and if ridden will mean a very tight or awkward turn to negotiate the next fence.

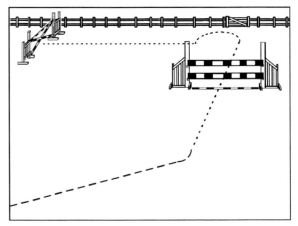

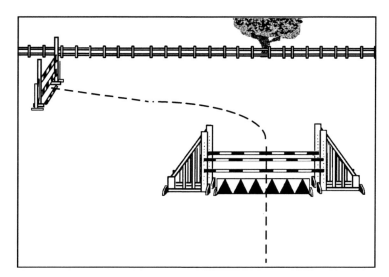

Here, though the first fence approach is straight, the turn is too quick and consequently the line towards the second fence is crooked. The second fence will either be jumped at an angle or near one of the posts. If the horse is not set up for the second fence he may even feel he cannot jump it and run out.

Although there is a great temptation to cut in (each fence seems to act as a magnet drawing both horse and rider towards it), the rider should use as much space as the line of approach allows.

The Course

Once the rider has inspected the fences, the course itself should be considered as a whole. It may help to make a rough plan on a piece of paper. This will help the rider to judge the track, turns and lines of approach and may help in memorising the course. Though riders will not fail for taking the wrong course, it can put both horse and rider off their stride.

The whole course is jumped from canter with periods of trot to enable the rider to change the leading leg. The horse must be under the control of the rider, progressing at an *active,* balanced, rhythmical pace. Taking a jump at too slow a pace is as dangerous as taking it too fast.

Ideally the horse should jump the fences within his stride, without having to take a long leap or a small half pace before the fence. If the rider sets up the approach and pace correctly, this will help the horse to judge the fence.

There may be times when the horse jumps a fence a little too far away or too close. If the rider sits correctly and does not interfere with the horse's action there should be no problem.

For the change of rein the horse should be brought forward to trot and, after a few strides, asked for the transition to canter on the correct leg.

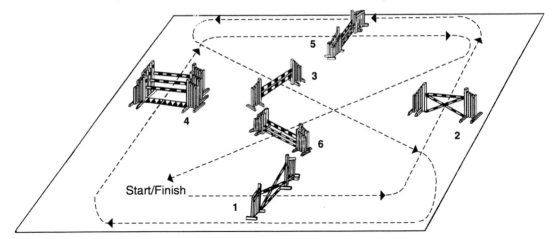

Figure 8: Example of a Jumping Course

The rider whilst keeping the horse active should take time to jump the course, using the space available to help set the horse up for each fence. Many candidates fail on the jumping section because their line of approach and turns are too tight and dangerous.

The Examiners will be assessing the rider's ability to ride a course of jumps as much as their riding position over the fences.

Exam Tips

In the warm up period, assess the horse by checking his manoeuvrability around corners. Ride some short bursts of lengthening stride at canter; this will encourage the horse to be more forwards going over the fences.

If the horse does knock a fence or pole down, do not look back. The Examiners will not penalise you for a knocking down a fence, provided you have presented the horse at the jump correctly.

If the horse should stop at a fence or run out, you must take the fence again, this time with stronger driving aids. If the horse has run out, changing the whip to the side in which he escaped may help.

If the horse refuses again then you must use the whip and chastise him. Do not become flustered, keep calm and ride the horse to the best of your ability.

Most important of all, smile! Relax and the horse will relax too and work more efficiently. With good instruction, regular practice around courses, preparation and a relaxed positive attitude on the day each, candidate will succeed.

CHAPTER 9
Care Section

The Horse Knowledge and Care at Stage II covers a wide variety of subjects. Some of these, as a continuation from the Stage I, demand a deeper knowledge and a greater degree of understanding. Other topics, such as Fittening and Roughing Off, are introduced for the first time.

The Care section includes Practical, Practical Oral and Theory sessions lasting about an hour each. Lungeing is also classed as part of the Care section and for this candidates are allowed fifteen minutes only. The Practical section includes preparing a horse for travelling and for a show or competition. The Practical Oral covers such subjects as clipping and types of clip whilst the Theory includes discussions on feeding and fittening. For the Lungeing, candidates will be expected to check the fitting and condition of the lungeing equipment and to lunge a quiet horse.

Horse Behaviour

Psychology was covered extensively in Stage I, but this is so essential to working with and handling horses that the subject will again be included in the Stage II. Candidates are strongly recommended to revise the section on psychology from the Stage I book.

Revision

Characteristics and instincts, body language, sounds, the importance of correction and reward, basic handling, approaching a horse.

Equine Perception

The horse perceives the external world through his senses of sight, hearing, taste, touch and smell. A horse's senses are, in many ways, different from and keener than humans.

Hearing

Equine hearing is keen. The external portion of the ear or pinna is large and kept erect. This increases the amount of sound waves that can be caught and directed into the inner ear. The ears are also very mobile. The horse has the ability to move each ear independently in all directions making it possible to pick up sound from a wide area.

Sight

The horse's eyes are positioned on the side of the head as with most prey rather than to the front as with predators. The horse has a greater peripheral vision with the ability to see all round him for enemies. This field of vision is increased by the movement of the horse's head; he will often turn, lower or raise his head to focus on an object with both eyes (bifocal).

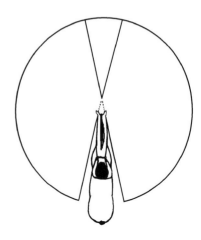

It is not certain whether horses see in colour but they can see different shades. They are often startled by a sudden movement, which humans cannot see.

Taste

The horse does have a sense of taste, testing food before swallowing it. He will also remember the taste of certain foods; rejecting those he does not like either by separating them in the food with his muzzle, or by dropping them out of his mouth.

Touch

The horse is sensitive to touch with his whole body, being aware of heat, cold, pain and pleasure. The part of the body that the horse actually *uses* for touch is the muzzle, which is covered in fine hairs connecting to nerves. The horse uses his muzzle by moving it to and fro; for example, when he sifts through his food or to 'feel' the grass when grazing.

Smell

This can be one of the strongest senses. Horses may often detect something by smell even before they see it. Smell is often used to recognise something familiar as well as sensing for danger. For instance, horses will often sniff at another horse's droppings.

My horse once refused to load into his brand new trailer. I could not understand this, as he was always excellent at loading and had never shown any hesitation before. I did notice however that whenever he was led to the ramp he would stop and sniff strongly. So I had an idea. I took some shavings from his stable, rubbed the trailer walls with a handful and put the rest on the floor. The next time he was introduced to the ramp, he sniffed and then walked straight in. I can only surmise that the scent was unfamiliar to him and, though he was used to trailers, his sense of smell was warning him of a possible threat.

Characteristics and Instincts

As well as his senses the horse reacts to influences that have been inherited from generations of his wild ancestors. For instance, he knows that keeping with the herd is vital for his survival. A horse on his own is easy prey; being one amongst many gives a greater chance of escape.

As well as his inherited traits, the horse also learns to associate situations with either pleasure or pain. The management and handling given to the foal or young horse will influence his behaviour in similar circumstances for years afterwards.

Horse Management

Trying to understand how the horse sees the world and realising this difference in perception is the basis of good handling and care. Handlers increase their proficiency by observation and experience. They learn to recognise the horse's body language and sounds so that they can anticipate his behaviour and reactions in different environments.

The horse at grass

In his natural environment the horse feeds on vegetation with the herd, wandering over the grasslands in search of food. The dominant stallion leads the herd to food and water and gives warning of impending danger. The rest of the herd has a 'pecking order', so that those higher up the order have the pick of the food, the first drink at the water hole.

In the domesticated animal this pecking order is still in operation. Seniority is usually decided by fighting or a show of aggression, and it is not always youth and strength that wins. Older horses, who can be quite assertive, may often be high up in rank.

This order of dominance can cause problems, especially when new members are introduced to the herd. Often a new horse or pony will take weeks or a couple of months to find his place. He may stand alone, dejected, picking at his food and possibly losing condition. More seriously, new horses are often kicked or bitten and suffer injury.

New horses should be introduced to herd members gradually. For the first few days the new horse should be turned out into a paddock with one or two quieter horses. Gradually over a period of weeks he can be turned out in the field with a few more of the herd. The different members of the herd will become familiar with the new horse and accept him.

There are other times when this dominant trait can cause problems, even with familiar members of the herd. Feed times for horses kept permanently at grass can be a particularly dangerous period. The horses are anxiously waiting round the area where the food is placed; there are kicks and squeals with the senior horses pushing to the front. The food should be placed quickly and quietly in the field, with enough space between the buckets or the piles of hay so that each horse is well out of kicking distance.

There should also be one extra feed or pile of hay for every six horses or ponies, so that they all have the chance to eat.

The Horse in the Stable

The domesticated horse has been taken from his natural environment and stuck in a stable with four walls. He is separated from his herd and fed on dry, manufactured foods at intervals during the day. Humans are constantly entering his box, grooming him and tacking him up for work.

Most horses accept this situation having become familiar with it from birth or soon afterwards. (Handling the foal is an important part of managing the adult horse.) Some horses though, either through bad handling or treatment, exhibit behaviour within the stable which the handler needs to recognise.

For instance in the stable, if the horse has his ears flat back when the handler approaches the door it would be a warning. If the horse then swings his hindquarters round to the door, he definitely does not want to be disturbed. Knowing how to deal with these situations is part of becoming a competent handler. In this case it would be wise not to enter the box. Instead, try to entice the horse's head round to the door by calling the horse's name and talking quietly to him. The promise of a treat may be successful. If not, find someone more experienced, preferably someone who knows the horse, to deal with the situation. It is dangerous for anyone who is nervous to enter the box of a horse who is frightened, aggressive or in a bad temper.

Another problem is when a horse or pony is difficult to catch in the box. He will keep swinging around out of reach, not actually threatening with his hindquarters, but evading the handler by turning his body so that his head and neck cannot be approached. This could be a sign that he will also be difficult to catch in the field. Some horses do give up after a while if the handler is calm and perseveres. Some horses or ponies may need their headcollar leaving on for periods in the box and out at grass. Though leaving the headcollar on in the stable or out in the field is not ideal, as the horse can become caught up and injured, over a short period of time it can help to train the horse and make him easier to catch.

Recognition of body language

The good handler learns from experience to recognise the horse's body language, anticipating how the horse will react to situations which can then be dealt with competently.

When a new horse is brought into the yard, he will often be nervous or frightened. This is new territory for him; he does not know the other horses; the surroundings are unfamiliar.

He will show his nervousness in several ways, his head will be held high, eyes wide, ears pricked, nostrils flared possibly blowing. His body will be upright; tense, ready for flight. He may dance round and possibly pass some droppings. His breathing may be rapid and shallow, his flanks heaving slightly. He may sweat and become agitated; he may quiver or tremble.

He should be taken to a quiet area of the yard and if possible given some hay in a net. The handler should remain calm, talking to him and patting him, until he is ready to be put into his stable.

Even horses familiar with the yard can be nervous. Different noises or smells, unusual activity within the yard, if his routine is upset, a visit by the Vet, all these can make a horse nervous. A calm, confident handler is essential. A nervous, frightened, flustered groom will only strengthen the horse's fears.

Talking to the horse in a calm but firm voice helps. The words are not important; it is the confident way in which they are spoken that will reassure him. The power of the human voice can have dramatic effects. At the same time patting or stroking the horse's neck will eventually quieten him.

Handling and Care

Handlers can influence a horse's behaviour from the time of birth by training and care. Some unfortunate animals learn fear and pain through cruelty or sheer ignorance and this can be a life-long memory influencing the horse's behaviour towards his fellow creatures.

Most horses fortunately are brought up with love, understanding and, most importantly, discipline.

All horses must be taught the principle of **correction and reward**. With fairness and consistency all horses learn to obey and respond to their handlers and riders, creating a harmonious working relationship that can result in mutual love and respect.

The horse must learn to trust the handler or, more correctly, the handler must gain the horse's trust by sympathetic understanding and by teaching the horse discipline through correcting bad behaviour and rewarding good.

Breeds and Types

There are many different pure breeds and mixed breeds of horses around the world. These developed characteristics according to their environment and the need for survival. The horse, as we know it today, evolved from a tiny animal that roamed the earth millions of years ago.

Fossil remains of the earliest ancestor of the horse (*Eohippus* or Dawn Horse) have been discovered in both Eurasia and America. The Eurasian species died out and the true evolution of the modern day horse apparently began in North America.

A descendant of *Eohippus* spread from North America to Europe, Asia, South America and Africa across the land bridges before they were submerged. The species in North America became extinct, for reasons that are still in doubt, and the horse did not exist there until the Spanish reintroduced it in the 16th century.

It took some 60 million years for *Eohippus*, the little fox-like animal with padded feet, four toes on the front feet and three toes on the back, to evolve into modern day horse (*Equus caballus*).

The Arab is the oldest pure-breed and the one that has had most influence on other breeds throughout the world. Originating from the Middle East, possibly as early as 5000 BC, the Arab's characteristics of speed, endurance, toughness and fine features have played a vital part in developing stock throughout the centuries. Even today the Arab is being used to improve the blood of many strains.

During the 17th century many oriental breeds, Arabs, Turks and Barbs were imported into Britain to improve the native stock. The British Thoroughbred itself is descended almost exclusively from three great stallions imported during the 17th and 18th centuries, namely the *Darley Arabian*, the *Byerley Turk* and the *Godolphin Barb*.

The Arabian strain has also played its part in influencing many of the native Mountain and Moorland breeds of Great Britain.

Native Mountain and Moorland Breeds

Some of the native breeds found in Great Britain date back to Prehistoric times, some stem from Celtic stock, whilst others originated during the Roman or Medieval periods. Most of these lines are not completely pure bred from ancient times, but are also influenced by the addition of other blood.

Characteristics of the Nine Native Mountain and Moorland Breeds of the United Kingdom

Name	Origin	Height	Colour	Physique	Use	Features
Shetland	Scotland; the Shetland and Orkney Islands. Dates from circa 500BC..	Around 9 hh up to 10.2 hh.	Black or brown and piebald or skewbald	Small head and concave face, short ears. Strong compact back	Children's pony, riding and driving	Hardy with a thick winter coat and full mane and tail. Can be very stubborn and wilful
Highland	An ancient breed possibly Celtic, from the Western Isles and the Mainland of Scotland	From 12.2 to 14.2 hh.	Varying shades of dun with dorsal stripes and zebra markings. Also black, brown or grey	Strong powerful body and legs	Riding, pack animals, children's pony	Strong and hardy with a docile nature. Two types-Island (Western Isles) and Garron (Mainland)
Fell	Western Pennines	From 13.2 to 14 hh.	Black, bay or brown	Sturdy with strong legs and good bone	Riding, trekking and driving	Hardy, strong with stamina. Feathers on legs, long mane and tail
Dale	Ancient breed possibly Celtic. From area of north-eastern England	Around 14 hh. to 14.2 hh.	Black, brown or bay occasionally grey	Strong sturdily built Cob type	Riding, trekking and driving	Placid nature. Feathers on legs and full mane and tail
New Forest	New Forest, Hampshire. Ancient origins but with additions of other blood including Arab and Thoroughbred	12 - 14.2 hh.	Any colour except piebald, skewbald	Two types: A lighter build under 13.2. B heavier build between 13.2 - 14.2 hands	Riding, jumping	Pleasant nature, hardy and versatile
Dartmoor	Dartmoor, Devon. Mixed with Exmoor and other blood	Up to 12.2 hh.	Black, brown or bay but not coloureds	Small head, strong body	Riding, driving, children's pony	Hardy, good stamina. Thick mane and tail
Exmoor	Ancient breed from Prehistoric times. Exmoor, Somerset and Devon	12-12.2 hh.	Bay, brown or dun with a mealy muzzle (lighter in colour) and a toad eye (lighter shading round the eyes)	Strong and powerful frame	Riding, children's pony	Hardy, strong. Thick winter coat
Connemara	Western Ireland	13-14.2 hh.	Predominantly grey, some black, brown or bay	Small, fine head. Sloping shoulder, strong back and quarters	Jumping, riding and driving	Pleasant nature. Hardy and strong
Welsh	**Five distinct divisions.**					
Section A Welsh Mountain Pony	Welsh mountains. Has mixtures of Oriental/Arab blood	Up to 12 hh.	Any colour except piebald or skewbald	Small, fine head with concave face. Good length of neck and sloping shoulder	Show pony, children's ride and breeding stock	Attractive appearance and movement. Strong, sturdy and spirited
Section B Welsh Pony	Additions of Welsh Cob and Thoroughbred blood	Up to 13.2 hh.	As in Section A	A little more heavily built than Section A	Riding, driving	Pleasant nature and active movement, more of a riding pony than Section A.
Section C Welsh Pony Cob	Similar to a small section D	Exceeds 12 hands but not 13.2	Colours as Section A	Cob type pony	Riding and driving	Good action, stamina. Fine feathers on legs
Section D Welsh Cob	With mixtures of oriental blood	Around 15 hh.	Colours as section A	Strong and powerful	Driving, jumping, riding and breeding stock	Strong with good stamina. Feathers on legs
Section E	Geldings only from above sections. Means of identifying non-breeding stock	Heights as in appropriate sections. Section D unlimited	Colours as section A	Powerful, hardy and strong	Riding, driving, jumping	As other sections

In addition to the Thoroughbred and the native Mountain and Moorland breeds, there are other breeds within the British Isles.

From the combination of Arab and Thoroughbred blood comes the Anglo-Arab, a cross that exhibits many of the finer features and characteristics of these two great strains. The **Shire,** the largest horse in Britain, is reputed to be descended from the 'Great Horse of England' of medieval times. The heavy **Clydesdale** from Scotland dates from the mid 18th century, when additions of Flemish blood were added to the native strain. The smaller **Suffolk Punch** dates from the early 16th century. Curiously enough every member of this breed now in existence, can trace its ancestry back in an unbroken line to one horse born in 1760. The **Cleveland Bay,** an ancient breed from Northern England and in particular Yorkshire, claims to be the oldest established breed of English horse. The **Irish Draught** is thought to have descended from the Medieval war-horse with additions of European blood. The **Hackney** contains Arab blood, being descended from the 'Darley Arabian' and the now extinct breed, the Norfolk Trotter or Roadster. The relatively new strain, the **British Warmblood,** dates from the 1970's and is a mixture of European Warmbloods and Thoroughbred horses born in Britain.

Hot, Cold or Warmbloods

Horses are referred to as hotbloods, coldbloods or warmbloods. Coldbloods are usually heavy, draught types such as the Shire or Clydesdale; whereas hotbloods originate in the East; Arabs, Barbs, Thoroughbreds. Warmbloods are a mixture of hot and coldbloodeds such as the Danish or Dutch warmbloods.

Stud Books

To qualify as a *'breed'* the horse or pony must be of pure ancestry and be registered in the Stud Book of that breed. There are two main types of stud book, 'closed' and 'open'. To qualify for registration in a 'closed' stud book, the horse must have both parents already registered in that book as members of that breed. A pure-bred Arab with registered Arab parents would qualify for registration in the Arab Stud Book.

In an 'open' stud book the horse must have parents that are of pedigree stock, but *not necessarily of that particular breed nor of the same breed.* Warmbloods are often descended from different breeds and will be registered in the 'open' stud book of that particular Warmblood Society.

Types

There are many crossbreeds resulting from mixtures and, as these cannot be registered in a Stud Book, they are referred to as **'types'.**

The designation of 'type' derives from the characteristics exhibited by a horse or pony whose ancestry is not known or cannot be proved. If, for example, a certain horse is not a pure-bred but in appearance looks very much like a Thoroughbred this may be classed as a Thoroughbred type. In the case of a pony, it may be a New Forest type.

Many horses and ponies of mixed origin do not exhibit particular traits of any breed and are then referred to as a **hunter type**, a **hack, cob** or **riding pony type**.

Hunter

The hunter type, height from 15.2 hands upwards, can be further divided into either **heavy, middle or lightweight** depending on the build. The best hunters are bred in the United Kingdom and Ireland and are usually a cross between a Thoroughbred and an Irish Draught. These horses may be half or three-quarter bred. A half-bred is a horse with one Thoroughbred and one non-Thoroughbred parent; a three-quarter bred has one Thoroughbred and one half-bred parent.

Hack

A hack is a lightweight type, in height 14.2 to 15.2, and is usually descended from Thoroughbred or Anglo-Arab stock. The Show Hack should be elegant with balanced, extravagant movement and perfect manners.

Cob

A cob type, in height around 15 hands, is distinguished by its sturdy, thick-set build designed to carry weight rather than for speed.

Riding Pony

Extending in height up to 14.2, the riding pony type is descended from a variety of bloods including the Welsh, Arab and Thoroughbred.

When classifying a horse or pony whose ancestry is not pure or is unknown, it is correct to call it a type, either as a breed type or as a hunter, hack, cob or riding pony type.

Exam Tips

The Examiners, as well as asking a few specific questions about horse psychology, will be assessing how each candidate handles the horse. You will need to show that you are competent and quietly confident when approaching, handling and working around horses.

Always make sure you approach the horse correctly, speak to him first to attract his attention; move around him with confidence, quietly and safely. Never walk behind the hindquarters, unless there is enough space to give him a wide berth, and avoid any potentially dangerous situation. Though in practical day to day contact with horses this is all second nature, in an Exam situation it is sometimes the automatic actions that cause hesitation.

If, during one of the practical sessions, you are required to hold the horse for any length of time, make sure that the horse is not ignored but frequently talked to and patted so that he does not become restless.

As part of your preparation for the Stage II you should learn to observe how horses behave, how they show their emotion through body language and verbal sounds.

You should also make a basic study of the common breeds and types of horse so that you are able to describe a horse as a Thoroughbred type or a Cob type. Practise by looking and distinguishing between breeds. In the Examination it is unlikely that you will know for sure whether any certain horse is a pure-bred in which case you will need to describe the horse or pony as a 'type'.

CHAPTER 10

Anatomy

Anatomy is the study of the physical structure of the horse, the skeletal frame and the organs of the body. Not only is this a fascinating subject but through anatomical study the student gains a deeper knowledge and understanding of how the horse is formed and how he uses his structure to move.

Points of the horse

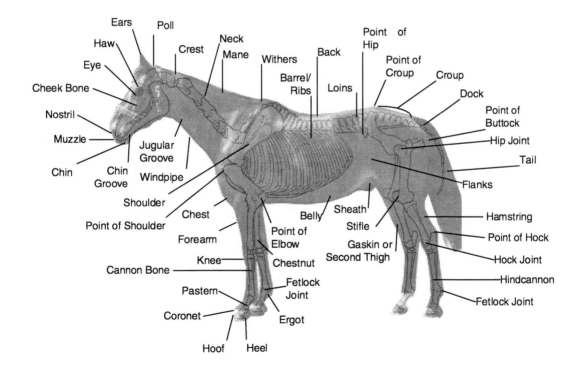

The skeleton is superimposed onto the horse's body to show that the majority of the points refer to areas of bone.

The Skeleton

The skeleton is the **framework** of the body; giving the horse its **shape, protecting** some of the **vital organs** and acting as a solid base to which **ligaments, muscles and tendons are connected**.

The adult horse's skeleton consists of **approximately 205 bones** of different shapes and sizes. It also contains **cartilage** (a gristly substance covering the ends of bones at some joints) and **ligaments** (fibrous bands that connect one bone to another).

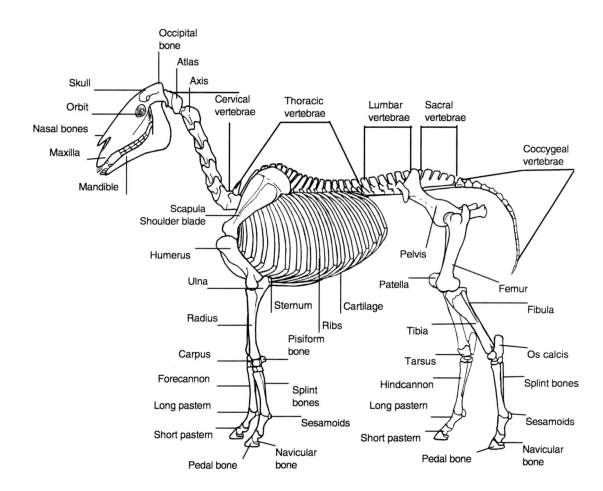

The skeleton of the horse is divided into two main sections:

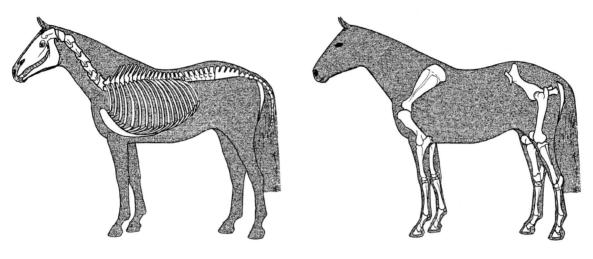

The **Axial -** the skull, the spine, the sternum and the ribs.

The **Appendicular -** fore and hind limbs.

The Axial Skeleton

Skull

The **skull** is a collection of bones many of which are fused together into immovable joints. This provides a solid **protection for the brain, the inner ear, parts of the eye and the nasal passages**. The **cranium** is the area of bone that surrounds the brain.

The eye itself lies in a cavity formed in the skull, the **orbit.** The **zygomatic or supraorbital process,** an arch of strong, prominent bone above the eye, gives further protection.

The **mandible** or lower jaw is hinged between the eye and ear to provide movement for chewing. It is one of the larger bones in the horse's body.

The **maxilla,** or upper jaw, together with the mandible contain the teeth.

The other bones in the skull include the **nasal bones,** and the **occipital bone** (pronounced oxypital) at the back of the skull. The occipital forms a joint with the top part of the neck.

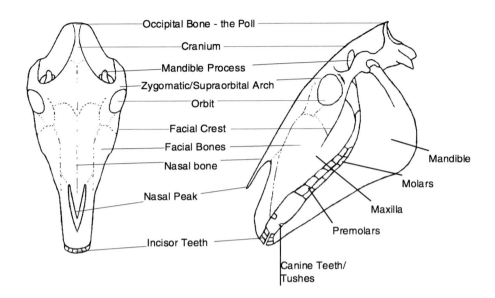

Spine

The spine or backbone is a collection of bones lying one behind the other to form a line from the back of the skull to the tip of the dock. There are *5 sections* within the spine starting from the back of the skull, the cervical, the thoracic, the lumbar, the sacral and the coccygeal (pronounced cockygeel).

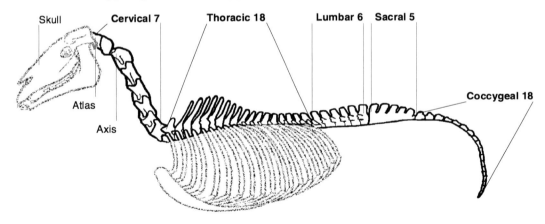

Cervical

There are **7 vertebrae in the cervical section.** The first is the **atlas,** which supports the skull and allows for nodding movements of the head. The second, the **axis,** allows rotational movement.

Thoracic

The **thoracic** section consists of **18 vertebrae**. Connected to each thoracic vertebra is a pair of ribs.

Lumbar

The **lumbar** region has **6 vertebrae.** These are large and rigid to cope with the transfer of thrust from the horse's hind limbs. (In some Eastern breeds, such as the Arab, there are only five lumbar vertebrae. In these cases there is an extra thoracic vertebra.)

Sacral

The **sacral section is made up of 5 vertebrae** that are **fused and joined together** to form part of the hip girdle.

Coccygeal

The **coccygeal is the tail section.** The number of vertebrae here **vary from 15 to 20,** on **average there are about 18.**

The numbers of vertebrae in the sections are **7, 18, 6, 5 and 18.**

The Vertebrae

Most vertebrae are shaped almost like a cross. The **vertebral body** forms an arch - **the neural arch**. Above this is bony projection - the **dorsal spinous process** that provides an attachment for the **supraspinous ligament**. This is one of a group of ligaments and muscles that holds the vertebrae, and therefore the spine, together. The spinous processes also act as anchorage for muscles which hold other bones in place, for instance the muscle that overlies the scapula or shoulder bone. On each side of the vertebra are the **transverse processes.**

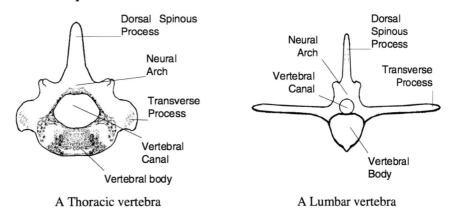

A Thoracic vertebra   A Lumbar vertebra

In different parts of the spine the **vertebrae vary in shape and size** because each section has a **different function and is subjected to different stresses.**

Both the dorsal spinous and the transverse processes vary in size and length. For instance, the processes of the neck vertebrae are much smaller to allow a greater range of movement in this area.

The dorsal spinous processes are longest in the wither region of the thoracic section to provide more anchorage for the muscles. The transverse processes are long and wide in the lumbar region.

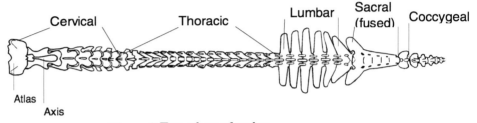

Figure 9:Top view of spine

Between each vertebra is an **inter-vertebral disc**, a flat shaped piece of cartilage, which is slightly compressible.

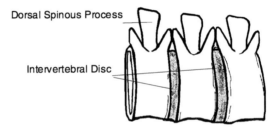

The Functions of the Spine

Besides **connecting the head and limbs** and **providing strength to support the weight of the body**, the spine has another most important function; **it holds in place and protects the spinal cord.**

There is a hole in the middle of each vertebra through which the cord passes. This cord contains the nerves running from the brain to all parts of the body, constituting a most vital area. Any damage to this part can result in paralysis or even death.

The spine or backbone contains;

- the vertebrae and discs that make up the **spinal or vertebral column.**

- the hole within each vertebra called the **spinal or vertebral canal.**

- the tissue containing the nerves, which is called the **spinal cord.** This emerges from the head and brain and extends the whole length of the spinal column. Nerves emerge from the cord, pass between the vertebrae at intervals and onto various parts of the body.

Ribs

The ribs, joined to the thoracic section of the spine, curve round and protect the heart and lung area. The ribs are thin flat bones of which there are **18 pairs.**

There are 8 pairs of 'true' ribs, which **connect directly to the breastbone or sternum** and **10 pairs** of **false** ribs that are **connected to the breastbone by strips of cartilage only.** The ribs are able to move slightly, in and out, to allow expansion and contraction of the lungs when breathing.

Sternum

The sternum or breast bone, a flat, boat shaped bone, forms the lower part of the rib cage.

The Appendicular Skeleton

This contains the four limbs of the horse, the two front legs from shoulder to toe and the two hind legs from hip to toe including the pelvic girdle.

Front Limbs

Each front limb is made up of a large shoulder bone or scapula, the humerus, the radius and ulna, the carpus bones in the knee joint, the cannon, the long and short pastern, the pedal and navicular bones in the foot.

Scapula or Shoulder Blade

The **scapula** or shoulder blade is **not connected by bone to the spine** but **by muscles and ligaments** only. **The horse has no collar bone (clavicle).** In other words the front part of the ribcage and its internal organs are held in a sling of muscle attached to the spine and shoulder blades. This, called the **Thoracic sling,** is designed so that the two scapulae have much more freedom of movement and that concussion, transmitted from the forelegs, is absorbed by the muscles, tendons and ligaments around the shoulder.

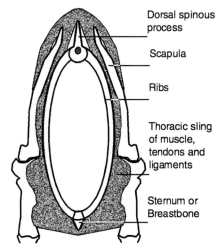

Dorsal spinous process

Scapula

Ribs

Thoracic sling of muscle, tendons and ligaments

Sternum or Breastbone

The scapula starts in the thoracic region of the spine and inclines downwards and forwards to the shoulder joint and **humerus.**

Humerus

Part of the humerus forms the **point of shoulder,** then the bone slants downwards and backwards to the **elbow joint.**

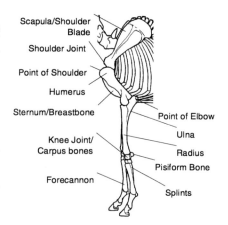

The Radius and Ulna

In the upper foreleg there are **two bones, the radius and the ulna.** The ulna, part of which forms the point of elbow, is a short bone fused to the radius. The longer radius stretches from the humerus down to the **knee joint.**

Knee Joint

The bones in the foreleg have to allow for a lot of movement and the knee joint itself is made up of **7 bones.** Six **carpus bones,** three on top of another three with the **pisiform bone** behind.

Cannon or Shin Bone

Below the knee are the **cannon bone (forecannon or shin bone)** and **two splint bones.** The splint bones start just below the knee joint, on the inner and outer aspect, and stretch down to about two thirds of the length of the cannon.

These splint bones are vestiges of the toes which, through evolution, became unnecessary and diminished in size allowing the horse to develop into the modern one-toed animal.

Pastern

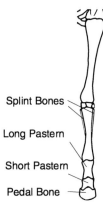

Below the cannon bone is the **long pastern.** The joint between these two bones is the **fetlock joint**. Behind this joint are the **two sesamoid bones.**

Below the long pastern is the **short pastern**. Part of this bone is included in the foot. Between the long and short pastern bones is the **pastern joint.**

The Foot

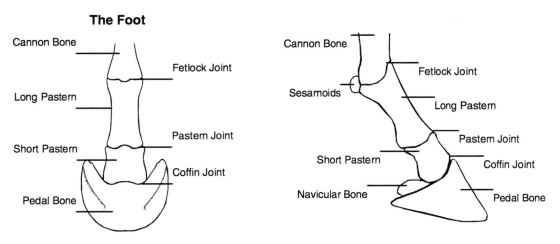

The foot contains part of the short pastern, the **pedal bone** (pronounced peedal) and the **navicular bone**. The joint between the short pastern and pedal bone is the **coffin joint**.

Hind Limbs

The hind limbs start with the pelvic girdle in the sacral region of the spine, and continues down with the femur to the stifle. Below are the tibia and fibula, the tarsus bones in the hock joint, the hindcannon bone, the long and short pastern, the pedal and navicular bones.

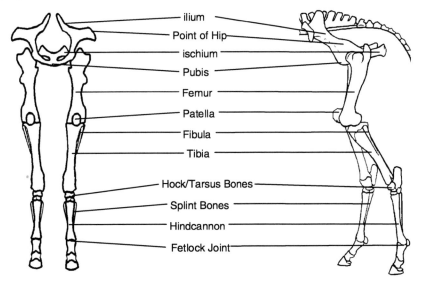

Figure 10:Pelvic bone and hind legs

Pelvic Girdle

The **pelvic girdle** is made up of the **ilium, ischium** and **pubis**, three bones which in the adult horse are fused together. **The pelvis is tightly attached to the lumbar and sacral vertebrae by ligaments (the sacroiliac ligaments).** These areas of connection, pelvis to spine, are called the **sacroiliac joints.** The pelvic girdle, through this close attachment to the spine, is extremely rigid and is able to transfer propulsion from the hind limbs to the trunk of the body. It also offers protection to the uterus in mares.

At the top of the pelvic girdle, the **tuber sacrale** forms the **point of croup.** At the back, the elongated piece of bone, the **ischium,** forms the **point of buttock.**

Femur

The **hip joint** connects the pelvic girdle and the femur. The **femur or thighbone** slopes downwards and slightly forwards from the pelvic girdle. At the lower end of this large bone is the **stifle joint.** Here there is a bone called the **patella,** similar to the knee cap in a human.

Tibia and Fibula

The **tibia** leads down from the femur to the hock. Extending about half the length of the tibia and parallel to it is a smaller bone called the **fibula.**

Hock Joint

The **hock joint** is made up of **6 bones**; five small **tarsus bones** and the larger bone at the back, the **tuber calcis,** or **os calcis**. This forms the point of hock.

Lower Leg and Foot

Below the hock joint is the **cannon or hindcannon** with the **two splint bones** and the **two sesamoid bones** at the back of the fetlock joint. Exactly as in the forelegs the order is the long pastern bone, short pastern bone, the pedal and the navicular bones.

Bone Structure

Bone is living tissue containing blood vessels and nerves. It is composed of proteins and certain minerals, in particular calcium and phosphorus. To encourage proper growth and maintenance, these two minerals should be available in the correct quantities.

There are many different shapes and sizes of bones; some are flat whilst others are round. The long bones, such as the cannon or radius, are structured in the same way, with a hard outer area, the **cortex,** and an inner area of spongy bone, the **medullary cavity**, containing **marrow**. In some bones new red blood cells are manufactured within the marrow.

The bone is covered with by a thin membrane, the **periosteum.** Tendons and ligaments are attached to the bone via this membrane.

Joints

The areas where two bones meet are called joints. Joints allow movement of the bones. The end of the bone at a joint is called the **articular surface** and is composed of denser bone to withstand friction. This surface is covered with **cartilage,** a strong elastic tissue which, by absorbing concussion, guards against possible bone fracture.

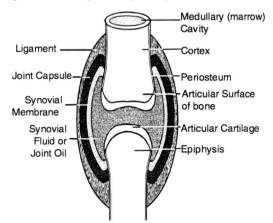

Behind the articular surface is the **epiphysis or growth plate** where the bone grows in length.

The whole joint is contained in a fibrous outer lining that acts like a ligament. Inside this is a **joint capsule.** Both the ligament and joint capsule are attached to the periosteum and give stability to the joint, limiting its movement.

The **synovial membrane** encloses the **synovial fluid** or 'joint oil'. This fluid lubricates the joint and nourishes the cartilage. In prominent bone areas, such as the elbow, these capsules are termed **bursae.**

There are three types of joint.

* **Immovable joints** - as in the skull.
* **Slightly movable joints** - as in the spine.
* **Freely movable joints**.

The last category is itself split into groups:

    1. **Hinge joint** - as in the fetlock.

2. **Pivot joint** - as in the atlas and axis vertebrae in the neck.

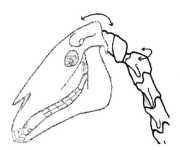

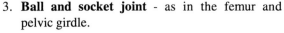

3. **Ball and socket joint** - as in the femur and pelvic girdle.

4. **Plane joint** - as in joints where flat-surfaced bones move over each other for example the carpus bones of the knee.

Ligaments

Ligaments are tough, fibrous bands that connect **bone to bone**, holding them together and in place. They are elastic to a point, allowing normal movement at the joints but not excessive or abnormal action.

The horse has developed another type of ligament; the '**check ligaments**' which connect some bones and tendons. These are present in the fore and hind limbs and, in conjunction with various muscles and tendons, are part of the horse's '**stay mechanism**'. They lock the limbs and joints so that the horse can relax and sleep in a standing position.

Tendons

Tendons connect **muscle to bone** and help to control the movement of bones at joints, and thus the horse's body, to a certain degree. This is shown particularly in both fore and hind limbs of the horse where there are **no muscles below the knee or hock**. All movement of the pastern and foot is transferred by tendons connected to muscles in the upper limbs and body.

The Horse's Evolution

The horse's skeleton has evolved over millions of years and understanding why this evolutionary process took place will aid in the study of the skeleton and its functions.

Eohippus or Dawn horse, a small animal about the size of a fox, had a small head and neck, an arched back and teeth shaped for browsing (eating the leaves from bushes). It had padded feet with four toes on its fore feet and three toes on the hind feet. The most marked change in its evolution was the growth and use of one toe on each foot. The other toes degenerated until only the vestigial splints remained. The toe, corresponding to our middle finger, grew in length and hardened.

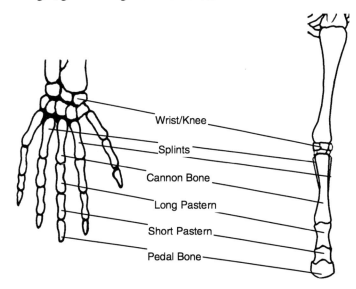

Wrist/Knee

Splints

Cannon Bone

Long Pastern

Short Pastern

Pedal Bone

This adaptation was necessary as the environment changed from a marshy, swampy land to harder ground. The horse could now take longer strides running on its middle toes and, with this extra speed, outrun its predators.

The skull changed shape, growing larger to accommodate a larger brain, and the position of the eyes altered to give greater all round vision. The teeth evolved as the food material altered, from those of the browsing animal to high-crowned teeth for grazing on grass.

The neck became elongated as the body grew larger so that the horse could graze on grass and, when necessary, raise his head higher to look for predators.

So the skeleton of the horse evolved as the environment and type of food changed. The horse became a larger, swifter, one-toed animal with the ability to graze on grass and the speed to escape predators.

Comparison of the horse with the human skeleton

The evolutionary process has developed the equine and human skeleton in various ways, forming structures for different functions. A comparison of these two skeletons shows the relative adaptations made by these changes.

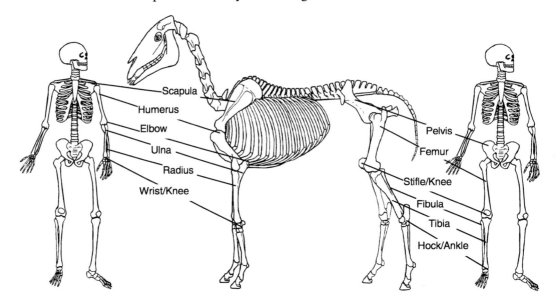

Exam Tips

During this section in the Exam, you will be asked to name a number of bones and possibly to point out their position on a horse. As some bones are not always obvious, for instance the position of the spine from the head to the withers, the whole skeleton needs to be studied carefully.

It is also possible for the Examiner to ask about the function of certain bones - the ribs protect the heart and lungs, the spine houses and protects the spinal cord. You need to know how some of the bones are connected, the difference between the connections of the scapula and pelvic girdle to the spine. There may be questions about the shape of bones or how bones move in conjunction with each other at joints. A practical understanding of the skeleton, how it works and why, is as necessary as the names of particular bones.

Some parts may be a little awkward to remember, so whenever possible relate areas to memorised phrases. For instance for the axis and atlas vertebrae remember that the 'T' in atlas comes before the 'X' in the alphabet or that Atlas was a God in Greek mythology who held up the sky on his shoulders just as the atlas vertebra holds up the skull.

To recall how many true and false ribs there are remember there are more liars in the world (10 false ribs - 8 true). To memorise the difference between ligaments and tendons, which connects bone to bone and which muscle to bone, remember that tendons 'tend on' muscle.

In preparation for this section, use the 'hands on' method on a live horse. Feel where the nasal bones are, feel the strength of the bone between the eyes (the horse will love it if you scratch him there anyway). Run your hand over the bony protuberance above the eye and feel the zygomatic (what a lovely word to get your tongue round) or supraorbital process; its strength and thickness protecting the eye. Follow the line of the spine from the back of the skull to the withers, remembering that this **does not follow the crest** but curves downwards through the neck. Whenever possible, observe the horse's movement; watch how he uses his joints to give him flexibility and motion.

Name	Structure	Function	Notes
Skull	A number of bones fused together	Protection for brain, inner ear, parts of eye and nasal passages	Mandible (lower jaw) Maxilla (upper Jaw) both contain teeth. Nasal bones Zygomatic or Supraorbital process protects the eye Occipital bone forms back of skull and joins top of neck
Spine	Collection of bones, vertebrae, lying one behind the other in a line from base of skull to tip of tail	Housing and protecting spinal cord Attachment for muscles, tendons and ligaments which support the weight of the body Connecting head and limbs	Cervical - 7 vertebrae - Atlas first bone in neck then Axis Thoracic - 18 vertebrae connection with ribs Lumbar - 6 vertebrae Sacral - 5 fused vertebrae part of hip girdle Coccygeal - average 18 vertebrae forming tail section
Ribcage	18 pairs of ribs each connected to a thoracic vertebrae	Protection for heart and lungs	8 true ribs connected to sternum or breast bone directly 10 false pairs connected to sternum by cartilage
Forelimbs Scapula	Shoulder blade - one either side of ribcage	Connected to spine by muscles and ligaments only allows freedom of movement and absorption of concussion	Horse has no collar bone, no fixed connection to spine of forelimbs
Humerus	Upper end forms point of shoulder	Connection of shoulder blade to forelimbs	Lower end joins forelimbs at elbow joint
Radius and Ulna	Upper part of foreleg	Ulna short bone forms point of elbow. Radius long bone stretches to knee joint	
Knee	Carpus bones and pisiform	Joint allowing movement in foreleg	6 carpus three on top of three. Plane joint allows movement. Pisiform bone at back

Name	Structure	Function	Notes
Cannon	Bone of lower leg	Weight bearing bone. Circumference of cannon just under the knee is a guide to the horse's ability to bear weight and do hard work. Often referred to as 'bone' e.g. the horse has 9 inches of bone	Stretches from knee joint to fetlock joint
Splints	Two bones either side of fore and hind cannons	Help to support some of the carpus bones of the knee but real function lost in evolution	In length about two thirds of the cannon bone Vestiges of toes
Sesamoids	Two bones behind Fetlock joint	Provide a groove to hold the tendons of the leg Also acts as part of the 'pulley system' for movement of the lower leg	
Pastern	Two bones in lower leg and foot	Connection between joints of the leg and foot	Long pastern between fetlock and pastern joints. Short pastern between pastern and coffin joint
Pedal Bone	Hoof like shaped bone of foot	Attachment for tendons and ligaments from muscles in the forearm	
Navicular Bone	Bone of foot		
Hind limbs Pelvic Girdle	Three fused bones - ileum, ischium and pubis	Tightly attached to spine allowing transfer of propulsion from the hind legs Protection of uterus	Joined to spine through sacroiliac joints. Ischium forms point of buttock
Femur	Large bone	connects with pelvis at hip joint and with hind leg at stifle joint	
Tibia and Fibula	Tibia larger of two bones from stifle to hock joint Fibula smaller bone	Forms upper part of hind leg	
Patella	Bone in stifle joint	Similar to knee cap in humans	
Hock	Tarsus bones and tuber or os calcis	Joint allowing movement of hind leg	5 tarsus bones and tuber or os calcis at back forming point of hock
Hind leg below hock	Hindcannon with splint bones. Long and short pastern Sesamoids, Pedal bone and Navicular	Similar to fore legs	

CHAPTER 11
Physiology

Physiology is the science concerned with the functioning of the anatomical parts and their relation to each other. With horses, as with other mammals, no single part or organ functions on its own, they all inter-relate with various other organs, coming together to form what is, basically, a miracle of life.

This chapter begins with a description of the main internal organs of the horse's body and continues with the study of the digestive system, its parts and functions.

Main Internal Organs of the Horse

There are various systems in the body which function for specific purposes such as the Central Nervous System or the Circulatory System. Each system is made up of a particular set of organs such as the brain and spinal cord or the heart and blood vessels.

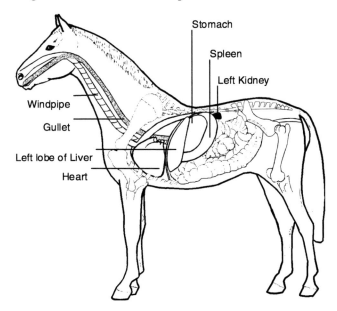

The heart is situated in the chest, slightly left of centre, just behind the elbow. The blood passes into and exits from the heart via the main veins and arteries. The left side of the heart pumps blood round the body whereas the right side of the heart pumps blood to the lungs only. The heartbeat is listened for on the left side because of the situation of the heart and also because this is the side where the greater 'pumping action' occurs.

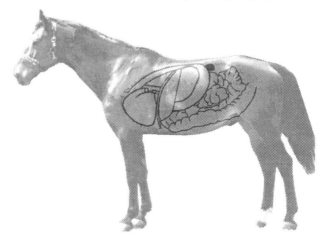

The horse inhales air through the nostrils. This passes through the nasal passages to the windpipe or trachea. The trachea, starting at the jaw, is a tube kept permanently open by rings of cartilage. It travels down to the chest and lungs. The lungs are enclosed within the rib cage and are roughly the shape of the cage itself.

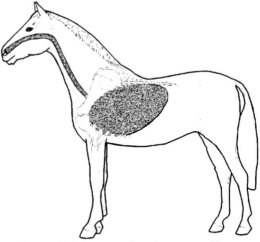

Figure 11:Diagram showing area of lung.

The diaphragm, a cone-shaped sheet of muscle lies directly behind the lungs. The positioning of the lungs close to the stomach emphasises the problems of working a horse directly after a feed, when the efficiency of the lungs and breathing can be affected.

The Digestive System

The digestive system is a muscular tube, divided into sections by sphincters or valves, in which food is digested and made into substances that can be used by the body for its various functions.

A sphincter is a ring of muscle at the opening of a hollow organ; which contracts to close it.

The whole system from mouth to anus can also be referred to as the Alimentary Canal. The term 'gut' can refer either to the whole system or to the intestines only.

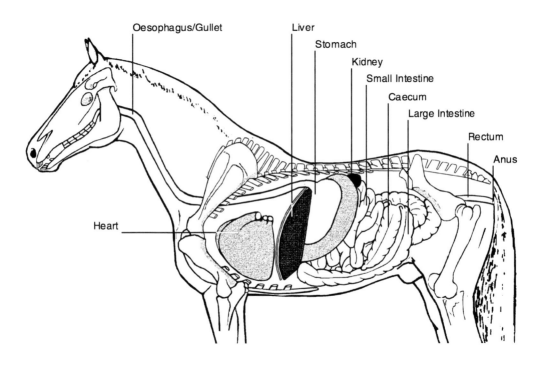

The digestive system starts at the mouth where the horse gathers its food conveying it to the teeth for cutting and chewing.

The gullet, behind or on top of the windpipe, passes from the jaw through the chest area to the stomach. The stomach is situated between the liver and the spleen. (Amongst other functions the spleen acts as a storage organ for blood.)

The kidneys, one either side of the spine, are just behind where the back of the saddle would reach, the loin area.

Muzzle   mobile part of upper lip, feels for and separates food.

Lips   gather the food in towards the mouth.

Incisor Teeth bite the food. In the adult horse there are twelve incisors, six at the front of each jaw, upper and lower.

Tongue   this muscular organ passes the food to the molar teeth at the back of the mouth. It also acts as the primary organ for the sense of taste with taste buds scattered over its surface.

Molars   the back teeth, grind or masticate the food.

Salivary Glands   release saliva into the mouth. This moistens the food, preventing the horse from choking. Saliva also contains enzymes which help in breaking down the food. Food is formed into a ball called the **bolus.**

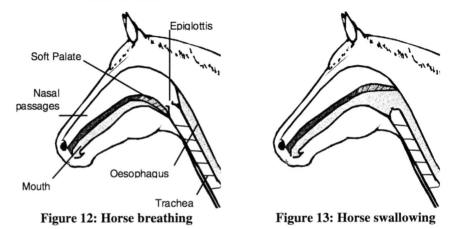

Figure 12: Horse breathing   **Figure 13: Horse swallowing**

As the horse swallows, the bolus is pushed against the **soft palate,** which rises to block off the nasal passages allowing the bolus to pass into the **oropharynx.**

At the same time the **epiglottis,** a thin flap of cartilage, closes like a lid covering the entrance to the upper respiratory tract. This prevents food from passing down the trachea into the lungs.

Oesophagus

Approximate length 1.5 metres (4 feet)

Starting from the back of the throat the oesophagus, or **gullet,** is a **muscular tube**. It is approximately 1.5 metres long and passes through the neck to the stomach. Food is squeezed through it by wave-like, muscular contractions called **peristalsis,** which can be observed when the horse swallows. Horses generally eat with their heads down so the food passes upwards.

The Stomach

Cardiac Sphincter

At the entrance to the stomach is a ring of muscle, the cardiac sphincter (pronounced sfinkter) that acts as a one way valve. So strong is this muscle that food cannot be regurgitated. Horses cannot vomit except in extreme circumstances. This is a disadvantage because the horse cannot eject through his mouth any foreign bodies or foods which, passing on into the digestive system, can cause problems.

Stomach

Average capacity 23 litres (5 gallons)

The stomach is roughly the size of a rugby ball and holds from 18-27 litres (4 to 6 gallons). This is relatively small for such a large animal.

The stomach is also rarely more than two thirds full. In the wild state the horse may need to flee enemies at any time so it is necessary to have a light stomach, not a large one heavy with food.

Gastric juices which include **hydrochloric acid** and the three **enzymes, pepsin, rennin and lipase,** are secreted from glands in the stomach wall. These begin the breakdown of **proteins and lipids (fats and oils).** The muscular contractions of the stomach mix the juices with the food until it is a soft mash called **chyme.**

Food stays in the stomach from 30 minutes to 3 hours depending on the type of food.

Pyloric Sphincter

The majority of feed passes through the stomach after 1 hour into the small intestine via another muscular valve, the pyloric sphincter.

Small Intestine

Approximate total length 23 metres (70 feet) average capacity 63 litres (14 gallons)

This is where the digestive system really gets to grips with the food! The chyme is pushed through this long muscular tube by peristalsis, whilst **fluids containing enzymes** (enzymatic fluids) mix with and break down the food. (Enzymes are groups of proteins that break down food substances.)

Products from the breakdown of **carbohydrates, proteins and fats** are absorbed here through the intestinal wall. These pass into the blood stream and are transported to parts of the body to be used for energy and growth.

The small intestine is divided into three sections.

Duodenum

Approximate length 1 metre (3 feet)

Bile enters via ducts (small tubes) from the **liver.** The bile disperses (**emulsifies**) the fats and oils into smaller droplets to aid the process of digestion. As the horse (in his natural state) feeds almost constantly, so bile is produced and secreted continuously. There is, therefore, no need of a bile storage organ; consequently a horse has **no gall bladder.**

Pancreatic juices, clear alkaline fluids containing enzymes, enter via ducts from the **pancreas. Enzymes** are also introduced from **intestinal glands.**

Jejunum

Approximate length 20 metres (65 feet)

Digestive juices continue to be secreted and mixed with food. Absorption of **amino acids, glucose, minerals and vitamins.** Little finger-like protuberances called **Villi,** along the intestinal wall, allow a greater absorption by increasing the surface area of the intestine. Nutrients pass into the blood stream.

Ileum

Approximate length 2 metres (6 feet)

Digestive juices continue to be secreted and mixed with food. The absorption of nutrients continues.

The small intestine is supported in coils on the left side of the abdomen by the **mesentery,** a double layer of **peritoneum.** Peritoneum is a smooth, moist membrane that lines the intestines and allows them to slide easily against each other. **The mesentery** is attached to the back wall of the abdominal cavity.

The ingesta (degenerated food) now passes through another muscular valve the **ileocaecal valve** into a part of the large intestine called the caecum (pronounced seekum).

Large Intestine

Approximate length 10 metres (33 feet)

This starts with the caecum and includes the large colon, the small colon, the rectum and the anus.

Caecum

Approximate length 1 metre (3 feet)
Average capacity 31 litres (7 gallons)

The cellulose in grass is broken down here by the **bacteria** which live in the caecum. These bacteria are divided into many types; each type deals with a specific food. Any change of feed necessitates an alteration to the numbers in the specific type of bacteria affected. As this takes time, changes in the diet must be introduced gradually to allow new development within the bacteria populations. **Nutrients** and a considerable percentage of **water** are absorbed within the caecum.

Large Colon

Approximate length 4 metres (13 feet)
Average capacity 90 litres (20 gallons)

Bacteria continue to break down foods. Water and nutrients are extracted and absorbed.

This part of the intestine is folded over on itself causing sharp bends. The food matter contained here is bulky and at one particular bend, the **pelvic flexure,** the intestine narrows to create an area that is prone to blockage. This can result in a condition known as impacted colic.

Small Colon

Approximate length 4 metres (13 feet)
Average capacity 16 litres (4 gallons)

Electrolytes (various kinds of salts) and **water** are extracted and absorbed.

Rectum

Waste matter passes from the small colon and forms into balls of dung that are stored here until ready to be evacuated.

Anus

This is a muscular valve or sphincter regulating the evacuation of dung.

Food usually passes through the whole system in about 40 hours but can sometimes take a little longer.

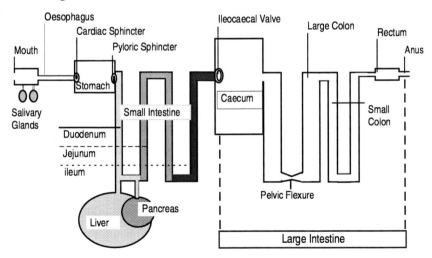

Figure 14:Flow Chart showing relevant parts of digestive system.

Accessory Organs

The Liver

This is a large gland situated in the abdominal cavity between the diaphragm and stomach. (A gland is a cell that produces and secretes substances into the body.)

The liver has many important functions including the production of bile which aids digestion.

Blood containing the substances from the intestines enters the liver via the **portal vein.** These nutrients are then converted into other substances for use around the body, stored for later use or turned into compounds for evacuation.

Because the liver is so necessary to the digestive and circulatory systems, any damage or malfunction within this gland can result in various and serious problems within the body, even resulting in death.

Pancreas

Situated in the abdomen adjacent to the duodenum and spleen, the pancreas produces alkaline fluid secreted into the duodenum. Enzymes within the pancreatic juices help in the digestion of proteins, carbohydrates and fats. The pancreas also produces the hormone insulin that controls the level of glucose in the blood.

Kidneys

Though part of the urinary system, the kidneys are involved in the digestive process. They lie either side of the spine just beyond the back of the saddle area, in the lumbar region. The kidneys filter waste products from the blood. This waste passes down the ureter to the bladder and is excreted as urine.

So the whole digestive system deals with the food taken in by the horse, breaking it down into easily digestible proportions. It extracts the nutrients needed for growth, to maintain warmth and for energy, and evacuates as waste products those substances not required.

Evolution

The horse is a herbivore, a vegetarian grazing on grass and plants. Vegetation can be difficult to digest and, to cope with this, the equine digestive system has evolved over millions of years. It is not a totally efficient system, however, and is prone to a variety of problems.

The horse eats mostly cellulose foods, grass and hay, which are bulky. Cattle, sheep and goats have a large first stomach or rumen where bacteria digest fibre. In the horse, however, the degeneration of cellulose food does not happen until it reaches the large intestine. Thus, bulky matter passes through a majority of the gut in a coarse state. If there is damage to the small intestine, for example through worm infestation, or if the food is particularly dry, blockages can occur resulting in colic.

Digestive Problems

All the separate parts of the digestive system work together and a malfunction in any single portion can result in problems throughout the system.

For instance, if a horse suffers from a tooth problem or his jaw is damaged in some way, the food will not be chewed properly. One consequence of this is **quidding** when the horse dribbles the food from his mouth. The result is a loss of condition through lack of nutrients. Another consequence is a condition known as **choke,** where food not masticated properly becomes lodged in the oesophagus.

Incorrect feeding can also result in a breakdown of the digestive system. There are various types of colic that occur in different parts of the alimentary canal; some can be mild; others can lead to death.

Giving too large a feed of concentrates can lead to distension of the stomach. Feeding dried foods without water can lead to a blockage (known as impacted colic) around the pelvic flexure. An excess of rich food can lead to diarrhoea or effect other systems, even leading to behavioural problems.

It is important therefore, because the horse's digestive system is not totally efficient and quite finely balanced, that the rules of feeding are observed and adhered to strictly.

Comparison of Equine and Human Digestive Systems

The equine and human digestive tracts have evolved in various ways to cope with different lifestyles and feeding habits.

The horse has a relatively small stomach where very little of the food is actually digested. Humans have a relatively large stomach where some of the food is digested.

The major difference is in the length of gut and the make up of the hind gut or large intestine. The equine digestion has to deal with a large amount of cellulose food and does this by having a bacteria population in the caecum.

Man, on the other hand, is omnivorous, being able to eat various foods, but not large amounts of grass or hay. So his gut has evolved without a portion to digest cellulose foods.

Exam Tips

During the Physiology section of the Exam, candidates will be asked to indicate on a horse the location of various organs of the body such as the heart, lungs, kidneys, liver, diaphragm, stomach, intestines. Study the diagrams then practise the 'hands on' method on a living horse. Feel the trachea and the rings of cartilage that keep it open. Watch as food passes through the gullet. Place your hand where the heart is situated and trace with a finger the shape of the lungs. Point to the stomach, kidneys, spleen and liver. This will help in memorising the exact location of these organs. It is not as simple as it looks.

The digestive system needs to be learnt thoroughly, though it is not necessary to know precisely the length of each section. It is more important to know the sequence of the system and to understand how and why it works. Candidates will be asked individually to name and perhaps indicate on a horse certain portions of the alimentary canal.

The Examiner may also ask where certain elements of the digested food are absorbed. Where and for what reasons certain substances are introduced into the system and in which part of the gut the bacteria live.

Compare the information given on the digestive system to the Rules of Feeding, for example having a small stomach the horse can only be fed small quantities. Candidates need to *understand* the functions of the gut and how these are related to the practical, daily routine of feeding the horse.

C H A P T E R   12
Health

One of the most important aspects of horse management is being able to recognise when a horse is suffering from ill health. At times this will be apparent, when there is a wound for instance, but in other cases ill health may only be detected by subtle changes in the horse's normal behaviour.

All horses must be given a close inspection at least once a day. For stabled horses, a quick check is performed as the first duty in the morning and a thorough check given later perhaps when grooming. For grass kept horses and ponies the daily inspection is even more vital to prevent ill health. Problems will then be detected as soon as possible and treatment, together with any necessary nursing, can be given immediately.

Report

When problems are discovered it is important to make a report either to senior staff or to someone in charge. In all riding establishments this is essential so that the horse can be given the appropriate care and attention. He may need to stop work or at least be worked lightly if suitable. It is far better to be safe than sorry; to act quickly before the horse becomes seriously ill.

Revision

Signs of good health in the stable and the field. The thorough check. Basic rules to keep a horse healthy. Signs of ill health in the stable and field. Daily routines and their importance.

A horse can suffer from ill health at any time of his life. In most cases this can be detected by signs shown through the horse's body language and by visible external abnormalities, for instance when a horse has a discharge from his nostrils.

Most handlers, when working around the same horse or horses daily, will become accustomed to their normal behaviour and recognise any differences that may signify ill health. **'Know your horse'** is a cliché resulting from centuries of experience and is an excellent basis for horse care.

The first rule in recognising ill health in a horse is to know the horse's normal behaviour and to be aware of any change in that behaviour. The handler should then make further inspections and checks, which may confirm the horse's condition.

Signs of ill health

There are physical signs that every horse will manifest when he is ill and of which every good handler should be aware.

- **Refuses to eat or drink**.

- Horse is unusually **lethargic**.

- **Ears droopy, eyes dull possibly showing discharge, nostrils showing discharge.**

- **Trembling, shivering with body 'tucked up'** (back arched, tail held tight into hindquarters).

- **Coat stary and dull.**

- Horse is **sweating abnormally** or coat shows **dried sweat marks**.

- **Kicking, biting his sides** or **lying down** and **rising frequently.**

- **Rug,** if worn, is **twisted and torn**.

- **Wheezing, breathing rapidly** or **irregularly, flanks heaving, coughing.**

- **Bedding tossed around** or **made into heap in the middle of box.**

- **Signs** of **kicking walls** and **doors.**

- **Abnormal droppings, too hard, too soft** or **none** at all. Signs of **scouring down hind legs (diarrhoea).**

- Keeping **weight off fore feet** or **pointing a foot** (toe kept on ground heel raised). Refusal to stand on all four feet equally for any length of time.

- In the field the horse **keeps away from herd** and **appears uninterested** in the **grass.**

Temperature, Pulse and Respiration

Once the horse has been diagnosed as being off colour his condition should be further monitored by taking his temperature, pulse and respiration, (TPR).

To make an accurate comparison, the horse's **normal TPR** should first be known. As each horse and pony is an individual, the TPR may be slightly different from the normal average. Readings should be taken when the horse is at rest and relaxed; not just after hard exercise when his temperature, pulse and respiration will increase. Also the readings can vary from day to day depending on such factors as weather conditions. It is important therefore to take readings over a period of a few days when the horse is healthy, in order to obtain the normal results.

The normal readings should be:

Temperature	**38° C or 100.5° to 101.0°F**
Pulse	**36 to 42 beats per minute**
Respiration	**8 to 15 breaths per minute.**

Ponies and young horses tend to have a slightly quicker pulse and respiration rate.

The temperature is taken by inserting an equine thermometer into the horse's anus. The pulse is normally checked from the facial artery under the cheek bone. The respiration can be assessed by watching the movement of the horse's ribcage; one rise and fall counts as one breath. Respiration rate is taken first as taking the temperature or pulse may affect the breathing rate.

Once the normal readings are known these should be written down in the horse's Health record, then if at any time there is a deviation in the TPR, this can be noticed quickly.

The Lame Horse

Thankfully most cases of lameness in horses result from simple injuries or illnesses rather than complicated or unusual ones. For stabled horses, lameness is normally detected first when the horse is taken out of the stable and appears to be limping or at least not putting his weight evenly on all four limbs. Sometimes it is noticeable even whilst the horse is in the stable; the horse may be 'pointing' a foot (usually one of the forelegs).

Hind legs are more difficult to assess as most horses at some time rest a hind. If the same hind is constantly rested though or held continuously off the ground, this would be sign of unsoundness in that limb.

Checking for Lameness

The horse should first be observed **at halt**. His legs should be inspected for heat, swelling and pain.

When the horse shows a lameness, even a slight limp, the first action is to inspect the horse's feet. The feet should be picked out and then checked. The shoes should also be checked. It may be something as simple as a small stone wedged between the frog and the bar of the foot. Though the feet are picked out after the horse has worked, sometimes small stones, pebbles or even a tiny puncture wound can be missed.

If the cause is the shoe, the horse should be seen by the farrier.

At other times there are obvious signs of injury to the leg, swelling, wounds, heat and pain. If the horse is showing signs of pain, or if the person in charge is in any doubt as to cause or severity of the problem, the Vet must be called.

Signs of Lameness

Providing the horse is not in pain; he is then walked on a solid, level surface and observed from the side, front and rear. He should also be turned in both directions; this usually emphasises any unlevelness. *If it is still unclear if the horse is lame he can then be trotted in hand on level ground.*

General signs

- ❖ **Limping** on any leg or **refusal to put the whole weight on a limb.**
- ❖ **Sounds of the hooves on the ground.** If the horse is lame this **will not be a rhythmical - 1, 2, 3, 4, beat at walk** or a **1, 2 beat at trot.**
- ❖ **Length of stride.** The length of stride on the lame leg will be shorter. The horse's stride will be unequal and may appear stilted.

Lameness in a foreleg

The horse will raise his head when the lame leg touches the ground to keep the weight off that leg. He will drop his head when the sound foreleg touches the ground. **Raised head when lame leg on ground - lowered head when sound leg** on ground.

Turns and Circles

The signs of lameness are often more clearly observed when the horse is led in hand around a turn or on a small circle. This should be performed on both reins on soft and hard ground to make a correct assessment.

Flexion Test

This is performed usually by the Vet who will hold each leg up for a minute in turn to 'flex' the joints. The horse is then trotted immediately the leg is released.

Ridden exercise

The horse can further be assessed when being ridden on a level surface. He should be allowed to move freely in a long, low outline without restricting hand pressure. His strides should be forward, equal in length with his hindquarters swinging and the hind legs stepping through underneath his body.

Minor Wounds and Basic Nursing

Horses, because of the work they do, are prone to wounds and injuries that need diagnosing and treating appropriately.

Types of Wound

The first action is to diagnose the type of wound.

Galls

Open or closed wounds, sores, swollen areas. Generally caused by dirty, ill fitting or worn tack, occurring particularly around the girth area behind the elbows.

Grazes

Top layers of skin scraped off. The wound may contain foreign particles which cause infection. Grazes can be caused by a fall.

Bruises (Contusions)

The skin is often unbroken but the blood vessels underneath are ruptured. Possibility of internal injury. Bruises are caused by blows, kicks or falls. Sometimes if there is no swelling, bruises can be hard to detect on a horse.

Lacerations (Torn Wounds)

Rough tears, damage to tissues, high risk of infection. Can be caused by barbed wire.

Incised (Clean Cut wounds)

A cut from a sharp edged implement, a knife or glass for instance, often profuse bleeding.

Punctures

Small entry to wound but can be deep, dirt and grit often become ingrained inside. Risk of infection high.

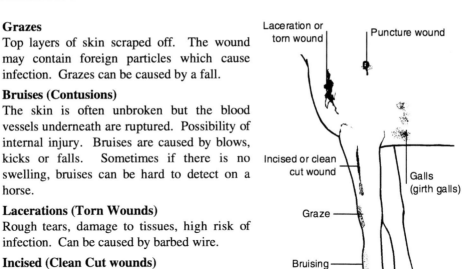

Taking the first letter of each of the wounds, **GGBLIP (Galls, Grazes, Bruises, Lacerations, Incised and Puncture - Gee, Gee, BLIP)** *helps to remember them.*

Basic Procedures

Most small wounds can be dealt with on the spot and provided there is no complications these can be treated quite successfully.

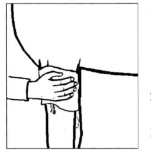

1) **Arrest bleeding**

   A slight loss of blood from a wound is Nature's way of cleaning the area and most simple bleeding will cease within twenty minutes. To stem the blood flow, apply pressure **directly** to the wound by holding a sterile pad or similar material firmly on top of the cut.

2) **Clean the wound**

   Cleaning *is an essential part of treatment as it is vital to avoid infection.*

3) **Dress the wound**

   The body has its own natural defences against germs and infections but these can be reinforced by the use of various dressings.

4) **Protect the wound**

   Some wounds will need protection to keep them clean, free of dirt and to prevent infection.

With minor wounds the sequence is - Arrest Bleeding, Clean, Dress, Protect. (AB, C, D, P).

Methods of Cleaning

By Hand

Use cotton wool and cool, boiled water or mild antiseptic solution. *Never clean wounds with disinfectant* as this kills off the body's natural defences as well as infecting germs. Use clean pieces of cotton wool each time.

Trim the hair around the wound if required with safety scissors. Cover the injury first to prevent hair entering the wound.

Cleanse the wound in a direction *away from the injury*, so that dirt or grit is not washed into the wound.

The groom should wash their own hands before cleaning wounds and certainly afterwards.

Cold Hosing

Effective for areas of swelling and bruising as well as cleansing an open cut.

Hose onto the hoof first to avoid startling the horse and gradually raise the flow of water up the body until above the wound. Hose for 10 to 20 minutes.

If the area surrounding the wound is very dirty or gritty, clean this by hand first so that no foreign particles are washed into the wound by the hosing.

Poultice

For puncture wounds and injuries where foreign particles are present within the wound. **Important point, these wounds must heal from the inside out,** otherwise foreign matter may be trapped inside.

A poultice draws out foreign matter and helps to keep the wound open allowing the matter to escape. It also increases the blood supply to the damaged areas, encouraging healing.

Different substances are used for poulticing. Clean around the wound first.

♦ *Animalintex*

This is a commercially prepared poultice similar to lint, with one side covered in a clear polythene. A piece large enough to cover the wound is cut and immersed in boiling water for a few minutes. The water is drained and the poultice allowed to cool. Excess water is squeezed out and the Animalintex placed over the wound, polythene portion on the outside.

Animalintex is quick, easy to use and very clean. It is also easy to check what sort of matter has been drawn out of the wound, as this is evident on the pad when it is removed.

◆ **Kaolin**

This is a clay bought either dry as a powder or moist in a tin. The powder is moistened in warm water until sticky. Tinned kaolin may be heated by putting the required amount in an oven or in a bowl. The bowl is placed in a pan of boiling water. When hand-warm, the kaolin is spread onto a plastic bag or a piece of brown paper and secured in place with bandages.

Kaolin should not be used directly on open wounds as it will make the area sticky and messy. Place a piece of gauze over the wound first and then the poultice.

◆ **Bran and Epsom Salts**

Used particularly for wounds in the foot. Mix together a couple of handfuls of bran, one handful of Epsom Salts and enough warm water to make a stiff consistency. Pack into and around the site of the injury and cover the whole foot with a strong plastic bag. Secure with a hessian sack, bandages and a poultice boot.

Poultices should never be used constantly over prolonged periods of time as this will do more harm than good; 5 to 6 days is about the maximum. Excessive use of poultices can cause worse conditions such as proud flesh or a suppurated wound.

A foot poultice should be discontinued after 2 days or the horn may soften.

If the wound is still not healing after ten days the Vet should be called.

Poultices should not be used on joints except on veterinarian advice. A poultice used for an open wound on a joint may draw out joint oil, especially if the joint capsule itself is damaged.

Though some poultices can be left in place for 24 hours (never any longer) most warm poultices lose their heat and effectiveness *after 12 hours* when they should be renewed.

Figure 15: Treatment boots

Dressing the Wound

There are a variety of products that can be applied to wounds and injuries to encourage the healing process. **Wound powder** for wet wounds to help them dry, **antiseptic ointment** for dry wounds that need to be kept moist so that the skin can heal and **antibiotic sprays** which penetrate into wounds. For girth galls *where the skin is unbroken*, surgical spirits can be applied to harden the area.

If the Vet has been called in to treat a wound or where there is a possibility that the wound needs stitching, *NO dressing should be applied*. The dressing will make inspection or suturing of the wound very difficult.

Protecting the Wound

For leg wounds, cover with a sterile pad or gamgee secured in place with a stable bandage. For horses confined to the stable the opposite corresponding leg must also be bandaged for support and to prevent strain. The horse may need all four legs bandaging to prevent his limbs filling with fluid and for extra warmth. For horses allowed out into a paddock, a useful alternative is a tubular bandage bought from a chemist's shop.

For wounds in the foot a sterile pad can be kept in place by a bandage. A poultice can be covered with a plastic bag secured with a bandage. Because bandages will rarely stand up to the wear and tear of a shod hoof, a treatment boot or poultice boot can be used for protection.

There are areas on the horse's body where bandages are impossible to fit, for instance the shoulder area or the mouth. Wounds in these areas will need keeping scrupulously clean by regular bathing and hygiene in the stable.

Basic Nursing

Some horses need 'box rest', being confined to a box through sickness or injury. In some cases box rest together with very light in-hand exercise is recommended. Some ailments improve with a period at grass.

In all cases nursing must include:

1. **A hygienically clean environment**.
2. **Regular care and attention**.
3. **Good ventilation without draughts**.
4. **Keeping the horse warm**. Heavy blankets should be avoided as these can be tiring for a sick horse. Layers of light rugs that trap warm air are preferable to one thick heavy blanket. Infra-red lamps can also be used if available.
5. **Dust free hay, feed and bedding**.

6. **A convalescence diet**. The feed should be changed gradually to a diet suitable for an invalid horse. Food can be offered more frequently in smaller amounts. (See relevant section in Feeding horse at grass and special cases.)

7. There must be **plenty of roughage.**

8. A **constant supply of fresh, clean water**.

9. **Follow the Vet's instructions**.

Grooming

In most cases horses off work will enjoy a groom, basking in the care and attention lavished on them at this time. Grooming will also help to improve circulation; keep the muscles toned; the skin and coat conditioned and shiny.

For a really sick horse though, grooming should be kept to a minimum as this will disturb him unnecessarily. A quick brush and wipe over with a stable rubber, feet picked out and nostrils, eyes and dock gently wiped will suffice.

The Cast Horse

Occasionally a horse may roll in his box and become 'cast', that is, he is down on the floor with his legs trapped in such a way that he cannot stand up. Even out in the field the horse can become cast with his legs trapped usually against a wall.

Initially the horse may thrash around and in attempting to rise injure himself. Some horses panic, kick out wildly and violently; others lie there placidly waiting for help.

With the use of strong ropes or lunge lines, two people can right the horse. Keep the horse quiet by gently holding his head and neck down and by speaking to him. Then pass the ropes over the horse's body and around the fore and hind leg nearest to the floor or wall. Gently pull the horse over, release the ropes and move out of the way. This operation must be performed gently and in unison to avoid any strain or damage to the horse's spine or neck area. Check for injury once the horse is quiet.

If there is no help available, it is possible for the horse to be righted by one person **with great care**. Quieten the horse first by talking to him and keeping his head and neck down until he is calm. Then flatten down the bedding around his back and shoulders. Carefully pass a rope around the hind or foreleg nearest to the wall and gently pull him away. Move and give him plenty of room to manoeuvre and stand up himself. Check him for injury.

When to Call the Vet

The rule of thumb here is; if in any doubt call the Vet. If a wound refuses to heal as it should or the horse is off colour for no apparent reason then the advice of the Vet should be sought. Sharing a visit is a viable proposition if the Vet is visiting the yard to treat another horse.

When a Horse Should be Taken off Work

As a rule, if the horse is well enough to work then he should work. Horses are healthier if they can be kept properly exercised. Most mild cuts or scratches once treated, cleaned and dressed will not prevent the horse from working. Taking a horse off work can create its own problems such as the formation of bad habits due to stress and boredom.

Where the horse is obviously ill, or is injured to such an extent that working will cause pain or make the injury worse, then the horse should be given time and rest to recuperate. For cases of lameness the horse should not be worked except under instructions from the Vet.

Exam Tips

At Stage II, you will not be expected to diagnose actual illnesses or know more than the basic reasons for lameness. You should though be able to recognise when a horse is suffering from ill health or is unsound.

You will not be asked to take a horse's temperature, pulse or respiration but the average normal readings should be memorised. On some occasions the Examiners may ask candidates to demonstrate how to trot a horse up when assessing for lameness. Though it is unlikely to be asked to actually assess the horse, candidates should know the basic signs that could indicate lameness in a horse.

You will need to know the different types of wounds and how to treat these, and have knowledge of basic nursing. The best way to gain a wider knowledge and experience, besides having your own horse, is to be observant around the yard, watching how staff deal with wounds and injuries.

C H A P T E R   13
Worming and Teeth

This chapter describes the problems caused to the horse by parasitic infestation, the importance of a worming programme and methods to reduce the worm population. This is followed by a section covering basic information on the horse's teeth and information about health records.

Worming

All horses suffer from internal parasites; this is an inevitable part of their lifestyle. The aim of a worming programme is to keep the infestation to a minimum, reducing the risk to the horse.

There are a variety of parasites which infest horses. The most common ones are; large red worms, small red worms, pin/thread or seat worms, tape worms, lung worms, white worms and the bot fly larvae.

Problems Caused by Parasites

When the parasitic infestation becomes severe, the horse will suffer. The consequences include damage to the digestive system, loss of appetite, anaemia, diarrhoea, colic, ruptured intestines, inflammation of the gut, loss of condition and even death. Some types of worm cause respiratory damage and illnesses.

Life Cycle of Parasites

The life cycle of worms is such that horses become reinfested regularly. Though some worms have a different cycle most, including the particularly virulent large and small red worms, reproduce in the same fashion.

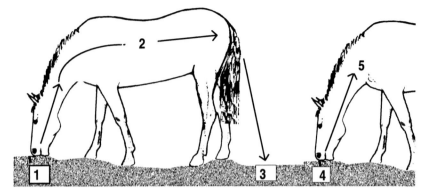

1. The horse ingests larvae from pasture and from bedding or hay on the floor of the stable.

2. The larvae, having migrated through various parts of the body, mature and lay their eggs in the intestines.

3. The eggs are passed out with the dung of the horse.

4. The larvae emerge from the eggs and migrate to the grass.

5. The cycle begins again.

The whole process can take from two to six months.

Though it would be impossible to completely eradicate worms from the horse and his environment, the worm population can be kept to a minimum. Dosing the horse at regular intervals with a commercially produced Wormer will control the internal infestation. Good stable management within the stable and fields will help to minimise the risk of reinfestation.

Worming Programme

There are many excellent Wormers on the market and research to improve these is taking place continuously. Wormers are a mixture of chemicals that kill the parasites within the horse.

There are three main points about a worming programme.

1) The horse should be wormed regularly, at least every **six weeks**. To create a good routine, many yards coincide their worming sessions with the visits from the Farrier so that both of these important jobs are done systematically.

2) Worms can develop a **resistance** to one kind of Wormer. It may be possible for worms to become immune to certain chemicals making that type of Wormer ineffective.

3) Whilst Wormers do deal with a **variety of worms,** *no one brand of Wormer deals with all types.*

To counteract the problems in points 2 and 3 one type of Wormer is used as a base Wormer for most of the year. This is then changed after twelve months and a new type of Wormer used to prevent resistance. To treat other types of worms a different type of Wormer from the base Wormer is used a couple of times a year usually Spring and Autumn.

Whilst these measures will deal with the problem of infestation in individual horses, to keep all horses and ponies on the yard as free as possible, other preventative measures should be taken as part of the overall yard management.

Yard Management

All the horses and ponies on the yard need protection against worm infestation. Good pasture management, an efficient stable routine and a strict worming programme will prevent the horses and ponies suffering as a result of worms.

1.   Worm all new horses and ponies that come into the yard soon after arrival.

2.   All horses and ponies should be kept in good condition. Animals in poor condition will be more prone to worm infestation.

3.   Keeping the horse or pony stabled for 24-48 hours after worming will minimise contamination of the pasture. Not all worms are killed after a Wormer dose, some will survive in the larval stage and, if the pasture becomes contaminated, these may be ingested by other horses and ponies.

4.   Worm all the horses and ponies on the yard at the same time, if possible, especially if all are out at grass. This will greatly reduce the risk of reinfestation.

5.   Practise good Grassland Management. Droppings in fields and paddocks should be removed or harrowed to reduce the number of worm larvae. Harrowing should be done in dry conditions.

6.   Pasture should never be overstocked, that is have too many horses grazing on it. Horses and ponies leave rough patches where they do their droppings and where, consequently, there will be worm larvae. If a field is overgrazed, the horses and ponies will start to eat the rough patches and thus ingest more worm larvae.

7.   The fields can be stocked periodically with other grazing animals such as cows and sheep. These ingest and kill off some of the larvae. Fields can also be 'rested' occasionally.

8.   Worm all horses and ponies before moving them into fresh pasture.

9.   Avoid spreading horse dung fresh from the stables onto the grass. This will infect the field.

10.   Worm all pregnant mares during pregnancy and both mares and foals 4 - 6 weeks after birth.

11. Feed horses and ponies in the stable from a bucket or skip. Avoid feeding directly from the floor to minimise the intake of larvae.

12. Keep all stables clean and free of dung.

13. Clean the dock area regularly to remove pinworm eggs. The pinworm sticks its tail out of the horse's anus to lay its eggs. These eggs appear as a kind of yellow wax around the dock and should be cleaned off. The cloth should then be burnt or disposed off hygienically.

14. Watch for bot eggs especially on horses and ponies at grass. These are apparent around April and May appearing as tiny yellow specks around the legs, shoulders and belly. Use a special bot egg remover (similar to a hard, rough sponge) or a bot knife, available from most tack shops. Picking them off by hand is possible but takes quite a time if the horse is heavily covered in these tiny eggs. It can help to wipe over the area with surgical spirits first.

15. The worm population in the yard and pasture can be tested for Wormer resistance, especially during spells of warm, damp weather conditions in which the larvae thrive. A worm count can be performed by a Vet, from samples of dung collected from the field or stable.

Methods of Worming

Wormers generally come in paste form or as granules and the amount given varies according to the weight of the horse.

Paste is contained within a syringe. Marked on the side of the syringe are approximate weights for horses and ponies showing how much paste to administer. The horse or pony should be properly restrained with an assistant holding the lead-rope. The cap is removed from the syringe and the nozzle inserted into the side of the horse's mouth, between the incisor and molar teeth. The plunger is depressed and the paste squirted as deep as possible into the horse's mouth. Once the required amount of paste has been given, the syringe is removed, the horse's head raised and his throat stroked downwards to encourage the paste to be ingested.

The granules are simply placed in a feed.

Controlling the worm population is a vital part of horse care. It should be part of the yard routine. Though Wormers are not a cheap commodity, especially in a big establishment, it is false economy to decrease the frequency of worming. Horses with heavy worm infestation need more food to replace the nutrients taken by the parasites and there will probably be Vet bills because the horses will suffer from ill health. Even years later, a horse whose gut has been damaged in the past will suffer digestive problems that can be extremely serious.

Teeth

Another important aspect of horse management is the inspection and care of the teeth. If the horse's teeth are not given proper and regular attention it can affect his condition and performance in work.

The horse's teeth are specifically designed for grazing. During the horse's life the root cavities shrink pushing the teeth out. This is balanced by the constant action of grazing and chewing which wears away the teeth.

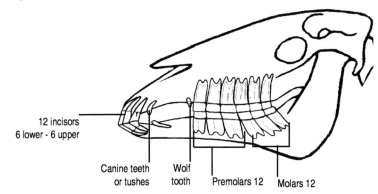

12 incisors
6 lower - 6 upper

Canine teeth
or tushes

Wolf
tooth

Premolars 12

Molars 12

Figure 16: Skull section showing the roots of the teeth

In the adult horse there are 12 incisor teeth at the front and 24 molars or grinding teeth of which the front three on the top and bottom jaws are termed premolars. All male, and some female horses, have 4 tushes, or canine teeth between the incisors and molars. Some horses also have wolf teeth that erupt in front of the premolars.

Teeth Problems

Horses rarely suffer from serious teeth problems. The most vulnerable period is between the ages of 2 and 4 years as the permanent teeth replace the milk teeth. Young stock need dental attention every 4 to 6 months.

Older horses, whose teeth have grown particularly long, can experience difficulties especially with tearing and eating grass. Their diet must be sufficiently soft and easily digestible to allow for this problem. Horses can also lose their teeth as they grow older.

Sometimes horses develop sharp edges on the *outside* edge of the *top* molars and the *inside* edge of the *lower* ones. The horse's top jaw is wider than the lower jaw and so the molar teeth of upper and lower jaw do not correspond exactly with each other. Consequently the grinding action wears down the molars unevenly.

If not treated, this will cause lacerations or ulcers inside the cheek or on the tongue. It will also affect digestion as chewing may be painful and eventually the horse may refuse to eat.

All adult horses are prone to uneven wear and a check should be made every 6 to 9 months when the teeth may need rasping.

Signs that the teeth need attention:

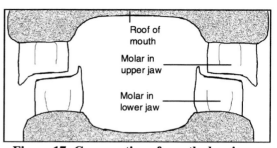

Figure 17: Cross section of mouth showing uneven wear on molars

♦ Pain in the mouth or around the face, this may be accompanied by swelling.

♦ Eating food more slowly; difficulty in chewing and swallowing; refusal of food and quidding, when the horse drops saliva and partially eaten food from his mouth.

♦ Loss of condition, the horse may begin to look thin and 'ribby'.

♦ A foul smell on the breath as rotting food becomes caught between the teeth.

♦ Performance will begin to suffer as the horse experiences pain and starts to evade the bit.

Inspecting the Teeth

The teeth can be inspected on a quiet horse by a competent person. If the horse is likely to be awkward or the handler is unsure of his skill, the inspection should be left to the Vet or Horse Dentist.

The horse is restrained by an assistant with a headcollar and lead-rope. The horse should not be tied up but held by the assistant for safety.

To check for uneven wear on the molars, stand to one side of the horse and, holding the horse's head still with one arm, slide the thumb only into the side of the horse's mouth.

Keeping the thumb close to the cheek, it is possible to feel for any sharpness on the outer edges of the top molars. If the top molars have sharp outside edges, it is likely that the corresponding inside edge of the lower molars are sharp too. This process may be repeated on the other side of the mouth.

Never insert a finger into the horse's mouth or attempt to feel the inner edge of the lower molars.

To make a visual inspection of the incisor teeth, the horse's tongue is *gently* but firmly grasped and held through the gap between the incisors and molars.

Age

As well as being an important part of the digestive system, the teeth provide one method of determining the age of a horse. Though this is not a totally reliable method, especially after about 8 years old, the appearance, size and shape of the incisor teeth give an approximate indication of age.

Age in young horses is determined by the appearance and disappearance of the milk or deciduous teeth. These are small in size and whiter in colour than the permanent teeth. The deciduous teeth are usually completely replaced with the permanent teeth by 5 years.

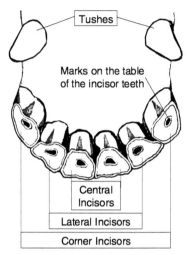

After that, the size and shape of the incisors, together with a mark on the top or table of the incisor teeth, gives an idea as to age. This can be quite difficult to assess though, as the wear of the teeth does depend on the horse's environment and food. For a horse permanently at pasture constant tearing at the grass will wear the teeth down more quickly than the stabled horse eating from a bucket. If a more precise estimate of age is necessary, this should only be done by an experienced person or a Vet.

Figure 18: Top view of the incisors in the lower jaw

A basic estimate of age can be achieved by looking at the incisors. The slant of these teeth alters with age. In particular the upper corner incisors change, with the appearance and disappearance of a 'hook' and with the lengthening of a groove. This groove, called Galvayne's groove, appears at around 9-10 years old and lengthens down the tooth from the top, extending along the whole tooth by 20 years.

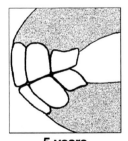 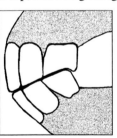 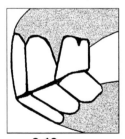 

5 years	**7 years**	**9-10 years**	**20 years**
Corner incisors meet	Hook developed on upper corner incisor	An indentation, Galvayne's groove, begins to appear on upper corner incisor	Galvayne's groove extends along the whole tooth. Teeth become more slanted

Health Records

A written record should be kept of the dates for worming, vaccinations and shoeing, together with descriptions of any medical treatment the horse has received. This acts as a reminder and gives an indication of the type of illnesses or injuries the horse has suffered in the past. This is particularly useful if any condition is likely to be recurrent, for instance laminitis. This information should be passed on to any new owner as it will assist in the care of the horse in the future.

In busy yards it is not always easy to remember which horse has been given what injection and health records in this situation are invaluable.

All records should be kept in a safe place for future reference. Many yards have these on computer now. A health record must not be mistaken for an identification/vaccination certificate that is normally required at BHS competitions.

Exam Tips

At Stage II level you should know why it is so important to maintain a regular worming programme. You will not be expected to know about each specific worm but you will need to understand the worm's basic life cycle and how this affects the horse. The Examiner may ask you basic information about Wormers, worming procedures and other measures that can be put into operation to prevent heavy infestations of land and animals.

You will not need to know a great deal about teeth only that they must be inspected regularly and rasped if necessary. It is a good idea though, and interesting, to start looking at horses' teeth and gaining experience in estimating age.

Keeping health records is common sense. Even for a person who owns one horse, dates can quickly be forgotten.

C H A P T E R   14
Watering

Water is essential to life. A horse's body consists of about 70% of water and most of the bodily functions take place within a water solution. If a horse is deprived of water for more than a few days, he can dehydrate and die.

Revision

The importance of water to the horse, factors controlling the amount of water a horse needs. The rules of watering, when not to water. Watering systems, in the stable and in the field, buckets, automatic waterers, troughs, rivers and streams.

Students of the Stage II will need to revise the systems of watering in the stable and the field as this was covered fully at Stage I and only a brief description is given here.

The Importance of Water

Water is necessary for:

Digestion   Water is present in the saliva and digestive juices. Lack of water can cause serious problems such as impacted colic.

Body Temperature Regulation
One of the methods in which the body regulates its temperature is to excrete sweat from the sweat glands. The moisture evaporating from the skin cools the horse down.

Lubrication   Water is present in the fluids that lubricate many parts of the body, such as the joints, the lining of the digestive system, the mucus membranes and the tear ducts.

Metabolism   Plasma in the blood consists mostly of water. Most chemical changes within the body occur in a water solution.

Waste Disposal
Waste products are evacuated from the body in a water solution; as in urine, droppings and from the pores by sweating.

On average a horse drinks about 36 litres (8 gallons) a day but in certain circumstances this can rise to 68 litres (15 gallons).

The factors that influence the amount of water intake are:

- **Diet**
  In a natural habitat, moisture is obtained from the grass. A stabled horse needs more fluid because his feed is almost entirely dry.

- **Temperature**
  The horse needs more water on hot, dry days.

- **Work**
  The horse will produce more sweat in hard work. Horses can also sweat when travelling.

- **Health**
  When ill the horse may lose fluids though abnormal faecal loss (diarrhoea), urinary loss or profuse sweating. When the horse is nervous, frightened or excited he will also sweat.

- **Milk production**
  Water is vital for brood mares when feeding their foals.

Rules of watering

1. **Horses must have a constant supply of clean, fresh water**

   Horses will drink polluted water if there is nothing else available.

2. **Cleanliness**

   All water buckets and containers should be kept **scrupulously clean** or they will cause disease.

3. **Water before feeding**

   It was traditionally thought that the horse should not drink after feeding as this washes the undigested food out of the stomach. However opinions are now changing on this subject. Personal experience shows that the horse can drink during and after a feed without any problems, *providing that he has constant access to water*. If a horse is denied water for a length of time, given a dry feed and then allowed a deep draught of fluid, this may cause problems. A full feed can swell quite dramatically when water is added and some horses are very prone to colic for this reason. In these cases dampening down the food, as well as constant access to water, does help to prevent digestive problems.

4. **Regulate water intake before and after hard work**

   A deep drink just before fast work will cause the stomach to swell putting pressure on the diaphragm and causing respiratory difficulties. During competitions, particularly long distance endurance rides or whilst eventing, the horse can be given small amounts between each phase.

After hard work, when the horse is hot and sweaty if he is given a quick draft of cold water this will provide a shock to the system and may result in colic. *The horse should be allowed to cool down before being given water.*

5.   **Provide efficient water containers**

All watering systems should be efficient. Automatic waterers are useless if they will not allow the horse a constant supply or a deep draught of water. Containers must also be **strong** enough for use, properly **secured and SAFE.**

6.   **Monitor the horse's intake**

Horses can suffer quite severely from dehydration, a state that is not always obvious. With buckets in the stable it is simple to check if the horse has been drinking because the bucket will need refilling. In the case of automatic waterers though, it is not always easy to observe how much the horse drinks. A layer of dust undisturbed on top of the water may be a sign that the horse is refusing to drink.

Dehydration test

If the horse is denied or refuses water for any length of time he will become dehydrated. This is made worse by excessive loss of fluids from the body due to sweating, haemorrhages, abnormal faecal or urinary loss.

Dehydration can be checked for quickly by the 'pinch test'. With the thumb and index finger pinch a fold of skin on the horse's neck. The skin should rapidly return flat. If the fold remains for longer than a few seconds, the horse may, to some degree, be dehydrated.

With an excessive loss of bodily fluids, the horse also loses electrolytes; various types of salts essential for certain chemical reactions within the body. Several companies now produce replacement electrolytes either in fluid form or as a powder. These can be added to the water or the horse's food. A salt lick in the box, or 25-50 grams (1-2 ozs) of salt added to the food, will also help in restoring the electrolyte balance.

Watering Systems

There are various ways of offering water to the horse in the stable and the field and all have their advantages and disadvantages. These are based on convenience, situation and availability of the water supply.

Providing water by buckets in the field or stable makes it easier to monitor and regulate the horse's intake. Buckets are also easy to clean and can be used when other systems are unavailable because of freezing, ice or poor water supply. Buckets though do take time and labour with the constant filling and refilling, are heavy to carry and may be knocked over by the horse.

Automatic waterers in the stable certainly have their advantages, especially in a large yard where they save time and labour. Though this system does offer the horse a constant supply of water, the bowls are often small and do not provide the horse with a deep drink. It is also often difficult to monitor or regulate the horse's intake and the bowls can be quite difficult to keep really clean. The bowls can sometimes ice over in winter or the pipes freeze.

In the field the most convenient and efficient method of watering is the self filling trough. This saves time, labour and provides a constant supply of sufficient water. However, the pipes leading to the trough can become frozen in winter and the trough itself may freeze over. Troughs that need filling by hose, whilst not as convenient, are more labour and time saving than buckets. Rivers and streams in the field are not suitable these days because of pollution. Also the area leading to the drinking point may become poached, that is muddy and dangerous. Rivers with a sandy bed can give the horse sand colic.

Positioning of water supply

In practical terms whatever the type of container used, it needs to be easy to fill, to keep clean and in a position that is convenient and safe.

The bucket in the stable will need to be large and strong enough to prevent it being knocked over and broken, but not too large or it will be heavy to carry. Ideally the bucket can be placed in a rubber tyre to secure it. There are buckets on the market now which include a moulded tyre shaped base. The bucket needs to be away from, but fairly close to, the door. Having to carry a heavy bucket over the bed is difficult and water could spill everywhere. It should also be a distance apart from the feed bucket to prevent the horse, as much as possible, dropping food into the water. Automatic waterers are ideally placed in a corner and boxed in to stop the horse banging his head on the bowl.

A trough in the field needs to be situated in a safe position away from the gate; the ground around the gate usually becomes very poached in wet weather. The trough should also be kept away from overhanging trees; as leaves, twigs and blossom may clog the water. Positioned against a fence or incorporated into the fence is safest. A trough in the middle of the field is a hazard; the horse may bump into it. If situated a little way from a fence, a horse may become trapped behind it and bullied by others. A trough that needs filling by hose or buckets, needs to be adjacent to a water supply.

Exam Tips

For the Exam you need to know why water is so essential to the horse, how much he needs and the variables that affect this amount. The rules of watering should be learnt thoroughly and related to the daily routine and health of the horse.

In preparation you should observe and study different methods of watering in the stable and field and decide for yourself which is most efficient and convenient. You should also be able to explain your reasons based on experience or observation.

C H A P T E R   15
Feeding

The subject of feeding horses is often an exhaustive and controversial one. Though there are variables that affect the amount and type of food to give, this is often made more complicated than it should be. If taken step by step, building on the information offered and with the knowledge of experience, this subject need not be confusing.

In its natural state the horse has a relatively 'simple' diet consisting of grasses, plants and herbs. The stabled horse lives in an alien and artificial habitat. Consequently the diet has to change to maintain the level of health and fitness required.

The objective of feeding the horse is *that energy input equals energy output.* If this ratio becomes unbalanced, the horse either loses condition and weight or becomes grossly overweight resulting in illness. Without doubt the maxim of **'know your horse'** applies, especially with the variety and scope of feeds available.

Revision
Rules and considerations of feeding, methods of calculating amounts of foods and percentages of roughage to concentrates.

The information given at Stage I is elementary. For Stage II, students will need a deeper knowledge and understanding of feeding.

Aims of Feeding

The horse needs food for **growth**, especially during the first five years of life when the horse's increase in body weight is at its highest. At this time he also needs a balance of nutrients to encourage proper growth of all body cells.

The horse requires food to **maintain his body temperature**, particularly important for grass-kept animals during the colder months. The body utilises food in the production of body heat.

Once the horse has matured he needs food to **maintain his correct body weight,** essential for horses in constant or hard work. During the winter in the field, horses must maintain their body fat for insulation.

Food is used to create **energy** so that the horse can perform his work efficiently.

For brood mares to feed and nurture the foetus and foal, and for stallions, food is essential in the **breeding** process.

Rules of Feeding

1. **Feed little and often**

    The horse's stomach is relatively small and, as he cannot regurgitate or vomit, any large intake of food may cause stomach distension or rupture. He is a 'trickle feeder', eating small amounts almost continuously. For these reasons a *feed of concentrates should never be over 4 to 6 lbs (2-3 kilos), depending on the size of the horse.*

2. **Feed plenty of roughage each day**

    A horse needs bulk food for the digestive system to work correctly and efficiently. Roughage slows the rate of digestion, allowing time for all the food to be broken down properly and for the nutrients to be extracted. Hay should always be offered with the first feed. The horse being without food for most of the night will need roughage with his first meal of concentrates.

3. **Feed the right amount of food**

    The horse should be fed the right amount for his size and work. Overfeeding causes problems. An obese horse will find it difficult to work properly and the weight he has to carry will put stress on his heart and lungs. Though slight underfeeding is more desirable, an undernourished or thin horse will be more susceptible to disease and infection, and will lack the energy to work efficiently. Muscle and tissue repair will be greatly reduced and the horse will be prone to accidents and injury.

4. **Feed the right type of food**

    There is a wide variety of 'hard' foods (concentrates) available as well as several types of roughage. It is essential to obtain the correct type of food to suit the horse. Too high an energy diet can be disastrous in a highly strung horse. Conversely a lack of certain nutrients can cause debility or problems of growth.

    It is quite feasible to experiment with foods to see which suits the horse best, as long as any change of diet is performed gradually (see Rule 6). Such aspects as breed, type, temperament and the work done by the horse are taken into consideration.

5. **Feed good quality food**

    Poor quality food is less nutritious and uneconomical as greater quantities will need to be fed. It could also be dusty or mouldy. To maintain his condition a horse needs good quality fodder.

6. **Make any adjustments gradually**

The horse's digestive system needs time to adapt to change (see Chapter on Digestive System). This is an important factor when considering any adjustment of diet, for example from concentrates to grass or from energy foods to a maintenance diet for an invalid horse.

7. **Allow one hour after feeding before exercise**

Too much food within the stomach will press against the lungs and impair breathing. This could also lead to colic. The horse should be allowed one hour without a feed before work and two hours before hard, fast work.

8. **After exercise allow the horse to cool before feeding**

A horse that is hot and tired should be given an hour to allow his circulatory system to cool and quieten down. During exercise the blood supply provides energy to the muscles; this needs time to be directed back to the digestive system.

9. **Feed in a routine**

The horse is a creature of habit and will expect his food at set times each day. No horse should be left for more than about 8 hours without food.

10. **Keep all utensils clean**

This is just as important for horses as it is for humans. Stale food, vermin and their excreta, remains of drugs, worm eggs or larvae can be lethal to the horse. All old, stale food should be disposed of and should not be fed to a horse.

The food should be kept dry and free from contamination; all food containers tightly covered and secured. A feed should never remain lying around uncovered whilst waiting to be fed. There has been a case where a feed prepared and left uncovered overnight became contaminated by rat urine. It was fed to the horse next morning with fatal results.

All food containers or storage bins should be cleaned regularly. The feed room must be clean to discourage vermin and insects.

11. **Feed succulents each day**

The horse will appreciate carrots, apples, swedes especially if the rest of the diet is dry food and hay. These will also provide some vitamins and minerals.

12. **Water the horse before feeding**

See Rules of Watering.

13. **Worm the horse regularly**

Worm infestation should be kept to a minimum as this does affect the efficiency of the digestive system.

Rations of food

There are three points to take into consideration when feeding;

- the daily amount,
- the percentage of concentrates to roughage,
- the types of food to give.

Amount

The daily total amount of food a horse or pony needs is based on his weight. To discover this precisely the horse will need to be weighed on a Weighbridge. Then the amount of food he needs is calculated. Traditionally the amount for a fully mature horse or pony is worked out at 2.5% of his body weight. With some manufactured compound foods however, the manufacturers suggest 2% of body weight.

If an accurate calculation is necessary, for racehorses or competition horses, another method is to use a weigh tape. The horse is measured around his girth area and a weigh table will then give the amounts of food required for different weights of horses.

There are other ingenious and wonderful calculations to work out the exact amount of food required but, being practical, the majority of owners make an assessment of daily food from the horse's height and build. The horse will then be monitored over a period of weeks and the food altered accordingly.

Estimation by Height

This is a fairly accurate calculation and is the method by which most horse owners work out the daily amount of food required. The kilo/pound conversions are not exact but are sufficient to work out the amount of food required.

Height of Horse	Daily Amount of Food
17-18 hands	15.5 kilos (34 lbs)
16 hands	13.5 kilos (30 lbs)
15 hands	12 kilos (26 lbs)
14 hands	10 kilos (22 lbs)
13 hands	8 kilos (18 lbs)
12 hands	6.5 kilos (14 lbs)

Variations

These amounts can be varied in relation to various factors.

Build

An important factor to consider is the build of the horse. This does, to some extent, depend on **type or breed**. The amounts mentioned in the previous section are for horses of medium build. Some horses are of a naturally lighter or a heavier build and will need a slightly lower or higher amount of food. For instance a Thoroughbred of 16 hands, a lighter build, can be fed up to a kilo less. Whereas an Irish Draught of 16 hands, being heavier, can be fed up to a kilo more.

Health

The amounts will vary according to the horse's physical metabolism. Some horses are 'good doers' that is they efficiently digest their food and consequently need less. Other horses are 'poor doers' who may need a fraction more.

Weight

If the horse or pony is already overweight he may need feeding a little less food to help him lose weight. If he is thin he may need a little more for weight gain.

Age

Young horses need more food per body weight because of their rate of growth. Older horses, too, may need more food as their digestive systems are not efficient enough to utilise the nutrients.

Environment

The environment is the horse's habitat, where he lives. If he is fully or partially stabled, the daily amount of concentrates and roughage will be the total calculated from weight and size. Where the environment factor really makes a difference is when the horse or pony is permanently out at grass. Then his daily amount of supplementary food will vary depending on such factors as time of year, quality of pasture, weather conditions and his workload. (Further information is available in the relevant chapter on feeding horses and ponies at grass.)

Percentages of Food

Food is basically divided into two categories - concentrates (hard food) and roughage (bulk food).

- **Concentrates provide energy and heat.**

- **Roughage provides the bulk allowing the digestive system to work more efficiently.**

The first consideration here is the horse's workload. This is divided into the amount of hours and the type of work performed. The more work, the higher the energy intake and the less bulk required though under *no circumstances should a horse be fed less than 30% roughage.*

Table for calculating percentages of foods to workload.

Workload	Description of Work	Percentages of food
Maintenance	No work or very light; walking, some trot work up to 4 hours a week	0-10% concentrates to 90-100% bulk
Light work	4 - 6 hours a week - light hacking or schooling	25% concentrates to 75% bulk
Light medium work	6 - 12 hours a week hacking, schooling with a little jumping	30% concentrates to 70% bulk
Medium work	6 - 12 hours a week includes hacking, schooling, dressage, show jumping	40% concentrates to 60% bulk
Hard medium work	12 - 14 hours a week schooling, show jumping, dressage, hunting once every one or two weeks	50% concentrates to 50% bulk
Hard work	12 hours and over, schooling, show jumping, eventing, hunting twice a week, point to point, racing, endurance riding. Concentrated work	60% concentrates to 40% bulk

Note: The current trend is to feed less concentrates and more roughage as too much 'hard' food can cause digestive problems.

These average examples are given as a guide, but all horses and ponies should be monitored and the feed altered accordingly.

Example; a 16.2 Irish Draught cross Thoroughbred (medium build) doing 14 hours a week schooling, hacking, jumping and going hunting once a week in the winter.

Work out total daily amount   =   13.5 kilos (30 lbs)

Type of work - Hard medium 50%-50%   =   6.75 kilos (15 lbs) hard food and 6.75 kilos (15lbs) roughage.

Weighing Food

Concentrates

Food can be weighed out precisely for each feed. Normally though, it is fed by scoop and the amount of each foodstuff is calculated in number of scoopfuls.

There are three considerations:

1)   *There are different sizes of scoops; from the small trowel scoop to the large round scoop.*

As a rule the small scoops give a ¼ to ½ a kilo (½-1 lb) of food whilst the larger ones can provide 1 to1½ kilos (2-3 lbs).

2)   *Weight of food will vary if fed as level or heaped scoopfuls.*

This can make quite a difference when feeding a number of scoopfuls in a day.

3)   *Different foods have varying weights.*

A small scoop of horse and pony cubes can weigh ½ kilo (1 lb) whereas the *same scoop* will measure out ¼ kilo (½ lb) of mix.

Here are some examples of feed weights from a small trowel scoop (level) weighed on kitchen scales;

1 scoop =	**Bran**	125 grams (¼ lb)
	Oats	250 grams (½ lb)
	Chaff	125 grams (¼ lb)
	Pasture Mix	250 grams (½ lb)
	Horse & Pony cubes	½ kilo (1 lb)

This shows the variation in different foods. When determining how much of each food to give from what type of scoop, the food should first be weighed correctly on some scales.

Hay

Hay can be weighed precisely in a haynet on a pair of hanging scales. More usually an approximate amount is estimated from the number of slices or wedges. Bales and wedges do however vary in size and weight.

On average a bale of hay weighs 18 kilos (40 lbs) but bales can vary from 16 kilos to 20 kilos (35lbs to 45lbs). There can also be from 10 to 15 wedges in each bale and these can differ in size and weight. The experience of feeding hay to horses gives a 'feel' for a wedge. A fat wedge can weigh up to 2 kilos (3-4 lbs) and a small, thin wedge can weigh 1 kilo (2 lbs).

Number and Frequency of Feeds

The number of feeds given each day will vary according to the total daily amount, the horse's daily routine and his environment. Most horses are fed at least twice a day, morning and at night, some have three or even four feeds a day to fit in with their work pattern.

The horse whose feed is split into four feeds a day may have the largest feed at night when he has time to digest it properly. Some owners prefer to give the larger feed in the morning or at lunch time if the horse is exercised in the morning.

The hay needs to be given when the horse will have sufficient time to eat and digest it. Most will be given for the last feed, some at breakfast so that this will aid digestion of the 'hard' food and some at lunch or tea depending when the horse works.

Simple feed charts

Feed charts are necessary particularly for the stabled horse for three main reasons;

- To ensure that the amount and type of feed is constant every day
- As a record of the horse's daily feeds
- To prevent confusion if more than one person is involved with feeding.

Depending on the yard and its requirements there are different methods of designing and displaying the Feed Chart. Some yards have a blackboard in the feed room with the names of the horses and their respective feeds. Other yards prefer to display a notice outside each box. Whichever method is used the chart needs to be **clearly visible**, **easily understood** and **adapted** if necessary.

A blackboard with chalk or a whiteboard with pen is quite efficient. Ensure that measures are all in the same denomination, that is weight or scoops but never a variation as this will cause confusion.

Sample Feed Chart (Summer) - All weights in kilos

Horse	Oats	Barley	Bran	Mix/ nuts	Chaff	Supp.	Notes	Hay
Harry 16. hh 13.5 kilos	1-1-2	½-0-½			½-½-½	Red Cell		2-2-3
Bella 13.2 hh 8 kilos				1-0-1	1-0-1	Biotin	At grass	2-0-2
Quinn 15 hh Cob 12 kilos				1-2-1	1-1-1		Part at grass	2-1-2

Exam Tips

All candidates will need to learn and *understand* the aims and rules of feeding. You should be able to calculate a total daily amount of food required for various horses and to divide these amounts up into concentrates and roughage depending on the horse's work.

When asked about amounts and percentages of food in the Stage II, candidates will need to answer with their estimations fairly quickly.

An Examiner may ask about the total amount of food to give a 16 hh Thoroughbred doing 10 to 12 hours a week schooling, dressage and a bit of jumping, taking part in Riding Club competitions during the weekends. A 15 hh Welsh Cob riding school horse doing mostly hacking with a bit of schooling for about 12 hours a week. Both of these are fully stabled with little grass time.[*]

Take each example step by step; height first, then the build taken from the breed or type. This will give the total daily amount. The work performed will decide the percentage.

Start by answering with the amounts and percentages as outlined. Then, if the Examiner should query the amount of concentrates, you can explain that the horse would be monitored for a few weeks and the diet changed accordingly if this was necessary.

You need to be able to relate the facts given in this chapter with practical examples. Prepare for this by estimating feeds for different types of horses and ponies in various situations.

When describing the amounts and percentages to be given to any one horse, this can be as pounds or kilos whichever you find easiest. You also need to relate these weights to number of scoops. A good tip is to take some scales down to your yard, weigh out different foods on different sized scoops and note down the weights of various food types. If you have your own horse or are feeding horses regularly, you may already be aware of how many scoops to each feed, but you will also need to know the weights that each scoop will hold.

* Answers on the next page (No peeking!)

Answers

16 hh Thoroughbred = fine build 13 kilos. Work; 10 to 12 hours a week schooling, dressage and jumping, taking part in Riding Club competitions at weekends = medium work = 40-60 = ~5 kilos hard food and ~8 kilos roughage.

15 hh Welsh Cob = heavy build = 13 kilos Work; hacking with a bit of schooling for about 12 hours a week = light medium work = 30% concentrates and 70% roughage = ~4 kilos hard food and ~9 kilos roughage.

C H A P T E R   1 6
Types of Food

Basically food is made up of **carbohydrates, proteins, fats and oils, vitamins, minerals, fibre and water**. Some foods include all of these in varying degrees whilst other foods include some but are deficient in others.

Revision

Advantages and disadvantages of foods, compounds and traditional. Cooked foods. Hay, types, advantages and disadvantages, vacuum-packed forage.

Nutritional Value of Foods

Carbohydrates, containing **sugars, starches and cellulose**, provide **heat and energy**.

Proteins are needed for **growth and repair** of cells and tissues.

Fats and oils provide **heat, insulation and energy**.

Vitamins and minerals are necessary for **growth, metabolism and bodily functions**.

Fibre provides **bulk** and **aids digestion**.

Natural Diet

In his natural habitat the horse grazes constantly for some 18 to 22 hours a day (trickle feeding). *Good quality grass at certain times of the year provides all the nutrients the horse needs for his maintenance.* A horse is said to be at maintenance level when he is kept in good condition whilst doing no work or, in some cases, light work.

Pasture containing a variety of grasses during spring, summer and early autumn will adequately provide a staple diet for horses at maintenance level. During the other seasons of the year this quality will vary and in winter all horses and ponies need their diet supplementing.

The majority of horses are worked to some degree whether they live out or are fully stabled. These will need extra foods in the form of concentrates and roughage.

Concentrates

The concentrate or 'hard' food portion of a horse's diet provides the energy needed for work as well as keeping him in good condition, maintaining his body temperature and providing nutrients for growth. Concentrates are divided into two categories - traditional foods and compound foods.

Traditional and Compound foods (sometimes known as 'straights')

Traditional foods are the cereals and grains used for centuries to feed horses; oats, barley, bran and maize. Compound foods, produced by Feed Merchants, are a mixture of traditional ingredients and other nutrients in one 'whole' food.

Compound Foods

In the last few decades equine nutrition has taken on a new dimension. Feed merchants and manufacturers employ professional nutritionists to research into the dietary needs of all horses and ponies at any stage in their lives.

Compound foods are produced as *nuts, cubes or wafers*, where the ingredients are ground, steamed and pelleted, or as *coarse mixes* which have a similar appearance to a traditional feed. Both types include varying amounts of cereals and grains together with added minerals, vitamins and usually molasses.

The great advantage to compound feed is that there is one food to give rather than weighing and mixing a variety of traditional foodstuffs. This means a saving in time, labour and storage space. Compound foods are also very easy to feed, an advantage if different people are making up the feeds. They are also dust free, of good quality and provide a standardised scientifically balanced food.

Some of the nuts or wafers can be dry but this can be overcome by moistening with water. They can be more expensive to purchase and, though two types of compound food can be mixed together if required, it is not easy to adjust by the addition or subtraction of one particular ingredient. Chaff and sugar beet can be added to the compound feed, but it should not be necessary to add any traditional foodstuffs such as oats to the food. This may cause an imbalance of nutrients.

It is easy to understand why compound foods have become very popular. They are simple and easy to feed yet at the same time guarantee a completely balanced nutritious food to suit horses and ponies in varying circumstances and environments.

Traditional Foods

In the days before compound feeding, horses were fed on a diet consisting of grains, seeds and roots as well as grass. Even today there are those who believe that the traditional feeds are the best.

Traditional Food Types and their Respective Values

Oats

Food value   Considered the best nutritionally, this grain is still used in some areas and countries as the main bulk of the horse's feed. Consisting of **carbohydrates, proteins, fats and oils**, oats also provide **fibre** and **vitamin B1**.

Deficiency   Oats are **deficient** in some minerals particularly **calcium.**

Quality   Oats should be **plump, golden** and **sweet-smelling**. Those which look small, dark or discoloured or smell musty should not be used. One of the best types to purchase are Scottish oats.

Form   They can be **fed whole,** though in this form may be **hard to digest**. Normally fed **rolled, crushed, clipped or bruised.**

Use   **Best source of energy without making the horse fat.**

Disadvantages They can cause a horse to **'heat up'**, become **hyperactive and hard to control**, particularly if the horse has this type of temperament. Oats should be **stored no longer than three weeks** or they will deteriorate.

Barley

Food value   Nutritionally **similar to oats** but with a **higher carbohydrate** level.

Deficiency   **Lower in fibre** than oats and **lacking certain minerals** such as **calcium**. Must be given as part of a mixed feed.

Quality   Barley should be **fat, round** and **golden in colour.**

Form   Fed either **bruised, flaked or micronized**, that is heat treated - a form of cooking which improves the digestibility without the loss of nutrients, and as nuts or rings.

Use   As an **alternative to oats**, as it is **less heating**. To **put weight on** a thin horse. Because barley is fattening it should never be fed in excess or to a horse in hard work.

Disadvantages Some horses are **allergic to barley** and develop an irritation of the skin called **barley bumps**.

Maize

Food value   Equivalent to a **combination of oats and barley**. It has a **high proportion of carbohydrate.**

Deficiency   **Low** in **protein and fibre**.

Quality   Appearance of **small corn flakes** which should be a **light golden colour, clean, dry and hard.**

Form   Maize is **usually fed as micronized flakes.**

Use   A **fattening** and **energy food**. Can be fed to **horses in hard work** though never in excess. Ideally the limit should be **25% of the total grain food.**

Disadvantages   **Very heating and fattening** if fed in excess. May also cause an **allergic skin condition**.

Bran

Food value   **High in fibre** (though lower than oats). High protein content but some of this is indigestible.

Deficiency   **Phosphorus/calcium ratio incorrect.** Bones contain certain minerals, including calcium and phosphorus, which must be digested in the correct ratio of approximately two parts calcium to one part phosphorus. Nutritional experiments have shown that bran is high in phosphorus and low in calcium. If bran is fed in large amounts, especially to young horses, without the addition of extra calcium, the result will be bone deformities.

Quality   Good quality bran should be **dry, floury crumbs**.

Form   Used **dry in feeds or wet as in bran mash**. Can be fed with addition of Limestone flour or sugar beet to replace calcium deficiency.

Use   **Bran mash** can be a good **tonic** for a **tired horse. Wet bran** can also act as a **laxative**.

Storage   When **stored for long periods**, bran absorbs moisture making it **sour and unfit** to use.

Disadvantages   Efficiency in milling process of wheat makes good quality bran **difficult to purchase.**

Wheat

Food value   Wheat as a grain has never really been considered a suitable feed for horses. The grain, when wet, **swells and can ferment quickly causing colic and other digestive problems**. Wheat can only be fed to horses as bran.

Linseed

Food value   Very **high oil content**, about 36% fats and oils.

Deficiency   Linseed contains some **24% of digestible protein** but the **quality** of the **protein is poor**; it lacks the essential amino acid lysine that is necessary for the horse's growth and performance.

Appearance   **Small, brown seeds**.

Form   This **seed of the flax plant** is **highly poisonous eaten raw** and MUST **always be cooked**. It can then be mixed in with the feed.

Use   The high oil content **improves hoof condition** and gives a **gloss to the coat**. It is also used as a **tonic in winter or for horses in poor condition.**

Disadvantages **Preparing** the linseed **takes time and labour**. *Linseed oil can be purchased ready made in bottles.* Because it is **rich and fattening**, linseed **should be fed sparingly**, no more than 100 grams (3 ozs) dry seed once a day, twice a week.

Sugar Beet

Food Value   **High in calcium, salt and potassium**. It also **provides fibre**.

Appearance   Sugar beet is available in dry form as **cubes or shreds**.

Form   The cubes look similar to horse and pony **cubes or nuts** but are **darker in colour**. The **shreds** look like **small, dried sticks** and are dark brown in colour.

Use   As a **'mixer' or 'opener'** added to feeds. It gives the food a sweeter taste; makes it **more palatable**. The fibre content **encourages the horse to eat more slowly** and **digest the food more efficiently**. Sugar beet should be fed in small quantities, no more than 1½- 2½ kilos (3 to 5 lbs) dried weight each day.

Disadvantages With some horses it has a **laxative effect** and in these cases smaller amounts should be given. **Sugar beet is slow to digest** and, because it is **bulky in the gut**, is **not suitable for horses in hard or fast work.**

Care must be taken that sugar beet cubes are not mistaken for pony cubes. If a mistake does occur this could have fatal results. When stored they should be clearly labelled.

Molasses

Food Value   Consists of **sugars**. Extremely sweet and fattening.

Form   **Black treacle;** it is the syrup remaining in the cane after the sugar has been extracted. Molasses mixed with chaff and bought commercially is added to the feed. Many compound foods include molasses.

Use   Provides **energy, good condition** and gives a **shiny coat**. Its **sweet taste** is tempting for fussy eaters, making food more palatable.

Disadvantages Can be too fattening. It should never be used to make poor quality fodder more palatable.

Peas and Beans

Food Value   High in protein including the amino acid lysine.

Form   They must not be fed whole but always split or crushed to make them more digestible. They must be fed in a mixture with other foods as they are too rich to be used alone.

Use   For very fit horses in hard work to provide protein in concentrated form. For maintaining muscle tone and providing energy.

Disadvantages They are heating and fattening and should be fed sparingly, up to ½ kilo (1lb) per feed maximum. Excess protein can cause illness.

Soyabean Meal

Food Value   **Very high protein content**. Low in fibre, fats and oils.

Use   Feed in **small amounts**, no more than ½ kilo (1lb) per day, as an addition to the feed for a horse in hard work. Soyabean meal **builds up muscles and provides stamina**.

Succulent Foods

Any additions such as carrots, apples, swedes, will add vitamins and minerals to the diet. As with everything, moderation is the key; feeding sudden large quantities can cause an imbalance of nutrients or digestive illnesses. Small amounts regularly will benefit the horse.

Openers or Mixers

These are additions made to the feed which encourage the horse to eat and offer extra nutrients. They can also help the horse digest his food more efficiently by slowing down the rate at which the food passes through the digestive system in the case of chaff. Foods such as sugar beet, molasses, linseed oil and chaff are all 'openers' or 'mixers'.

Supplements

There is a bewildering variety of supplementary foodstuffs available for purchase. Herbal mixtures including Comfrey, garlic and nettles, or vitamin and mineral supplements. There are supplements to heighten performance, to add iron to the diet and some which quieten the horse down making him more placid. Visit any feed merchants and look at the supplementary section, it will be a case of 'you name it, they've got it'.

Adding any supplement to the horse's diet is mostly down to personal preference but there are two important points that should be remembered.

1. No supplement should really be given without the advice of a Vet.
2. Under normal circumstances a horse who is getting a nutritionally balanced diet should not need supplements.

Salt is an essential part of the horse's diet and can be provided as a salt lick or as rock salt in the manger.

Cooked Foods

Oats, barley and maize can all be cooked by being boiled gently in a double quantity of water until the grains soften. This provides a damp, easily digestible meal.

Bran is made into a bran mash by the addition of water - two thirds of a bucket of bran and up to one third of a bucket of warm water. The water is added until the bran is a damp and crumbly consistency, not too wet. It is fed when cooled and may be mixed with other foodstuffs such as boiled barley, limestone flour or sugar beet.

The two foods that **must be prepared before being fed** are **linseed** and **sugar beet.**

Linseed - cover 100 grams (3 ozs) of seed with cold water and leave to soak overnight. Add more water and boil for 4 to 6 hours. Allow to cool and add to a feed or an oat, barley or bran mash. Linseed can be cooked with other foods as long as the seeds are cooked thoroughly.

Sugar beet - soak the shreds in double the amount of water for 12 hours and the cubes in three to four times the amount of water for 24 hours. Both should be fed as soon as possible, and certainly within a few hours after soaking, as sugar beet ferments. For this reason cold water is used for soaking as warm or hot water will make the sugar beet ferment more quickly.

Any or all of these can be mixed together to give a restorative meal for a tired horse or to provide a sustaining feed for an invalid or aged horse.

Roughage

For the stabled horse hay is the main source of fibre. For animals permanently at pasture, during the spring, summer and early autumn, grass is the main bulk food. During the late autumn, winter and possibly early spring though, they will also need hay to supply the roughage in their diet.

There are two main types of hay;

Seed hay, which contains specially sown grasses such as rye, timothy, cocksfoot, fescue and clover. This is fed to horses in hard work as it is of a higher quality and more nutritious.

Meadow hay, taken from natural pasture, varies in quality depending on the grasses it contains. It is sweeter and softer than seed hay and suitable for all horses.

Wet Hay

In the past few years there has been a greater number of horses suffering from respiratory problems. All seed and meadow hay, regardless of quality, contain fungal spores that may be inhaled into the lungs causing an allergic reaction. For horses that are susceptible the problems range from a simple cough, a discharge from the nostrils to a chronic respiratory disease.

Most yards, establishments and horse owners wet the hay before feeding for the following reasons.

- The spores, as they become wet, stick to the grass stems. This prevents them from being inhaled into the lungs.

- When wet, the spores swell in size making it more difficult for them to pass down the windpipe and into the lungs.

- Some of the spores are washed away with the water after draining.

Methods of Soaking Hay

If the hay is to be weighed then it must be done before soaking.

Soaking

Place the hay into a haynet and the net into a container; a plastic dustbin used for this purpose is ideal. Cover with water so that all the hay is fully submerged. If soaking a whole bale, a larger container is necessary, such as a water tank.

Steaming

Place the filled haynet into the plastic bin and pour a kettle of boiling water over it. Cover and leave until cool.

When the hay is soaked thoroughly the bin is tipped over and the water allowed to drain. The wet haynet should then be hung up over a bar or on a hook to drip off before feeding. (A thoroughly wet haynet is very heavy to carry, will wet the clothes of the person carrying it and soak through the horse's bedding in the box.)

Time

Hay needs to be soaked for a sufficient time to allow the spores to swell. Wetting the hay down by merely passing the hose over the haynet, is not effective.

On the other hand, immersing hay in water for long periods decreases its quality. Hay contains some water soluble nutrients and over a period of time these are washed out and lost. This is evident by the dark-brown, beery water that is poured down the drain.

Research shows that soaking hay in water for twenty minutes is sufficient time.

Alternative Bulk Food

For the past few years, hay has been in short supply, difficult to obtain and consequently expensive. Vacuum-packed forage, commonly known as HorseHage[*], is an alternative. This type of roughage is made from grass that is cut, baled and vacuum-packed within a few days so that it retains moisture. The grass slightly ferments giving a sweet smell and taste.

There are about six different types on the market. These include a high protein forage for horses in competition work, a lower protein/higher fibre kind for horses in medium work, and a type which is low in protein/high in fibre for ponies or horses in light work.

The most important point about vacuum-packed forage is that it is dust free and is very useful for horses with respiratory problems.

It is quite rich though for some horses and ponies and, because of its taste, tends to be devoured quite quickly even from a 'HorseHage haynet' with smaller holes. Even Fibreage, produced to be less rich and higher in fibre, will be eaten more quickly than normal hay.

Under normal circumstances this type of forage is more expensive than hay. However, because hay has risen in cost recently, the two are now comparatively similar in price.

Extra fibre can be offered as an addition to the concentrate feed. Sugar beet, chaff, Mollichop or specially manufactured high fibre mixes are all used to add bulk to the horse's diet. The most important bulk food is grass. This provides fibre as well as other nutrients and was, after all, the food for which the horse's digestive system evolved.

Haylage and Silage

Haylage and silage are semi-wilted grass with varying moisture contents. Haylage is baled and silage is treated and sealed in airtight bags. Haylage is occasionally fed to horses but is not as popular as hay or HorseHage. Silage is not considered suitable for horses as cases of Botulism (bacterial poisoning) have been reported.

---

[*] HorseHage is the trade name of Marksway HorseHage

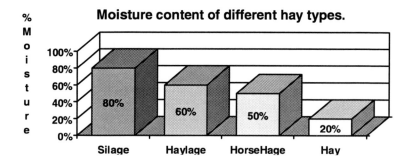

Moisture content of different hay types.

Exam Tips

During the examination you will be handed one or possibly two samples of food and should be able to give a description of that food, its basic respective values and its use as a feed.

Observe the sample of food closely, take it out of the container and smell it to check the quality. The container itself will give you a clue as to the freshness of the food. If the container is a plastic cup or bowl, it may be fresh off the yard that day. If it is a dusty jar obviously used for samples of food, the food is more likely to be older. The food may look and smell musty and in this case you can state that this particular sample of food is unsuitable for feeding.

Collect booklets and leaflets from Feed Merchants to discover the different types of feed available. Ask your Yard Manager what food is given to the horses, why some horses are on different foods, ask about feeding traditional foods. Make a study of various foods given to horses even if you have your own horse and are familiar with feeding. It does no harm to ask other people's opinion to gain a fuller comprehension of this subject. You can even contact the feed manufacturers and request leaflets on nutrition and feeding.

You will need to know the different types of hay and vacuum-packed forage and when to feed these. Make a study of hay quality, especially in a yard where this can vary and understand why hay varies in quality and how to recognise good hay.

Feeding Horses at Grass and Special Cases

Feeding horses and ponies at grass is a varied and extensive subject dependent on many factors. These basic guidelines are a good starting point but the horse or pony, especially those permanently at pasture, should always be monitored and their feeding regulated as necessary.

To simplify this section it is split into two parts, horses and ponies partially at grass and those permanently out at pasture.

Horses partially at grass

Pasture time is important for all horses no matter what their workload as it allows them time to relax and mentally recharge.

Fit horses

Most fit horses or those in medium to hard work should be allowed pasture time during the day or a least a couple of days per week.

The important point is that a fit horse or one in hard work should not be allowed to gorge for hours on rich grass. This will give him a 'grass belly' restricting his ability to work properly. About 2 hours a day or one to two half days a week is generally long enough especially during the months when the grass is at its richest. It is better to restrict pasture time and feed more hay, than to allow an excess of rich grass.

If the horse is out a couple of hours a day, his feed will be almost normal. He may not need his lunch time ration of hay if he goes out in the afternoon. If the grass is good he will probably refuse his hay at lunch time anyway, in anticipation of the juicy pasture which he will prefer.

Horses on light to moderate work

If the horse is not in hard work and his pasture time is longer, around six hours a day, he will still need his concentrates to suit the work. His hay though, can be reduced by a couple of wedges per day.

Horses and ponies permanently out at grass

This subject is little more complex because of the variety of scenarios.

The first question is to ask what **type of horse** would be kept permanently at grass? Whilst it is possible for Thoroughbreds or competition horses to live out successfully, in this country the majority of those at permanent pasture are native breeds; ponies and cob types of around 14 to 15 hands high. These can withstand wet springs and autumns with spells of cold in winter.

The next consideration is the **seasons** of the year and closely allied with this is the **workload** of the horse or pony. Unlike stabled animals who generally are worked fairly regularly all year, especially if the establishment has an indoor school, the grass kept animal's workload is dependent on weather conditions and hours of daylight. Even when there is an indoor school available, if the horse or pony is wet he will not be able to be ridden until dry. (A saddle should not be put on a wet horse.)

Quality of pasture is partly dependent on the season but also on the standard of grassland management. The types of grasses, the soil, altitude, weather and the efficiency of the farmer, can all affect fields. Pasture can vary from being rich, with plenty of clover, to sparse or poor. A horse at rich pasture will need less additional feeding than a horse on poor pasture.

All these factors must be considered in relation to each other when calculating a correct quota for feeding a horse or pony at grass.

- **Type of horse or pony**
- **The time of year**
- **Quality of pasture**
- **Type and amount of work**

The Seasons

Winter

All horses and ponies living out need supplementary feeding in winter. At this season there is little or no grass, and what there is has lost its nutritional value, yet the pony now has to maintain his body temperature and condition through cold, wet weather. He now needs the same ration as the stabled horse. During very cold spells he may need a little more.

Hay

Feeding extra roughage starts around mid October if the weather is bad, but certainly by November. This is vital if the horses and ponies are to stay in good condition and winter out the next few months successfully.

Hay is put out into the field in increasing quantities during the winter months. Small amounts are offered at first. During October if the grass is still nutritious this may be left uneaten. When the animals are consuming all the hay, the quota must be increased to provide the roughage necessary.

In the depth of winter the amounts will be about 7 - 9 kilos (15-20 lbs) per pony and 9-11 kilos (20-25 lbs) per horse.

Concentrates

The amount of hard food given should be related to the workload. For the horse or pony performing more than 4 hours a week or harder work such as cross country rides, the concentrates must match the workload.

Normally the horse or pony will be worked less as the nights draw in and the weather worsens; the work becomes sporadic, usually only during weekends and holidays. A low energy diet can be given as 10% of the total daily ration with a slight increase during the times when the horse or pony is worked.

Example New Forest pony mare 13.2 hh increasingly needs up to 9 kilos (20 lbs) per day, most of this is hay in the field. As she is exercised only at weekends and holidays, she will need a basic 10% concentrates increasing to 15-20% hard feed when working, the remainder is hay. This equals 1-2 kilos (2-4 lbs) hard feed and about 8 kilos (16-18 lbs) of hay.

Spring

Around mid March the hay quota in the field will be refused in favour of the new spring grass. It is at this time and for the next few months that the horses and ponies need watching. If left to gorge on the lush, spring growth they will quickly become fat and soft. This can lead to various digestive problems and illnesses including laminitis when an excess of rich grass leads to painful inflammation in the sensitive laminae of the foot. The laminae swell and press against the hoof causing intense pain. This usually occurs in the forefeet but can also affect the hind.

If the grass is rich all the horses and ponies, particularly those prone to laminitis, will need their pasture time restricting. They can either be brought in and kept in a stable for a few hours or put in a starvation paddock during the day. Large fields can be divided or have a portion fenced off, so that the horses do not have access to large amounts of pasture.

Being brought in for a few hours a day, lightly exercised and then given a small feed of a Pasture mix or cube will help. The compound food will be less rich than the grass, and feeding before turning the pony out in the field may prevent him from gorging himself. And can they gorge themselves! What appeared to be a well-proportioned pony will, in three to four hours, take on a roundness that is unbelievable.

Though April, May and June are the danger months, ponies can develop laminitis during March if the winter has been mild and the grass comes through early. For horses and ponies in full work during spring, good quality pasture will provide all the roughage needed. Concentrates must be fed as per workload.

Example Our New Forest mare is doing well, too well to judge from her shape! She is being exercised more regularly but will certainly need her pasture time restricting. She is brought in and put into a box, given a small feed of pasture mix about 1.5 kilos (3 lbs) with carrots. She stays in the box for about four hours then is put into a paddock. She is allowed out in the big field at night, but her waistline definitely needs watching.

Summer

Basically a horse or pony feeding from good quality grass during the summer months, working up to four hours a week will need no further food. The pasture will provide all the nutrients necessary for him to maintain his condition.

Summers, though, can be hot and dry and result in arid pasture with little or no grass. In these circumstances horses and ponies will certainly need feeding with hay for roughage and the appropriate hard food.

The grass kept horse or pony is exercised more often during the summer. The evenings are lighter, the weather warmer and drier; there are competitions and shows on at the weekends. The horse or pony may hack out each day or be schooled and have riding club work on Saturday or Sunday. In this case he needs some hard food. Whilst he can maintain his condition quite satisfactorily on good pasture, even coping with light work, for a larger workload his diet will need supplementing. The workload and hard feed are gradually built up late spring and early summer, so that the concentrate percentage is equivalent to the amount of work performed.

Example Our pony is doing more work now, hacking each day, light schooling, a little jumping and small competitions and gymkhanas some weekends. She obtains all the roughage needed from grass and refuses to eat hay.

She has maintained condition well but as she is working 6-10 hours a week, is now being fed 2 kilos (4 lbs) of mix and carrots per day after work to contend with the workload. If she works longer at weekends she will be given 2.5 kilos (5 lbs) per day split into two feeds morning and in the evening before she goes out to pasture.

♦ Native horses and ponies convert grass into energy more efficiently than non-native breeds. So our New Forest is being given a little less concentrates than if she was fully stabled.

Autumn

The grass begins to lose its goodness in early autumn, though there can be a second surge of growth in September. By October, hay should be put out in the fields at a rate of 4 kilos (10 lbs) per pony. The horses and ponies should have put on a little weight over the summer period, which will act as insulation and food reserve during the winter.

The workload is probably decreasing but there is now little or no nutrition in the grass. In order to avoid any sudden alteration to the diet, food should be altered gradually during the autumn period.

Example The workload is dropping off with the dark nights and colder weather. Our New Forest pony is making full use of the last growth in September and by October is eating the hay put out in the field. Her workload is decreasing and we gradually decrease her concentrates to follow suit. She will be brought in every day and given a feed, which starts off at 2 kilos (4 lbs) reducing to 1 kilo (2 lbs). If she is worked at weekends she will be compensated with a larger feed.

Summary

This is the basis for feeding horses and ponies at grass, but there must be complete flexibility as so much depends on the type of pony and his general health throughout the year.

Though horses and ponies fare well at grass, and sometimes seem healthier and happier than their stabled counterparts, they are individuals and changes may occur which need to be dealt with promptly. The rule is to **monitor the animal's condition constantly.**

Feeding special cases

Young horses

Foals grow at a much faster rate than adults, especially during the first year of life. Until 5 or 6 years of age they need more protein, vitamins and minerals for growth of bones, teeth, muscles and all bodily systems. Deficiencies arising during this time will affect them in later life.

With compound foods there are special feeds for brood mares, foals and young stock such as Creep Pellets, Yearling Cubes and Stud Mix. Foals kept at pasture must have good quality grass including some clover.

Invalid horses

The first consideration for a horse who is off work or on light exercise only, is to reduce the percentage of 'hard' feed.

Convalescence diet

The sick horse will need the same daily amount of food but the concentrate portion will be reduced gradually whilst the amount of roughage is increased. The type of concentrates given can also be changed to a low energy food.

The horse will need proteins, fat and oils, extra minerals and vitamins to aid his recuperation, to encourage the replacement of lost cells and the growth of new bodily tissues.

Method

The concentrate portion is reduced to convalescence level by the third day.

> For horses on a low amount or percentage of concentrates, this can be achieved by halving the concentrates on day one and again on day three.

> For horses on a higher amount of concentrates, decrease the feed on day one, two and three.

> The rate of decrease is performed gradually and the level of 20% concentrates to 80% roughage is reached by the third day.

At the same time the type of food can be altered. Oats can be stopped almost immediately. In the case of Compound feed, the Competition Mix or similar can be replaced with Convalescence Mix.

Roughage must be increased in conjunction with concentrate decrease.

The type of roughage can be changed from HorseHage or seed hay to meadow hay, which is softer, easier to digest and less rich.

Food can be mixed with sugar beet pulp or dampened down to minimise dust and to make the feed easier to chew.

Smaller feeds can be offered more frequently. Hay can be given ad lib. (This should be soaked hay preferably, to prevent any respiratory problems. The horse may be more prone to this when ill).

Succulents should be offered especially if the horse has no access to grass.

Molasses or sugar beet may be used to tempt a fussy eater or a horse that is off his food.

Cooked foods are especially beneficial being easier to chew and digest. These can be fed little and often. Alternatively there are compound feeds especially designed for invalid horses such as Convalescence Mix or Cooked Cereal Meals. If possible, take the horse out to nibble some grass. There is nothing that encourages recuperation so swiftly as 'Dr. Green'! In some cases the Vet may advise a special diet and supplementary vitamins or minerals.

Older or aged horses and ponies

As with invalid animals, older horses and ponies are likely to have a lighter workload. There is also the possibility that they may have problems digesting the food or find it difficult to chew. The teeth may be too long or missing; the digestive system is not as efficient. It is important that the food contains proteins, vitamins and minerals to replace the accelerated loss of body cells.

Food for older horses needs to be easy to chew and digest. Cooked foods are useful as they do not need a lot of chewing. Compound cereal meals are also useful especially when dampened.

Exam Tips

Feeding horses and ponies at grass is such a wide and varied subject. Even if you have personal experience, you will need to know the basic rules for the average type of horse or pony at grass. You will need to understand how these are affected by the seasons, quality of pasture and workload.

For feeding special cases you will need to know the general rules about growth rate, special foods for horses that cannot chew their food efficiently and those that need food when ill. Again a visit to the Feed Merchant will give you an idea of what foods are available for these special cases.

C H A P T E R   18
The Horse's Foot

The foot is of vital importance to the horse. **'No foot, no horse'** is a very true cliché. The foot bears the horse's weight, absorbing the concussion and providing the essential foothold to prevent slipping. Watching a horse in action, it is astounding that the tiny area of the foot takes all the weight of the horse, rider and saddlery absorbing the immense concussive jar, making it look smooth and amazingly simple. This is particularly evident in jumping when the horse initially lands on one foreleg!

The Hoof

The hoof is made up of the horny portion or **wall** of the foot that grows down from the **coronet** at the top of the wall just under the hair. With an average monthly growth of about 1cm (approximately three/eighths of an inch), it can take between 9 to 12 months for a whole new hoof to grow. The hoof wall is made up of tubules of horn and, having no blood vessels or nerves, is insensitive; rather like a human nail.

The wall surface is covered with a varnish-like substance called the **periople** that regulates the amount of moisture entering and leaving the foot.

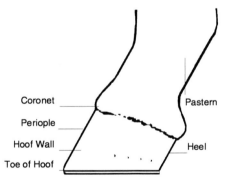

The thickness of the wall varies, from the thickest area at the **toe** to the thinner parts of the **quarters,** that is the sides of the hoof wall, and the **heels**. The wall is strong and tough, **providing protection to the inner, sensitive parts**. It also **carries most of the horse's weight**.

In appearance the wall of the foot should be **healthy and shiny**, with no cracks. The quality of horn depends on the health of the horse; poor health creates poor growth.

The wall should be an **even shape** all round. Both **forefeet should be similar in size** as should both hind feet. Incidentally, colour does not affect the strength of the horn. There is no proof that white hooves are weaker than black; they just have less pigmentation (colour).

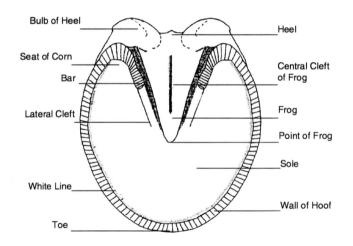

The Bars

The wall of the hoof continues right around the foot and turns inward either side at the heel. These are the bars. They are situated between the wall and the frog and merge into the sole before the point of frog. Between the bar and the wall is the seat of corn, a sensitive area that should not come into contact with the ground as it is prone to bruising. The bars, together with the frog and the grooves between, act as a non-slipping device. They provide a foothold rather like the ridges on the sole of a hiking boot.

The Frog

This soft, rubbery portion underneath the foot is triangular in shape, starting at the heel and decreasing to a point. It has four main functions.

- **Absorbs concussion** on contact with the ground acting as a **superb shock absorber.**

- Provides **grip** through its shape and the clefts, one in the centre and the lateral clefts at each side.

- **Pumps blood and lymph** back up the leg by putting pressure on the inner part of the foot. As the frog comes into contact with the ground it spreads under the weight. This affects the digital cushion inside which in turn compresses, forcing the blood back up the leg. It is, therefore, essential for the circulation in the foot and leg.

- Helps to **bear the horse's weight.**

To fulfil these functions properly, it is vital that the frog comes into contact with the ground when the horse is moving.

The Sole

The sole surrounds the frog and extends to the hoof wall. The external part is hard and protects the inner sensitive, fleshy sole. The outer layers are constantly growing with old growth paring off at intervals. New growth is provided by the inner sole.

The shape of the sole is important to provide a better foothold and to prevent bruising. It needs to be slightly concave. Too flat and the sole may suffer from bruising, injury, increased concussion and lameness. Too concave a sole may prevent the frog coming into contact with the ground. The sole also helps to bear the weight of the horse on its outer rim, adjacent with the wall.

The White Line
Along the inner edge of the foot, between the wall and the sole, is the white line. On the outside of this line is the insensitive part of the foot, the wall and the insensitive laminae. Inside the white line are the sensitive parts, the blood vessels, bones, sensitive sole and laminae.

Interior Structure of Foot

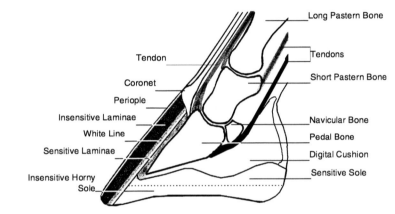

Laminae
The insensitive laminae are just inside the hoof wall. The sensitive laminae are attached to the pedal bone in the foot. The insensitive and sensitive laminae, thin leaf-shaped projections, interlock with each other rather like interlocking fingers and thus help to hold the pedal bone in place. So, if due to acute laminitis the blood supply is disturbed and some laminae are damaged, this interlocking breaks down. If enough laminae become diseased, the pedal bone is no longer held in place. The tendon at the back of the bone pulls upwards and this causes the bone to rotate. Eventually the tip of the bone can penetrate the sole.

Bones
There are strictly speaking **two and a half bones** in the foot. **Part of the short pastern bone,** the **pedal or coffin bone** with the **coffin joint** between and the **navicular.**

Tendons
The tendons, attached to muscles in the forearm, run down the leg and are connected to the bones in the foot. All movement within the foot is controlled by muscles whose actions are transmitted via these long tendons to the foot. **There are no muscles beneath the knee or hock.**

Ligaments
Attach bone to bone and help prevent over extension of a joint.

The digital or plantar cushion
This is situated above the frog and is similar in shape. It is thick and, because of its elasticity, acts as part of the shock absorbing mechanism.

The lateral cartilages
The cartilages hold and support the digital cushion. They also help to absorb concussion.

Table showing functions of the various parts of the foot and leg

Function	Part associated with function
Weight bearing	Wall, part of sole, frog
Anti-concussion/shock absorber	Frog, digital cushion, lateral cartilages, suspensory ligament in leg. The shoulder area
Grip/foothold, anti-slipping device	Frog, cleft of frog, bars, sole
Circulation of blood	Frog, digital cushion
Protection	Wall of foot, sole, rubbery exterior of frog

Horses rarely have perfect feet but there is no doubt that if a horse is born with, or develops through life, a poor foot he will inevitably suffer from physical problems.

A good Farrier is therefore an essential asset to all horse owners. The Farrier can keep the horse's feet in a good condition, minimising as far as possible many problems. He or she can also perform remedial shoeing, which helps to improve incorrect conformation or faulty action due to injury or disease.

Angle of the Foot

The slope of the foot has a specified angle between the horizontal floor surface and the slope of the front of the foot. Ideally this should be **45 to 50 degrees in the forefeet** and **50 to 55 degrees in the hind.**

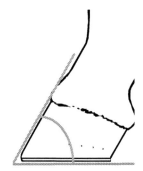

Front foot

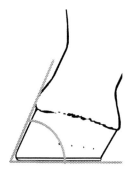

Hind foot

To assess these angles stand the horse on level ground and view the foot from the side. The slope of the foot should follow through the **pastern to the fetlock**. *In other words the angle of the foot should be the same as the angle of the pastern.* This is referred to as the **Foot Pastern Angle or FPA.**

The heel of the foot should be **parallel to the front of the foot,** that is **it should have the same angle.**

Incorrect angles

Horses who exhibit an incorrect FPA do so for two main reasons, conformation or bad shoeing.

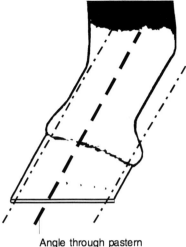

Angle through pastern to fetlock.

1) Conformation

Horses are born with an incorrect angle of foot.

a) If a horse has naturally upright feet and pasterns, he is said to have 'boxy feet'. The feet are usually too small for the horse's size. Because the frog is small, the heels upright and the angles of the joints too straight, concussion cannot be absorbed efficiently.

The results will be increased concussion to the joints and consequently a bumpy ride.

b) If the horse has long, sloping toes and pasterns with low heels, the result is flat feet prone to bruising of the sole.

This conformation also results in tendon strain because the angle is sharp around the fetlock.

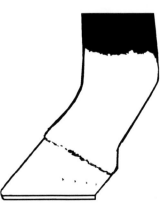

2) Bad Shoeing or Bad Foot Care

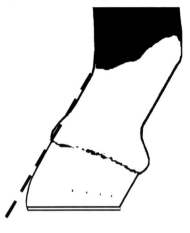

a) **Foot too short.** The foot is made to fit the shoe; the toe of the foot has been cut too far back (dumped). The results are damage to the toe and possible cracking of the horn.

b) **Toes allowed to grow too long**. The horse is either not shod frequently enough or is shod incorrectly. The heels are worn down causing tendon strain and possibly navicular syndrome (a degeneration of the navicular bone in the foot). A horse with an overlong toe can also tend to trip and possibly injure himself.

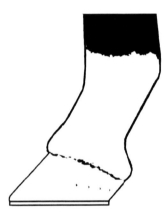

In the case of a horse with bad conformation, shoeing can to some extent reduce the problems. In the case of bad shoeing or bad foot care this may take a good Farrier months, even a year to correct.

Exam Tips

For the Stage II you will need to learn the external and internal structure of the foot. Start to observe a variety of horses' feet and learn to judge the Foot Pastern Angle, relating this to the slope of the shoulder, the two should be similar. Learn also to recognise those horses with upright, boxy feet and those with long, sloping feet. Then watch their action and observe how the feet can influence the horse's movement. The more you understand about the problems that can result from an incorrect slope of foot the easier it will be for you to explain this to the Examiner.

CHAPTER 19
Shoeing

The horse's feet should receive attention from a Farrier every four to six weeks depending on the horse's foot growth, condition of his feet, his work and environment. **The horse should never be left longer than six weeks,** even those resting at grass should have their feet inspected regularly. To leave a horse longer than six weeks can result in problems.

Reasons for Shoeing

1. **Protection** for the foot - to prevent wearing down and damage of the horn from work.

2. **Grip** - to provide a more efficient foothold particularly in difficult conditions, occasionally with the assistance of studs.

3. To aid in the **reduction of concussion**.

4. To keep the feet in a **healthy condition**. The feet need to be **correctly trimmed and balanced** to avoid many problems from injury or illness.

5. To **improve the condition** of poor feet. Good shoeing can work wonders on problem feet.

6. To **protect against bad conditions**; wet conditions can soften the feet; hard, dry conditions can damage the feet.

7. To **improve defects** in conformation or action. Problems with the feet can affect the whole horse.

8. For **medical reasons**, in conjunction with veterinarian treatment.

9. If the shoe does not need renewing, the old shoe should be removed and the foot trimmed. The old shoe can then be replaced. This is called a **'remove'** or a **'refit'**.

The foot will need attention when;

- the shoe is **cast**.
- the shoe is held on by one nail or a clip; it is **sprung**.
- the shoe is **loose**.
- the **clenches are raised** and stand out from the wall.
- the shoe is **worn thin** in areas, is cracked or snapped.
- the **foot has grown too long**, usually happens at the toe.
- there is a **medical problem** that needs remedial shoeing.
- there is a problem such as **nail bind or nail prick**.
- the horse develops an **incorrect action** such as **over-reaching**; hitting the front foot with the hind, or **brushing**; when one foreleg hits the other foreleg.

Figure 19: Over-reaching   **Figure 20: Brushing**

Hot and Cold Shoeing

Shoes are generally bought ready made. Some Farriers can fashion their own shoes from a bar of steel that is already concave and fullered. This type of shoe is necessary in special circumstances, for instance if the horse or pony has an unusual shaped or sized foot.

In the majority of cases, a specific sized shoe is shaped to fit the foot.

In hot shoeing a furnace is used to heat the metal and then the shoe is hammered into shape.

Cold shoeing is a little more restrictive because the shoe cannot be remodelled to a great degree. The feet need to be measured accurately and the Farrier given the measurements before his visit.

Measuring A Foot

Measure the foot heel to toe and from side to side.

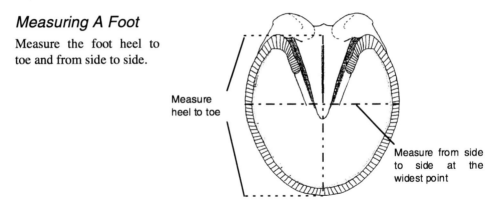

Measure heel to toe

Measure from side to side at the widest point

The Farrier's Tools

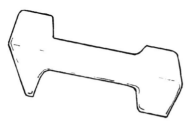

Buffer

Made of steel this is used in conjunction with the driving hammer to raise the clenches when removing the shoe.

Driving Hammer

Together with the buffer this hammer raises the clenches. It is also used to drive the nail into the foot securing the shoe, and to twist off the point into a clench.

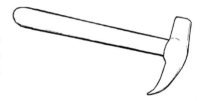

Pincers

These are used to lever off the old shoe.

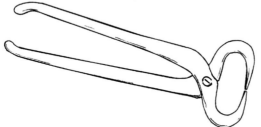

Hoof cutters

Similar in shape to pincers but having one thin, sharper blade and a thick, flat blade. Hoof cutters are used to trim the hoof.

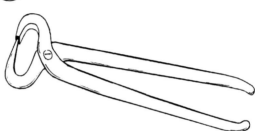

Rasp

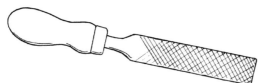

Used to rasp level the surface of the foot and to finish off the foot and shoe. One side is rougher than the other.

Drawing knife

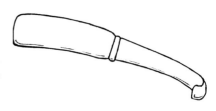

Has a curved blade with a slightly bent end. This knife trims the horn, frog and sole. It is also used to cut the hoof to provide an indentation for the clips.

Anvil

A large piece of metal on which the shoes are hammered into shape.

Fire tongs

Long bladed, pincer type tool used to place the shoe in, and remove it from, the forge.

Pritchel

A steel bar with a pointed end. The Farrier sticks the sharp point of the pritchel into a nail hole of the shoe and carries the hot shoe to the horse's foot for fitting. The pritchel can also be used to place holes into the hand made shoe.

Shoeing tongs

Used to hold the shoe when being hammered on the anvil.

Toeing knife

A small steel knife with a short flat blade. Trims excessive hoof growth.

Tripod

A three legged stand used for placing the hoof on when rasping and finishing off.

Nail Clencher

Used to flatten the clenches against the hoof wall.

(Also known as the 'smiling crocodile'!)

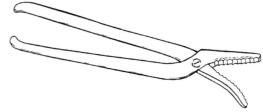

Shoeing procedures

There are different stages in the shoeing process. The Farrier removes the old shoe, trims and shapes the horse's foot, fits the new shoe and secures it with nails.

The horse is properly restrained first with a headcollar and lead-rope to a securing ring. Most horses and ponies are used to being shod and will stand quietly but, if the horse decides to fidget, an assistant may have to hold him whilst the Farrier works.

1. Removing a Shoe

Facing the hindquarters, the Farrier picks up the horse's foreleg and places the hoof between his knees. The Farrier holds it firmly by turning his (the Farrier's) toes in slightly. The hindleg is not placed between the knees in case the horse kicks. The Farrier bends his knees slightly and rests the hindleg across his thighs.

Buffer and Hammer. One of the thinner ends of the buffer, either the wedge end or the more pointed portion,is placed under a clench and the blunt end is tapped with the hammer until the clench is clear of the wall and straight. All the clenches are straightened out in this way.

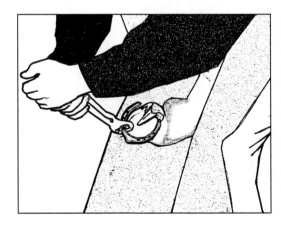

Pincers. The shoe is levered off with the pincers. This is done carefully to avoid ripping or tearing off any hoof wall. Starting at the outside heel the Farrier grips the shoe with the pincers and gently levers *towards the centre of the foot*. This is repeated on the other heel, again levering towards the centre of the foot. The pincers are then used in exactly the same way on the quarters of the shoe and the toe. At the toe, the shoe is levered towards the centre of the foot and then removed cleanly.

The foot is inspected to check that all the nails have been taken out.

2. Trimming

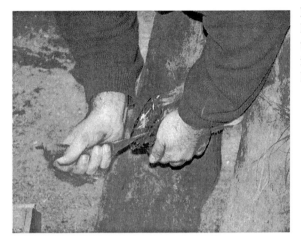

Excess growth is cut off with the **hoof cutters**. The hoof wall tidied up and ragged pieces of sole or frog trimmed with the **drawing knife**.

3. Preparing the Foot

The surface of the foot is levelled off with the **rasp**.

Small indentations may be made with the **drawing knife** for the clips. Front feet have one toe clip in the centre. Hind feet have two 'quarter' clips, one either side. A toe clip placed on the hind foot may cause damage if the horse overreaches.

4. Preparing the Shoe

Cold shoeing
With cold shoeing the foot should already have been measured and the shoe will either fit or be close to fitting. A cold shoe can be hammered into shape to a certain extent but not nearly as precisely as in hot shoeing.

Hot shoeing
The Farrier will check the shoe against the foot first. Then he will place the shoe in the **forge** for heating. Most Farriers have a portable forge these days.

5. Fitting the Shoe

The **pritchel** is used to carry the hot shoe to the foot. The shoe is held against the surface of the hoof, which will burn slightly. This is to check the fit; any uneven discoloration will give a clear indication as to where alterations must be made to the shoe. This is not meant to create a better surface for the shoe by burning off any bits of hoof. The shoe should never be too hot nor held against the hoof too long. If a portion of the hoof is burnt too much, it will disintegrate in time and break away.

The hot shoe may be hammered into shape and tried again on the foot. When the Farrier is satisfied the shoe is immersed into cold water.

6. Securing the Shoe

Normally the amount of nails used is seven, three on the inside of the foot and four on the outside. There are no hard and fast rules about this; the number may vary. If the horse has a badly split hoof, the Farrier may choose to use fewer nails. If the horse has a habit of casting his shoes then a greater number of nails may be necessary. Nails come in different weights and sizes, the decision which to use is dependent on the type of horse and the work he does.

Nails are shaped with a flat bevelled end and a sharp pointed end. The nail is slanted slightly to one side so that it can be driven in correctly between the white line and the outer edge of the wall.

This slanting design ensures that the end of the nail emerges from the hoof pointing away from the wall. Pricking the sensitive parts of the foot can cause numerous problems from soreness to an infected puncture wound.

The first nail is usually driven in at the toe to secure the shoe. All the nails should emerge from the wall about 3-4 cm (1½ inches) from the lower edge of the hoof. The driving hammer is used to drive the nails in.

The claw on the other side of the head is used to twist the point of the nail off; leaving enough to create a clench.

It is important that the nail is driven in correctly to avoid problems:

Nail bind   the nail is driven in too close to the white line causing soreness and pain.

Nail prick   the nail is driven into the sensitive areas of the foot causing a puncture wound.

Coarse nailing the nail is driven too high up the wall.

Fine nailing   the nail is driven in and emerges too low down the wall. The shoe is more likely to come off and the hoof more prone to splitting.

7. Finishing off

The sharp point of the nail is smoothed with the rasp. A small indentation in the hoof may also be made with the rasp or the drawing knife to create a 'bed' for the clench. The point of the nail protruding from the wall of the hoof is flattened down with the nail clencher. Alternatively the Farrier may use the hammer to make a clench.

The clenches are rasped to make them flush against the wall. The front toe clip and hind quarter clips are gently tapped into place with the hammer. The rasp is then run around the lower edge of the hoof where it meets the shoe to reduce any gaps and make the hoof flush with the shoe.

Most riding establishments prefer hot shoeing. The shoe can be made to fit the horse's foot more precisely than with cold shoeing. The only drawback to hot shoeing is that some Farriers may burn the foot too much. On the other hand there is a greater temptation when cold shoeing to make the foot fit the shoe rather than the other way around.

Inspecting the Newly Shod Foot

Though some problems are not always apparent until a couple of days later, all newly shod horses should be checked straight away. Any correction can then be made by the Farrier whilst he is still at the yard.

Checks to be made.

1. The shoe has been made to fit the foot and **not the foot to fit the shoe**. In some cases the hoof is left too long to fit a large shoe or the foot is dumped to fit a smaller shoe.

2. The **shoe is the correct size**. The shoe must not be too small or parts of the foot will be liable to bruising particularly the heels and seat of corn. Too large a shoe and the horse may start brushing and cause injury.

3. The **shoe fits properly** and **is flush with the hoof**. There should be no gaps between the foot and the shoe.

4. The **feet have a regular, even shape** all round. The forefeet should be similar in shape to each other as should both hinds. One foot should not be bigger or smaller than the other unless this is a fault in the horse's conformation.

5. The **correct amount of hoof has been trimmed off**. The toe should definitely not be too long or conversely too short.

6. The **Foot Pastern Angle is correct.**

7. The **heels of the shoe must be the correct length**, not too short nor too long. Sometimes if the heels of the foot wear down too quickly or the horse suffers from contracted heels, the Farrier may make the shoe a little longer for protection. If the heels are too long the shoe can easily be ripped off.

8. The **clenches are the correct height on the foot**. This should be approximately one third up the hoof.

9. The **clenches are level**, in a line on the foot.

10. The **correct number of nails are used**. Normally 4 on the outside, 3 inside, but this can vary.

11. All **clips and clenches are flush with the hoof wall**, not standing out or prominent.

12. There has been **no undue rasping** of the hoof especially above the clenches. The periople may be damaged.

13. The foot is **balanced from heel to toe** and **from side to side**. The surface of the foot on the shoe and the shoe on the ground should be level; no part should be higher or lower than the rest of the foot. An imbalance will cause incorrect action, strained tendons, muscles and joints. It may even cause deformities in the joints of the legs if not corrected in time.

14. The **correct weight or type of shoe has been used**. This is particularly important. A light shoe on a heavy horse can wear out more quickly and a heavy shoe on a light footed horse can cause action problems or tripping.

15. The **frog comes into contact with the ground.** The foot needs to be picked up to check. Lay the hand flat against the sides of the shoe; the frog should just be felt. The frog should not be over trimmed nor the wall of the hoof left so long that the frog cannot come into contact with the ground when the horse is moving.

16. Most importantly, **the horse should be sound**.

The horse may be trotted up before the Farrier leaves the yard. This does not show distrust of the Farrier but it may save him a return journey if the horse does need attention.

Daily Care of the Foot

The horse's feet should be cleaned and checked daily and picked out after he works. As much dirt as possible should be removed including in the clefts of the foot and around the heel area. If the horse lives out at grass his feet should be cleaned and, if wet, allowed to dry out every day.

The use of a hoof ointment or vegetable oil assists in keeping the feet in good condition. The thick, black hoof oil is not recommended these days as it prevents the osmotic action of the horn, that is, the interchange of moisture to and from the hoof.

The stable and bedding should be kept clean and dry. When hacking the rider should avoid stony or really hard areas as well as deep, soft, muddy ground, which may put a strain on the foot and shoe.

Common Types of Shoe

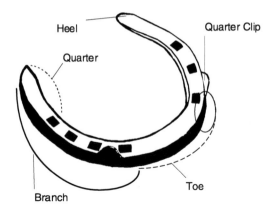

Figure 21:Parts of a shoe

Concave Fullered Shoe

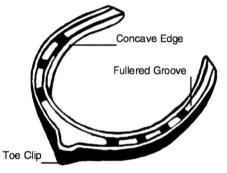

This is the most usual type in use. The inside edge of the shoe is concave, sloped to match the shape of the hoof wall, and grooved on the ground surface (fullered). This makes the shoe lighter, provides extra grip and reduces suction in soft ground.

There is one toe clip for the forefeet and two quarter clips for the hind. The heels are usually pencilled, that is made with a slimmer shape at the heel. This is designed to minimise the risk of the shoe being trodden on by the horse or another horse and ripped off the foot. The shape of the fore shoe will be fairly circular and the hind is slightly oval.

Plain Stamped Shoe

This has a flat, level surface all round and, as it is stronger and hard wearing, is generally used on heavy horses performing roadwork. The nail holes are designed in the shape of the nail head to hold the shoe more securely. These holes can also be varied along the surface of the shoe to suit different shapes of foot. The plain stamped shoe is heavier and does not provide the grip or anti-suction properties of the concave fullered shoe.

The Hunter Shoe

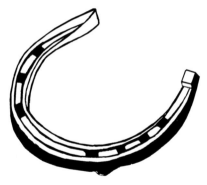

This can be made from a plain stamped shoe but is usually of a concave fullered design. It has the additions of a **calkin and wedge**. A **calkin is a square raised portion on the outside heel** whilst the **wedge is a slimmer raised portion on the inside heel**. (Remember the **in** is **out**; calk**in** is on the **out**side.)

These provide grip, especially in soft ground. The wedge is smaller than the calkin to prevent the horse wounding himself should he happen to catch the opposite leg. Nowadays the calkin and wedge have been replaced by studs of which there are a variety of shapes and sizes to suit the conditions of the ground.

Grass Tips

These are modified shoes specially fitted for horses at grass. They cover the **toe region only** and prevent splitting or other damage to the hoof. They are also used for a horse who may kick in the field. The normal shoe is removed and replaced with grass tips then, should the horse kick another, the risk of injury is reduced.

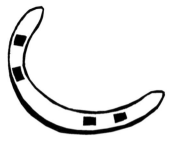

Exam Tips

Look at as many horses' feet as you can so that you are able to tell when a horse has been newly shod and when he needs shoeing. Check some horses who have just been shod and learn to look out for the points of good and bad shoeing. Look at horses with problem feet and ask the Farrier the methods he uses to correct any defects.

In the examination each candidate will be given a shoeing tool and asked to name, describe and talk about its function. Candidates may then have to give a *practical demonstration on how to remove a shoe*; not actually removing it but showing how this is done.

There is really no substitute to watching and talking to the Farrier. It is amazing how much can be learnt from observing and asking relevant questions. He may even be willing to allow you to remove a shoe - on a quiet horse, under supervision. If you have never taken a shoe off it is worth practising once or twice. The Farrier makes it look simple, but it is harder than it appears.

C H A P T E R   20
Bridles

Bridles are available in various patterns and designs, but one of the most important points is to purchase a bridle made of good quality leather.

The leather should have good 'substance' that is thickness and strength; good quality English leather is the best. There are foreign makes on the market, some of these are of good quality but the cheaper ones made of inferior leather may break easily. The most important areas are the cheekpieces and the reins; these need to be tough and strong for safety.

Bridles are sold in three main sizes - full size, cob or pony and sometimes in a small pony size. Normally the bit is bought separately.

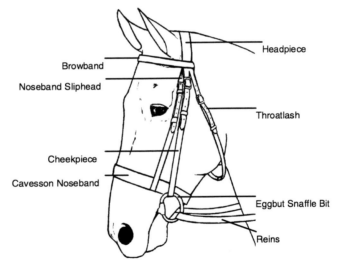

Figure 22: Points of the bridle

Revision

The snaffle bridle, snaffle bits, single, double jointed and straight bar, different bit rings, parts of the snaffle bridle. Nosebands, Cavesson, Drop, Flash, Grakle and sheepskin. How to put on and remove a bridle. How to fit a snaffle bridle with different types of noseband.

Fitting the bridle

As well as being of good quality, the bridle needs to fit the horse correctly. A quick assessment can be made first by holding the bridle up to the side of the horse's head. This will give a good indication of whether the bridle will fit and whether it needs to be lengthened or shortened.

If the bridle appears to be the right size and after any adjustments have been made, the bridle can be assessed on the horse. Remove the straps from the runners and keepers first so that any alterations can be made quickly.

Once the bridle is on, check the position of the bit. A snaffle bit should be high enough in the mouth to cause a wrinkle around the corners of the lips. Too low and it may come into contact with the canine or incisor teeth; too high and it may knock against the molars; at best it will be uncomfortable for the horse.

Alter the cheekpieces if necessary. Check that they are fastened at the same level on either side of the headpiece, usually two or three holes from the top, so that the bit is level in the mouth.

The browband should fit fairly snugly, not too tight to pull the headpiece forward, yet not too loose allowing the headpiece to slip backwards.

Fasten the noseband and check the fit. The position of the cavesson should be about two finger's width below the projecting cheekbone. It should be tight enough just to fit two finger's width between the noseband and the horse's nasal bone.

Fasten the throatlash so that there is the space of one hand's width between it and the horse's cheek. If the throatlash is too tight it may restrict the horse's breathing; too loose and the bridle may come off if pulled forwards.

The reins are important and should be the right size for horse and rider. So many times long reins are used for ponies and the excess loop can be seen wrapped around the child's foot. Often then the child has to knot the reins, which is not ideal. Alternatively if the reins are too short this will make the rider lean forward or pull on the horse's mouth. Reins vary from pony to full size.

The reins should also be the right thickness for the hand. If the reins are too thick this is uncomfortable. Too thin and they may break more easily.

Reins are manufactured in a variety of materials such as; plain leather, plaited or laced leather, rubber covered or webbing.

Nosebands

Nosebands, used in conjunction with the bridle, for the most part help the action of the bit. The cavesson is mostly cosmetic helping to 'shorten' the appearance of the horse's face. It can be used with a standing martingale.

The Flash, Drop and Grakle all have similar functions. They help to keep the bit in place in the horse's mouth and to prevent the horse opening his mouth or crossing his jaw and evading the bit. The Grakle is the strongest as it acts over a larger part of the face applying pressure to the nose area.

The Flash, Drop and Grakle are fitted so that a lower strap fits under the bit. This is fastened quite firmly to have an effect but not too tight to clamp the horse's mouth shut.

The Kineton noseband is rarely used nowadays. It helps to control a strong horse by transferring some of the rein pressure from the mouth to the nose. It can however restrict the horse's breathing if incorrectly fitted.

The front of the noseband is very similar to the frontal part of the Drop noseband except that it can be adjusted by a buckle. Connecting the front section to the sliphead is a U-shaped piece of metal that fits behind the bit.

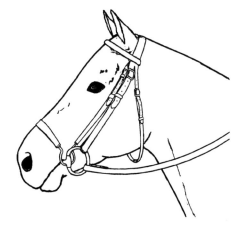

The front part of the Kineton must be four fingers width above the nostril and fastened tight enough to employ pressure upon the horse's nose when necessary.

The Bit

There are so many different views and opinions on bitting that choosing a bit for a new horse can be confusing. Sometimes finding the most suitable bit comes through experimenting and experience; trying different types and feeling how the horse responds.

The different families of bridles and bits are:

1. The snaffle
2. The gag
3. The pelham
4. The Kimblewick (normally included in the pelham family)
5. The bitless bridle
6. The curb
7. The double

Materials

Bits are constructed from a variety of materials. The most popular is **stainless steel**; it is durable, relatively rust proof and safe in the mouth as it does not tend to break or bend. **Chromium plated steel** again is durable and safe except that, occasionally, the chrome can flake off, resulting in a roughened surface. Bits can also be manufactured from **alloys,** a mixture of stainless steel, copper and nickel. **Pure nickel** is not safe; the metal is weak and can snap. A nickel bit can be recognised by its dull, yellow colour. **Copper** bits are used for horses who suffer from dry, fixed mouths as it encourages salivation making the mouth moist and more relaxed.

Rubber, though soft in the mouth and therefore mild, is easily bitten through. Any rubber bit must have a metal interior, a metal bit or a metal chain, to give it strength. **Vulcanite bits** (made from rubber hardened by heat) though kind in action, tend to be thick and heavy. This type of bit can sometimes give very little 'feel' in the mouth.

Nylon is a material that is strong and durable but at the same time is light in weight.

Nathe is a pale yellow, rubbery plastic covering a chain of metal. This can be beneficial for a horse with a tender or sensitive mouth. Nathe bits are easily bitten through and in some cases do not last long.

Principles of Bitting

Bitting is choosing a suitable bit for the horse and fitting it correctly. Basically the aim is to find a suitable bit in which the horse will perform well.

This choice depends on several factors,

a) **Type and breed of horse or pony**.

b) The **conformation** and **size of his mouth** and **tongue**.

c) The horse's **age** and **size**.

d) His **temperament**.

e) The horse's **standard of training**.

f) Any **mouth problems** - whether the horse has a **dry mouth**, if he has any **sensitivity in the mouth** or problems with his **teeth**.

g) Whether he is **strong**.

h) The **rider's capabilities** and **experience**.

i) The **work the horse is to perform** and his level of training.

j) Whether or not the horse **competes**. At certain competitions, only specified types of bit are allowed.

Action of bits

Each type of bit has a particular action and influence on the horse. Bits act by **movement and pressure** on different parts of the horse's head.

- the **tongue**
- the **bars** (the space in between incisor and molar teeth)
- the **lips**
- the **corners of the mouth**
- the **sides** of the **cheeks**
- the **palate or roof of the mouth**
- the **poll**

With special attachments pressure can also be transferred to

- the **chin groove** (curb chain)
- the **nose** (some types of noseband)

A mild or soft bit gives a light pressure especially when used by kind hands. A more severe bit either has a more definite action or applies pressure to another part of the horse's mouth or head.

The Snaffle

The most popular bit is the snaffle. This bit is made up of the mouthpiece and the bit ring. The main types of mouthpiece are the single jointed, double jointed, the straight bar and the mullen mouth. The bit ring varieties are the loose ring, the eggbutt, the D ring and those with long cheeks, the Fulmer and the long cheeked snaffle.

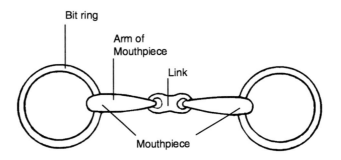

Figure 23: French link bit (double jointed) with loose rings

Single Jointed Bit

* Applies pressure to **the tongue, the bars of the mouth, the corners of the mouth and the lips.**

* 'Nutcracker' effect when the two arms increase and decrease the angle at the joint.

* Acts to **raise the horse's head**.

* **Thicker bits** are generally **milder than thinner bits**, but this does depend on the size of the horse's mouth. A large bit in a small mouth could be uncomfortable.

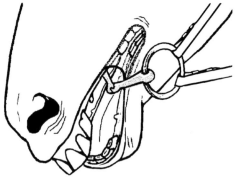

* Some variations can provide a stronger pressure such as the twisted snaffle with its twisted mouthpiece, which is a sharp, severe bit.

Double Jointed Bits

* The link between the arms of the mouthpiece provide two joints.

* Acts on **the tongue, the bars, the corners of the mouth and the lips**, but **without the nutcracker** effect of the single jointed.

* Three types of double jointed. The **French Link** is **mild** as the link lies flat on the tongue. The **ring type** has a small ring instead of a link. The **Dr. Bristol,** similar to the French Link, is more **severe** because the **link is set at an angle** and **puts pressure on the tongue.** The angle is caused by the arms of the mouthpiece being slightly twisted.

Straight Bar Bits

* Acts on the **tongue, the bars of the mouth and the lips**.

* **Mild action**, though with **little movement** in the mouth so the horse can learn to 'lean' on the bit.

* The **vulcanite** and **metal straight bar** can be **heavy**.

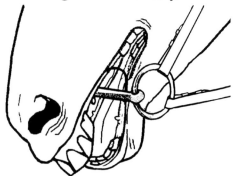

* The **mullen mouth** bit has a **raised portion above the tongue** reducing the pressure in this area.

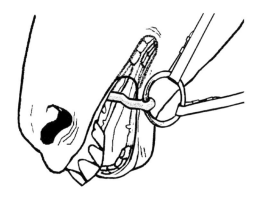

Bit rings

Different types and designs of bit rings also affect the action of the mouthpiece.

The Loose Ring

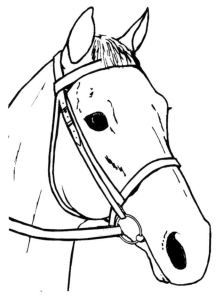

* Freedom of movement through the arm of the mouthpiece, so the rider's rein aid not as direct as the eggbut.

* Suitable for horses who tend to 'lean' or be 'heavy' on the bit.

♦ The movement can wear the metal thin where the ring passes through the mouthpiece. This can become sharp and pinch or injure the horse's mouth.

The Eggbut

* Designed to prevent pinching around the mouth.

* Suitable for a horse who has a 'fussy
mouth'.   Ring fixed to mouthpiece
making rider's rein aid more direct.

* Limits the movement of the bit in the
mouth and can consequently give a
rather 'fixed feel'.

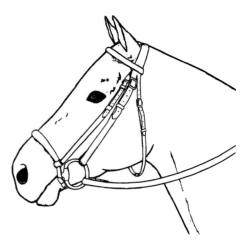

The D ring

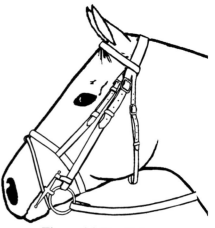

* This type of ring prevents the bit from
being pulled through the mouth.

* Helps steering by applying pressure on
the side of the mouth.

The Fulmer and the Long Cheeked Snaffle

* Both have long cheekpieces either attached
to the mouthpiece or as part of the ring.

* Useful for young horses because the bit
cannot be pulled through the mouth.

* The cheekpieces aid steering by pressing on
the cheek.

* All long cheeked bits should have **leather
keepers** to hold the cheekpieces in place.
This keeps the bit still in the mouth. Some
horses can, however, learn to 'lean' on the
long cheekpiece.

Figure 24:The Fulmer

Size of Bit

To obtain the correct size of bit use a piece of strong string or twine. Place it in the horse's mouth (with the horse correctly restrained) and keeping it straight, hold it either side just by the corners of the lips. Take the string out of the horse's mouth and measure the length. A bit should be approximately half an inch longer than the width of the mouth.

Bits are still measured by inches. They are usually sold in measurements increasing by half an inch. As a guide 4½ to 5 inches is pony size; 5" to 5½" is medium size; 5¼" to 5¾" is fine horse size and 5½" to 6" is full hunter size. Should the horse or pony not quite fit into these categories, purchasing a slightly larger size will cause no problem. It is better a little large than too small.

Checking the Size of Bit

To check the bit in the horse's mouth, the bridle should first be fitted correctly and the bit held straight and level. There should just be a thumb tip width (¼ inch) either side of the bit between the bit ring and the horse's lips (without depressing the lips). If the fit feels tight and the thumb is pressing the horse's lips inwards, try a larger size.

Overbitting

'Overbitting' is using a harsher bit than is necessary. This may happen when a rider, who is not proficient enough to use a milder bit, has to use a severe bit to gain control. The bars of a horse's mouth contain nerve endings that can become numb to any feeling through overbitting or bad, hard riding. The results are a 'hard mouth' and a horse who is unresponsive to the bit.

There are times when a stronger bit is necessary and this, in capable hands, can improve the horse's performance. A strong bit though, should never be used to force the horse into submission or to compensate for the rider's lack of skill.

Bit attachments

Bit guards are circular pads of rubber placed on the mouthpiece just inside the rings. They lie either side of the horse's mouth. These protect the mouth from any rubbing or chafing from the bit and rings. Bit guards must be kept clean. Dirt stuck to the guard will cause rubbing and sores on the horse's face.

Brush pricker. Similar to bit guards but with the addition of bristles on the inside of the pad. This is placed on the horse's stiff side in an attempt to encourage him to move away and stop him leaning on that side of the bit. A brush pricker should only be used for a short time.

A **Tongue Grid** is used to prevent the horse from putting his tongue over the bit. Placed on the mouthpiece, this rubber attachment can also help a horse with a dry mouth as it encourages mouthing and salivation. Some horses object to it quite strongly. Metal tongue grids are connected to a separate headpiece and fitted into the horse's mouth above the bit. This has the same function as the rubber tongue grid but is safer, as the rubber grid may become detached from the bit and be swallowed by the horse.

Australian Cheeker. Shaped as an inverted 'Y' this attachment, made of rubber, helps to keep the bit in the correct position in the mouth, and stops the horse from putting his tongue over the bit. It is attached to the headpiece and is positioned centrally down the horse's face. The separate arms are attached to each side of the bit. Used mostly for racehorses.

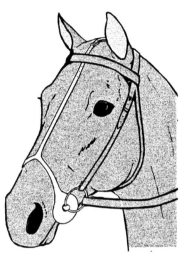

Grass Reins are fitted to ponies who have a habit of putting their heads down to graze when being ridden by children or on the lunge. Small children generally do not have the strength to pull the pony's head back up so grass reins are fitted to prevent the pony from suddenly putting his head down to nibble the grass. The reins can be made from leather, nylon, cord or improvised from strong twine. They are fastened onto the saddle 'Ds' or attached around the girth straps. The reins are threaded through the browband loops and attached to the bit or crossed over the neck of the pony.

Poor Fitting or Dirty Tack

A bridle that does not fit the horse will result in soreness around the face and head. A sore poll is often caused by a bridle that is too small. A dirty bridle could chafe the skin leading to open wounds which may become infected. Visible signs of problems would be bare patches or sores around the face, poll, cheeks or in the region of the noseband or browband. If the horse is reluctant to have his bridle or headcollar put on this would be another symptom of injury or soreness caused by the bridle.

Bits

A bit that does not fit will cause chafing, sores, pinching, result in pain and damage to the mouth and surrounding areas. Bits that are clogged up with old dried grass and saliva will not only be unpleasant for the horse but will result in friction sores.

Wounds can develop on the bars, the roof of the mouth, lips, corners, cheeks and even the chin groove. The symptoms of such problems would be redness around the mouth and on the tongue, bruising, soreness, splitting at the corners of the mouth, or rubbing in the chin groove. Any damage to the mouth area can take a long time to heal and it can be even longer before the horse's resistance is overcome.

Exam Tips

Candidates will need to know the various types of snaffle bit and their respective action on the horse's mouth and head. Look at as many different bits as you can and ask people the reasons for using one bit as opposed to another and how they feel the horse goes. Be careful not to take people's opinions too literally. There are as many different views on bits as there are bits, but this will give you a wider and more varied knowledge of bits and bitting.

CHAPTER 21
Saddlery

Saddles are available in various shapes and sizes to fit different horses, ponies and riders. There are also different styles to suit various types of work.

Revision

General purpose, dressage and jumping saddles. Materials used in constructing a saddle. Points of the saddle, assessing the condition of a saddle. Checking for a broken tree. Putting on and checking the fit of saddles. How to fasten the girth correctly. Checking the fit in use. Ill-fitting saddles and the consequences. Numnahs and saddle cloths, putting on and correct fitting. Removing the saddle.

Saddles

The **General Purpose saddle** having a medium cut flap is used for all disciplines, dressage, jumping and hacking.

The **Dressage saddle** is designed with a straight cut flap and a deeper seat encouraging the rider to sit deeper into the saddle with a straighter leg. Some dressage saddles feature longer girth straps which fasten below the saddle to a Lonsdale girth. This allows the rider's leg to come into closer contact with the horse's side.

The **Jumping saddle,** with its forward cut flaps, accommodates the rider's shorter stirrup length and the knee and thigh rolls secure the leg position. The seat of the saddle is generally flatter to allow more movement of the rider's seat when jumping.

The **Cross Country saddle.** Some 'event' saddles are similar to a GP saddle and can be used for dressage as well. Most advanced event riders though, will have two saddles; one specifically for the cross country and one for the dressage phase.

The **Child's saddle** has various designs but all are small and light. Some are made of felt which, being soft, are particularly good for a fat pony or one whose weight and shape fluctuates.

The **Show saddle** is fairly straight cut, particularly around the shoulder area, to show as much as possible of the horse or pony and his movement. It is usually quite light with quite a flat seat.

The **Long Distance saddle** needs to spread the rider's weight over as wide an area as possible on the horse's back so that pressure points are minimised. This is achieved by extending the panelling so there is a greater surface area. Specially designed, thick numnahs can also be used.

The **Side saddle,** used traditionally for ladies, keeps the legs to one side. Gaining in popularity, it is now used mainly for Showing classes.

The **Racing saddle** is small and light to minimise weight.

The **Western saddle.** Western riding is becoming more popular in this country. The high pommel and deeper seat are designed for riding for long periods in an upright position.

Size of saddle

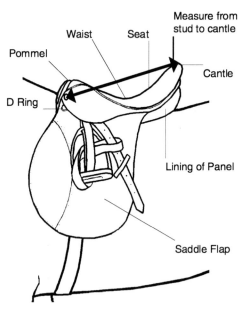

Saddles are produced in various lengths and widths to accommodate the shape and size of both horse and rider.

The length of a saddle is measured usually from the stud to the middle of the cantle. The length can vary from 10 to 14 inches for ponies, extending up to 17 or even 18 inches for a large horse. This length is important both for horse and rider.

Horses and ponies not only vary in size and therefore length, there are also differences between animals of similar size. Horses can be 'short-backed' or 'long-backed' and this will influence the length of saddle required.

Too long a saddle on a short-backed horse will rest on the loin area and could bruise or damage the kidneys. If the saddle is too small the rider's weight will be concentrated in one area causing pressure points.

Riders too come in difference shapes and sizes and it is just as essential that the saddle fits the rider for comfort, safety and to aid their riding ability.

The width of the saddle is judged by seeing the saddle on the horse's back. Most good Saddlers will come to the yard and try some saddles on the horse.

If the horse is difficult to fit, however, a template measurement can be taken from his back. A piece of wire is placed just behind the withers where the front arch of the saddle would sit. The wire is 'moulded' round the horse to fit his shape. The wire is then placed on a piece of paper and the shape drawn by pencil along the inside of the wire.

Fitting the Saddle

The saddle should be checked without a numnah or saddle cloth. The girth is fastened on the same number holes of the girth straps on both sides and to the same corresponding straps. This should be either the first and second straps both sides or the first and third. (The girth should never be fastened to the second and third straps as these are connected to the same webbing and this would be unsafe if the webbing came undone.)

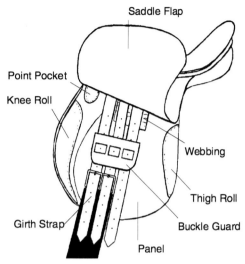

The girths ideally should fasten about half way up the straps. A girth that is long enough to fasten on the top hole, is too long.

Assess the length of saddle on the horse and the size of the saddle flaps. These need to be large enough for the rider's legs and the correct size for the horse. If the saddle flaps are too large or cut too far forward, the horse's shoulder movement will be restricted. Too small and the rider will be uncomfortable.

Now check the space between the pommel and the withers. This should measure at least four fingers' width (10 cm or 4 inches). Any less and the saddle will press on the horse's spine with a rider mounted. Check the gullet behind the pommel. Some horse's have high withers and if the saddle dips in this area it may touch the spine.

Run a hand under the saddle from the pommel down around the wither and horse's shoulder. The saddle should fit firmly but not tightly. There should be no pressure on the top of the shoulders. A narrow saddle will pinch.

The cantle should be slightly higher than the pommel. If the cantle is lower the saddle will be too low on the horse's back. If it is too high the rider will be tipped forward into an incorrect position. Lift the cantle up and down; too much movement will mean that the saddle does not fit. When the horse is moving, the saddle and rider will bang down on the horse's back.

From the rear of the horse, the gullet should show a clear space all the way through. The saddle should not at any point come into contact with the horse's spine.

When the horse is standing square, evenly on all four legs, the saddle should be level, not slanting to one side.

Once the saddle has been checked for fit, it should now be assessed with the rider mounted. The gullet should still show a good clearance from the horse's spine.

The saddle should be checked from the side and rear with the horse and rider in action. There should be no excessive movement of the saddle up and down or from side to side. The horse should move freely and happily. The rider should be comfortable.

Maintaining the saddle

The saddle is such an important piece of tack that it must be maintained and cared for properly. If the saddle is damaged in any way it may cause injury to the horse's back. A broken tree may result in open, raw sores along the horse's spine. Any rubbing or friction from the saddle will also cause sores, pressure points, lumps and pain. The horse can suffer from mental trauma that can last for years.

Saddles should be periodically checked for a broken tree. This will be evident by a grating noise or excessive movement when the cantle is pressed towards the pommel. When stored, the saddle should be put away on a saddle rack in a dry, airy room.

Problems of an ill fitting saddle

A correctly fitted saddle is not only essential for the horse's health but also for the rider's benefit. A saddle that is too high at the pommel or cantle will make the rider sit incorrectly. A saddle that is lower on one side will encourage the rider either to sit on one side or to lean over in an attempt to compensate. This can cause pressure points or sores on the horse's back and also make him work incorrectly. He will need to balance himself to carry the rider.

There may even be permanent marking of the skin and hair; many old injury marks caused by saddle friction show up as white markings along the back or within the saddle area. An ill-fitting saddle not only causes pain but results in long lasting implications to physical and mental health.

Saddles will need re-stuffing normally about every six months or so, but this does depend on the amount and type of use the saddle receives. A saddle that needs re-stuffing may be a little flat on the horse's back, the cantle may drop below the height of the pommel or one side will be lower than the other.

A good saddle, well fitted and maintained will last for years helping both horse and rider work correctly and comfortably.

Girths

The purpose of the girth, together with the girth straps, is to keep the saddle in place and secure.

Sizes

Girths are measured from the ends of both buckles and are available in measurements increasing by 2 inches. The smallest normally measure 920 mm (36") to the longest at 1470 mm (58").

Types of girth

There are different designs made out of various types of materials - leather, webbing, nylon and synthetic fibres.

Leather girths

- *The Three Fold girth*

  This is a piece of leather folded over into three layers. It is strong and reliable but expensive to buy and more difficult to clean than a modern synthetic girth. It needs cleaning after use with saddle soap and kept supple by regular oiling. It is fitted with the open side of the folds facing away from the horse's elbow.

- *The Atherstone girth*

  This girth, usually of leather, is shaped so that it narrows behind the elbows to prevent girth galls forming in that area.

- *The Balding girth*

  Designed for the same purpose as the Atherstone. This leather girth is shaped by splitting the leather into three and crossing over the outside portions.

Figure 25: Girths: Three Fold, Atherstone, Balding, Nylon String, Cottage Craft & Lonsdale

The Lampwick girth

Made of webbing material, Lampwick girths are soft and comfortable for the horse. They do have a tendency to stretch or fray.

Nylon string

Not as popular now, this girth is strong and durable though sometimes the strings can fray and break. The nylon material has a tendency to make the horse sweat in the girth area. The strings can also pinch the horse's skin. The thicker German Cordstring girth is similar but much better to use.

Cottage Craft

A recent design of girth made from nylon and cotton with an interior foam padding. This girth is strong yet soft, durable and very easy to clean by hand or in a washing machine. The softness of this girth lessens the risk of girth galls.

Lonsdale

This is a short girth used in connection with long girth straps. Most dressage saddles have this feature but other saddles also have this style. Designed to reduce the bulk beneath the saddle so that the rider's legs can stay in closer contact with the horse's sides. Because the girth fastens below the saddle flap, the buckles are padded underneath to prevent rubbing or galling the horse's sides.

Care of the Girth

The girth is a vital piece of saddlery that needs to be kept clean and in good condition.

* A girth should be cleaned after every use to remove grit, mud and sweat.

* The girth and its buckles should be checked frequently for any worn or split areas.

* Any girth that is not 100% reliable should be replaced immediately.

* The girth straps on the saddle should also be checked. This is another area where weakness can occur and cause accidents.

Dirty girths cause sores, galls and infected wounds. The consequences of a worn girth breaking in the middle of a long gallop or on a cross country course are horrendous.

Saddle Accessories

Numnahs, Saddle Cloths and Pads

Technically, a numnah or saddle cloth should not be necessary with a saddle that fits well. However, numnahs and saddle cloths are popular and provided they are fitted correctly can be useful. For instance, when a horse has not been ridden for some time his back may be 'soft'. He may suffer from a 'cold back'. A numnah or saddle cloth can act as a form of protection to the horse's back. One advantage of numnahs and saddle cloths is that they keep the underneath of the saddle clean.

The front of the cloth should *fit well up into the pommel*. It should not be flat and taut around the withers as this will put tremendous strain on the spine as well as cutting into the skin and creating bald patches through friction. In size the numnah should be about one inch (2-3 cm) larger than the saddle all round. The saddle cloth should be large enough to extend beyond the saddle but not too large that the cloth flaps around.

Both numnahs and cloths should be fastened correctly and firmly with all straps secured to the saddle. A numnah or saddle cloth should never be used unsecured under a saddle; it will move under the saddle and cause sore areas.

Numnahs and saddle cloths should be washed after use, in a non-biological washing powder, and dried thoroughly before being used again.

There are now various types of pads on the market that fit under the saddle. There are 'shock absorbing saddle pads', 'gel pads', 'waffle pads' and 'poly pads' all designed to protect the horse's back.

Girth Sleeves

Girth sleeves are often used to reduce the possibility or recurrence of girth galls. They are made from various materials such as synthetic wool or expensive real sheepskin. A piece of rubber inner tubing cut to fit can be just as effective though this may cause sweating in warm weather or if the horse is worked hard.

Girth sleeves are often used during a fittening programme to save the horse's soft skin.

All types of girth sleeve should be kept absolutely clean. A dirty girth sleeve can cause friction sores and infected wounds.

Crupper

A crupper is designed to prevent the saddle from slipping forwards. This is particularly useful on small fat ponies whose shape makes the saddle prone to sliding. When the pony lowers his head to nibble at the grass, the saddle slips towards the pony's ears and off comes the child.

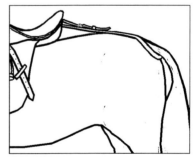

At one end of the crupper is a padded and rounded leather loop that fits firmly underneath the dock. At the other end is a leather strap that attaches to the saddle by passing through a ring at the cantle. The crupper is then adjusted to fit snugly. If the saddle does not have a crupper ring, this can be easily fitted by a Saddler.

Cruppers are available in different designs but in all cases the tail loop must be well padded. It must also be kept clean; the area under the tail is vulnerable to rubbing and sores.

Surcingle Girth

Often called an 'over-girth', 'jumping surcingle' or simply a 'surcingle', this is a special 'extra' girth fastened around the horse over the saddle. Necessary for cross country jumping as a safeguard if the normal girth breaks or gives way for some reason. This girth must be secured through a breastplate, a martingale or at the girth to prevent it from slipping backwards.

Seat Saver

This is a cover that fits over the saddle. Normally made of sheepskin this makes the seat of the saddle more comfortable for the rider. The seat saver is not allowed in dressage competitions.

Exam Tips

In the practical session, candidates may be asked to tack a horse up and comment on the fit of the tack. You need to have the ability to check the fit of a saddle on the horse. If the saddle does not fit you should point this out to the Examiner, giving your reasons and considered opinions. If there is any doubt, inform the Examiner and explain that to assess the fit thoroughly the saddle should be checked with a rider mounted.

Practise as much as you can before the exam on fitting saddles. If you can gain experience at looking at and judging badly fitting saddles as well, you will learn to differentiate between the good and bad points.

C H A P T E R   22
Martingales and Breastplates

As with all attachments, the first consideration is whether or not it is necessary. The fewer accessories used the better for the horse and rider. However, should the horse have a problem that cannot be solved by any other method or it becomes dangerous, it may help to use certain artificial aids even for a short period.

Martingales

It can be a frightening and dangerous experience to ride a horse who is constantly tossing his head about, especially when the head comes so high that it hits the rider's hat or face. A martingale can minimise and hopefully, in time, cure this problem.

There are several varieties of martingale, but the three main types are the Running, the Standing and the Irish. There is also the Bib martingale, which is a variation of the Running martingale.

Running martingale

This type of martingale was covered in Stage I so only a brief description is given here.

Revision

Running martingales, fitting, putting on, functions.

Description

This is a leather strap with a loop at one end through which the girth is passed. The strap divides into two thinner straps each of which has a metal ring at the end through which a rein is passed. A neck strap made of leather is attached via a rubber loop near the area where the single strap divides.

Functions

Prevents the horse from raising his head beyond the angle of control and from tossing his head from side to side. Also helps to lessen the affect of excessive movement from a novice rider's hands.

Fitting

The martingale may already be attached to the bridle. The neckstrap may be put over the horse's neck together with the reins. If not, the martingale is put on first and then attached to the bridle. There should be one hand's width between the neck strap and the horse. Check the fit by holding the rings up to the withers on either side of the horse; these should just reach the level of the wither. (The two straps may be fitted a little shorter but never more than one hand's width below the withers.) At all costs the martingale *must never restrict the horse's normal action or put pressure on the jaw*. Alternatively, the straps can be measured by holding the rings to the horse's jaw; the straps should just reach the throat.

There should always be a rubber stop on each rein between the martingale ring and the bit to prevent the martingale from interfering with the bit.

The running martingale is often used in jumping competitions but is not allowed for dressage competitions.

Standing martingale

Description

A single leather strap with loops at both ends passes from girth to noseband. A neck strap secured by a rubber loop or stop holds the martingale in place.

Putting on

The standing martingale should only be attached to a cavesson noseband or the cavesson part of a flash. The neck strap is placed over the head and onto the withers. The girth is passed through the girth loop and the noseband fits through the other loop.

Fitting

With the neck strap and girth loop in place, the other end of the strap should just reach the horse's throat. If the strap is too short, the horse's head and neck movement will be severely restricted. Too long and the martingale will have no effect.

Functions

1. Prevents the horse from raising or throwing his head up out of control.

2. Discourages rearing, especially for younger horses.

The standing martingale may be used for jumping and on polo ponies.

Irish martingale

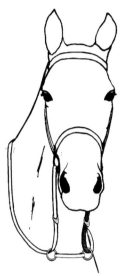

Description

A single strap, usually 4 to 6 inches (10-15 cm) in length, with rings either end.

Putting on

This martingale is attached to the reins, one rein passing through each ring, under the horse's neck.

Fitting

The strap should be long enough so that it does not interfere with the rein action. Stops should be placed on the reins to prevent the martingale from slipping forward and interfering with the bit.

Functions

1. Stops the reins from being flung or slipping over the horse's head, for example if the horse shakes his head dislodging the reins.

2. Prevents the reins from being dragged over the head, for example, in the event of a fall.

This type of martingale is generally used for racehorses.

Bib martingale

This is a modified Running martingale, which has a piece of leather connecting the two front straps. It combines the functions of the Running and Irish martingales.

It is particularly useful on a horse that grabs at one of the front straps and for one who, when excited or overbent, may get his head tangled in a Running martingale.

Breastplates

There are two main types, the Hunting and Aintree breastplates.

Hunting Breastplate

Description

Similar in design to the Running martingale with the omission of the two front straps. A single looped strap fixes to the girth at one end and to the neck strap at the other. At the top of the neck strap are two leather straps which are fastened, one on each side of the withers, by buckles to the D rings on the saddle. The neck strap lies along the top of the sloping shoulder blades.

Fitting

The neck strap should allow enough space for the width of one hand between the strap and the horse. The ring connecting neck strap and girth strap should fit centrally at the base of the neck. The bottom strap should not be too short or it will pull on the neck strap.

The two saddle straps should be long enough to avoid distorting the neck strap at the withers. The whole breastplate should fit securely enough to prevent the saddle slipping, but not so tight as to cause friction sores.

Function

Prevents the saddle slipping backwards whilst riding up and down hills, hunting or riding cross country on sleek, fit horses or those with poor conformation.

A martingale attachment may be fitted to the centre ring on the chest.

Aintree Breastgirth

Description

A wide band, usually of webbing or padded leather, passes around the horse's chest and is fastened either side to the girth by adjustable straps. This band is sometimes covered with sheepskin and elasticated.

A narrow leather strap passes over the horse's neck just in front of the withers and is attached to the webbing band to keep the breastgirth in place.

Function

As with the hunting breastplate, to prevent the saddle from slipping. Used for the same reason when training and lungeing young horses.

Fitting

The breast girth must be the correct height on the chest. Too high and it will lie against the horse's gullet and may restrict breathing. Too low and it may interfere with the horse's shoulder and foreleg movement.

Untacking martingales and breastplates

With martingales, unfasten the girth first and remove the martingale girth loop. Most martingales are removed at the same time as the bridle. The neckstrap and reins are held together and taken over the horse's head as normal.

To remove the breastplate the saddle straps are unfastened first. The girth is unfastened and the breastplate removed.

Cleaning tack

The bridle, saddle and leather accessories such as martingales, should always be cleaned directly after use when grease, dirt and dust can be removed more easily. (Saddle soap, normally purchased as a bar, is now available in a spray and this is very easy to spray on and wipe over for a quick clean.) If the tack is wet, the leather should be allowed to dry before cleaning. The bit should be rinsed with clean water to remove saliva.

Every week leather tack should be taken to pieces and given a good cleaning with saddle soap. Metal work, *except for the bit*, can be cleaned with a metal polish.

Generally if tack is cleaned properly with saddle soap, the leather will stay supple and should not need oiling frequently. If the leather is dry, however, it should be given a dressing of leather oil. New bridles and saddles will need oiling about three times to soften the leather and make it supple. On saddles the oil should be applied to the underside of the leather not along the top of the seat or the saddle flaps as this will make the saddle slippery.

Synthetic tack can either be washed in warm water or thoroughly rinsed through with a hose. Smaller items can be put in the washing machine with a little non-biological washing powder.

It is imperative for the horse's health and for the rider's safety that the tack is kept clean and in good condition. An hour or so every week spent cleaning could prevent accidents, injuries, illness and expense.

Exam Tips

The subject of martingales and breastplates may be included in the Practical/Oral when candidates will be asked to describe each type, their uses and functions. In the Practical session candidates will be asked to tack up a horse and this may include a martingale or a breastplate.

When untacking a breastplate, always remember to unfasten the saddle straps at the withers first. Trying to remove a saddle with these still fastened is not only embarrassing but potentially dangerous.

CHAPTER 23
Grooming and Care of the Horse after Exercise

Grooming

For the Stage II candidates will need to know the procedures for strapping and quartering, when these types of grooming are done and how long each takes. Each candidate may be given two items of grooming kit and asked to name them and describe their use. During the Practical session, candidates may be asked to give a horse a quick grooming, pick out his feet and show how to use a wisp.

Revision

Reasons and aims of grooming, equipment and its use. Grooming procedures, quartering, strapping, brushing off and setting fair. The tail bandage, uses and method of putting a bandage on. Washing the mane and tail. Grooming the grass kept pony. When not to groom.

Grooming is covered extensively at Stage I and students should revise this if necessary.

Grooming is an essential part of the horse's daily routine. It keeps him clean, improves his appearance, massages his muscle and skin, prevents skin diseases and infections. Most importantly it gives the groom time to inspect for injury and build up a rapport with the horse.

Quartering

This is the first grooming of the day given to clean the horse before exercise. The horse's body, mane and tail are brushed quickly and any stable stains brushed or wiped off with a damp sponge. The feet are picked out and the eyes, nostrils and dock sponged. Quartering takes around ten to twenty minutes.

Strapping

This is the main grooming of the day given preferably after exercise when the horse is warm and the pores are open. Depending on the efficiency and speed of the groom, strapping can take from 30 minutes up to 1 hour.

It includes picking out the feet and cleaning them with a damp water brush; brushing the body, mane and tail and sponging the eyes, nostrils and dock. Wisping can be included or a massage with a special massage glove. The hooves can be oiled and the horse given a last wipe over with a stable rubber or clean cloth.

Wisping

This is a traditional part of grooming which is not so popular now as it takes time. Some people also feel that wisping may bruise and damage muscle fibres particularly if not done correctly. Others believe that a daily wisping hardens and tones the muscles, encourages the circulation and gives the coat a shine by activating the oil glands in the skin.

The best wisp is made of straw or hay but there are now leather wisping pads on the market that can also be used.

The wisp can be dampened down if required. The horse is restrained with a headcollar and lead-rope.

If the horse is unfamiliar or not accustomed to being wisped, it is safest to find out first if he will accept the vigorous action of wisping. Begin by slapping gently with a hand on his neck, his shoulder and hindquarters. Slap a little more strongly and then try the wisp with a gentle slap.

The wisp is used on the muscle areas only, the neck, shoulders and hindquarters. *The wisp should never be used on bony areas.*

Starting on the neck and shoulders, slap the wisp strongly onto the muscle in the direction of the coat about a dozen times. Repeat on all muscular areas on both sides of the horse.

Some grooms wisp and then use a stable rubber (a clean cloth or tea towel) to wipe the horse after each stroke. With the wisp in one hand, slap the horse then, with the stable rubber in the other hand, wipe over that area so it becomes a slap - wipe - slap - wipe action.

Caring for the horse after exercise

The main aim of caring for the horse after exercise is that he cools down gradually to his normal body temperature. He also needs to calm down mentally, be cleaned, checked for injury, watered and fed in relation to his physical needs.

✔ If the horse is being ridden back to the yard, walk him home for the last ten to fifteen minutes. This should help to cool him down.

✔ If the area is safe, allow the horse to stretch his neck on a long rein. This should not be done on the Public Highway. *(A long rein is when the rein is allowed to lengthen but there is still a contact. A loose rein is when the reins are let out to the buckle and there is little contact.)* The girth can be loosened by a hole five minutes from home, providing again that the area is safe.

✔ If the horse arrives back at the yard hot and sweaty straight after the ride, he must be cooled down before being put in the stable. Similarly if the horse has to travel home by box or trailer, he must be cooled down before being loaded.

✔ Dismount as soon as possible and loosen the girth. The saddle should be left on for a couple of minutes, so that the circulation can return to this area before exposure to cold air dilates (contracts) the blood vessels.

✔ In warm weather cover the horse with an anti-sweat rug, a cooler rug or a light summer sheet. In cold conditions a stable rug should be used.

✔ Walk the horse around for ten minutes to prevent his muscles stiffening up and to stop him cooling down too rapidly. After ten minutes his temperature can be tested by feeling the base of his ears. These should be body warm, not hot. If he is still hot, he should be walked around for another five minutes and checked again.

✔ If the saddle patch is dirty and sweaty this can be sponged down with warm water and excess water removed with a sweat scraper. If the horse is covered in mud or dirt, he can be bathed in warm water and the excess removed with the sweat scraper. He can then be covered with a cooler rug and walked around until dry.

> ✖ Cold water should never be hosed straight onto a horse's body or back when he is hot and sweaty. This will cause muscle spasms that can be painful.

✔ Inspect for injuries when he has relaxed a little. Any knocks or bumps can be covered with an ice pack or cold poultice to minimise swelling. Pick out the horse's feet and check for stones, bruising or puncture wounds.

✔ Offer the horse some water after ten minutes. This should be 'chilled' water, that is water with the chill taken off, by the addition of a little hot water. Give him 2 litres (½ gallon or about a quarter of a standard bucket).

NOTE when travelling away from home, it is wise to take water and a bucket. Horses drinking from a communal trough are at risk of disease. Also water is not always available at some events. On warm days the water will usually warm up enough in the container to be given to the horse. At least it will not be icy cold.

Most horses cool down within twenty minutes.

✔ Once the horse is cool and dry, take him into his stable and give him a quick brush down. Wipe his eyes and nostrils with a damp cloth. Put his rugs on. If travelling he can be dressed in his travelling clothes ready for loading. His legs may be bandaged to minimise any strain and keep him warm. A tired horse is more susceptible to cold.

✔ He can now have a drink, a haynet and after an hour, his feed. This can be a bran mash with boiled barley and linseed that is easily digestible, palatable and warming. Alternatively he can be given his normal food mixed with warm water.

The horse should be watched carefully as he may 'break out' that is, sweat again. If this happens he must be walked around until dry. Keep checking his ears for heat, and around his chest, elbow area and flanks for sweat.

Next day

The horse may be a little stiff the next morning.

✔ Walk him round in hand to loosen any stiffness. He may be trotted up to check for lameness, which can then be dealt with promptly.

✔ Watch his body language, if he seems bright, maybe a little tired but quite happy he will benefit from a day off in the field. This will give him rest, time to relax and the light exercise will help to prevent his muscles from seizing up.

✔ Check for any further injuries, cuts, punctures wounds, bumps, bruising, swellings, areas of pain or heat. Clean out his feet thoroughly with a wet brush. Check each foot by gently tapping the sole and the shoe (not the frog or heel) with the hoof pick. He will flinch if he has a sore spot - call the farrier.

Importance of Care

There is a cliché *'take care of the horse and the horse will take care of you'*. A horse properly cared for will enjoy good health and fitness and be capable of giving the owner or rider countless hours of enjoyment.

There is another old cliché *'take care of the horse first, yourself second'*. This was constantly drummed into us as working pupils and, fortunately, has become second nature. Many a dark winter's night have I spent, after a day's hard riding, with the wind howling and the rain crashing down; weary, hungry, thirsty, covered in mud and grit, clothes cold with dried sweat and rain.

Then I take that moment when my horse is finished to stand in his box watching him. In the warm, soft light of the stable there is a peaceful haven. Rugged up for the night, he is groomed, fed, watered, standing in a deep bed of straw, one hind leg resting. I listen to the harmonious munching of hay, the occasional snort and know I have achieved a happy, relaxed horse. Then he turns his head, breathes warm air over me as if to say, 'Go on you can go home now, I'm fine.' I sometimes wonder who is top dog around here!

Exam Tips

Candidates will need to know the basic procedures for caring for a horse after exercise and the reasons for these procedures. You will need to know how to cool a horse down, when to water and feed. If you can speak from experience this will certainly help.

Taking a horse out to shows, competitions, long hacks or cross country rides, and caring for the horse afterwards, will give you the experience necessary. If you do not have the luxury of owning a horse, then ask if you can accompany a friend or someone at the yard on their outing. They will probably be only too pleased to have someone else around to help. There is always a lot to do even at the smallest show. It is a pleasure and relief to return tired out from a ten mile cross country ride to find hordes of helpers just eager to do their bit!

Just a tip when grooming, never groom with your gloves on. Though in normal practice gloves are not worn when grooming, so that any areas of swelling and heat can be detected, in the Exam it is all too easy to forget that you are wearing gloves.

C H A P T E R   24
Fittening and Roughing Off

Fittening

This is the process whereby a horse is brought up from pasture and, over a period of weeks, made fit again. The fitter the horse needs to be, the longer the period of fittening. Muscles, tendons and ligaments need to be stretched and made supple. Respiration and heart rate need to be conditioned to the faster work required and the digestive system needs time to become accustomed to the change of diet. The skin needs to toughen so that wearing tack will not cause galls.

The time taken to return a horse to fitness will depend on certain factors.

1. **Time out at grass**. The longer the period of rest the more unfit (softer) the horse will be.

2. **Condition of pasture.** A horse will be in a softer condition after a wet summer than a dry one because the pasture will be richer.

3. **Time of year**. The horse will generally come in fitter after a winter rest; he may even have been brought in at night in very cold weather. A summer on lush grass will create more fat.

4. **Weight**. This will relate to the time of year the horse is out and the quality of pasture. The fat horse will take longer to return to fitness.

5. **Fitness of the horse.** Some horses keep themselves remarkably fit when at grass whilst others lose their fitness within a few weeks. Also horses who have been kept in the peak of fitness before being turned out or who have undergone the fitness programme before, will return to fitness in a shorter period.

6. **Type or breed.** Some breeds take less time to become fit, for instance a Thoroughbred will become fit more quickly than a heavier type of horse.

7. **Age**. Older horses and young horses who are being fittened for the first time can take longer to return to fitness.

8. **Whether the horse was worked at grass**. Some horses are exercised or lunged once a week just to keep them ticking over.

9. **Work expected to do in future**. The harder the work the horse will be expected to do, the longer the period he will need to reach that standard of fitness. Building up stamina needs more time. Endurance riding demands more stamina and this will take longer to achieve than the short bursts of energy needed by the show jumper.

Depending on these variables the fittening programme can vary from 6 to 20 weeks and needs careful thought and management if the horse is to progress satisfactorily. Some horses will be brought in to prepare for a specific event and will need to reach the peak of fitness by a certain date. Hunters will start their fittening programme with a view to full hunting by November. Cub hunting starts in September and this will be integrated into a hunter's fittening programme. Eventers will need to reach fitness for the first competition of the year, which is usually early March.

Timetable for fittening

Type of Horse	Work	Length of Fittening Programme
Riding club	Small cross country events, Prelim. dressage competitions at weekends, hacking.	6 to 8 weeks
Hunter	Cub hunting in September - full hunting in November 1 - 2 days a week. A light weight Thoroughbred will probably need 8 weeks, the heavy hunter up to 10 weeks.	8 to 10 weeks
Dressage	Dressage competitions.	8 to 10 weeks
Show Jumper	Show Jumping.	8 to 10 weeks
Long Distance	Endurance riding, long distance hacking. Needs to build up stamina.	10 to 12 weeks
Novice Eventer	Novice dressage, show jumping and cross country.	10 to 12 weeks
Three day Eventer	Dressage, show jumping, steeplechasing and cross country.	12 to18 weeks
Golden Horse Shoe	Endurance riding over greater distances.	12 to 18 weeks

The times given are a good basis for a fittening programme but should be adaptable for each individual horse. The horse may still be fairly fit when he is brought in or he may be grossly overweight. He may suffer injury during the fittening period and need extra time. The periods may need adjusting to suit each horse.

Preparation

Ideally the preparation can start a week before the fittening programme. The stable can be thoroughly cleaned out and disinfected; tack cleaned and oiled; clothes brought out of storage, checked and cleaned if necessary. Food bins, buckets, hoppers and scoops can be cleaned and made ready. Food, bedding and hay can be bought and stored. (Old food should never be used.)

The horse can be given his inoculations if these are due and have his teeth checked. He can be wormed towards the end of the week, a day or two before he starts work. The Farrier will need to visit either to check the feet or to shoe before fittening starts.

The horse can be brought into the stable during this time for a short period each day. He can be given small feeds, 1 kilo (2-3 lbs), of low energy food such Horse and Pony cubes or Pasture Mix with carrots. Hay can be offered 2 kilos (4-5 lbs) though this may be refused if he prefers the grass.

To reduce the risk of tack sores, surgical spirits can be rubbed gently into his back and girth areas to hardened up the skin.

Method of Fittening

Once the actual programme of fittening begins the horse must be reintroduced slowly to his new lifestyle.

The three major aspects of fittening are;

1. **Stable management.**
2. **Feeding.**
3. **Exercise.**

These must all be considered in conjunction with each other; relating exercise to feeding and stable care. The fittening programme is designed to prevent problems which can result from too rapid a change.

Arnie Horsenegger

Programme for fittening

At first work begins by walking on the flat, perhaps in a field, progressing onto roadwork to build up the muscles and harden the legs. Slow, steady work for a longer duration rather than short fast work is best.

Example of a fittening timetable for a 16 hh middleweight Hunter over 8 weeks. Total daily food required 13.5 kilos (30 lbs).

Week	Exercise	Hay	Concentrates	Notes
1	Ridden at walk on the flat starting with 15 minutes and increasing daily to 45 minutes by the end of the week.	90% Start with meado w hay.	10% Start with low energy compound or barley, bran, sugar beet and chaff. *Oats should not be offered.*	The horse can be turned out to grass a few hours daily. Check saddle, girth and bridle areas. Light grooming (quartering) can be done. Pull mane and tail.
2	Walking increased each day to 1 hour or 1½ hours. Watch breathing and sweating.	85%	15%	Include some road work to harden up legs and muscles. The horse can still have some pasture time.

3	Include walking up and down hills. Short trot work (1 minute, two or three times) gradually introduced. This should be a steady slow trot, not a jog. If the horse jogs this is an evasion.	80%	20%	Keep checking saddle and girth areas. More concentrated grooming; strapping can be introduced.
4	Walking as week 3. Increase trot work and if horse progressing well, may introduce short canter by end of the week. Some schoolwork for about 10 minutes.	70%	30%	
5	Work time: 1½ hours per day. Walking, trotting and slow canters up hills. Some work over small fences.	60%	40%	Check shoes and feet. Farrier may be needed.
6	Increase work time to 2 hours a day (one hour twice a day). Include longer canters. Jumping, schooling and lungeing on some days.	60%	40% Oats if required, can gradually be introduced into the feed.	Worming will need doing now. Farrier will need to attend to shoes and feet.
7	As week 6 with one fast canter or gallop (pipe-opener).	60%	40%	
8	In full work.	60%	40%	Percentage of feed depends on the horse. Can now feed seed hay if required.

Some owners prefer to add an extra week onto the programme to compensate for unavoidable events, such as the horse being kicked in the field.

The horse should be monitored closely throughout the programme and adjustments made as and when necessary.

Hazards of the Fittening process

Most of the problems experienced when bringing a horse up from grass are entirely due to lack of consideration, negligence or ignorance.

The fittening programme is designed to prevent;

- *Colic and digestive problems*
  The horse must adjust gradually from a diet of roughage to one that includes concentrates. Digestive problems can occur if the diet is not changed gradually in relation with exercise. Illnesses such as colic, azoturia (muscles spasms and stiffness caused basically by too rich a diet and too little exercise) or lymphangitis (swollen, fluid-filled legs). The horse may become over-heated and excitable with too much hard food too soon. Allowing the horse some pasture time during the fittening programme regulates the change of diet and prepares the gut. He should have his one rest day a week as normal.

- *Coughs, colds and other respiratory problems*
  The ventilation in the stable must be maintained; it is better to rug up than stop the flow of air. Poor ventilation, dusty atmosphere, dry hay containing fungal spores may cause respiratory problems.

- *Chills*

  The horse should not be allowed to sweat profusely. (If he is obese *slight* sweating will reduce his weight.)

- *Tack sores*

  The use of soft numnahs and girth sleeves at first will minimise the risk of saddle sores and girth galls. The tack must kept clean. Exercise will begin with walking on level ground to help prevent the saddle rubbing.

- *Weariness*

  Exercise is introduced slowly and built up gradually so that the horse does not do too much too soon.

- *Accidents and injury*

  Accidents can be a result of tiredness. If the horse is asked to perform work for which he is not yet fit enough, for instance jumping, he may make a mistake and fall. Strain is put on the muscles, tendons and ligaments when asking the horse to work again after a period of rest. If these are not made supple over a period of time, excess or sudden exercise will tear, pull or injure these tissues. Overreach injuries can also be caused by asking the horse to work too fast before he has developed his balance.

- *Physical illness and stress*

  An incorrect feed/exercise ratio can make the horse over excitable. Standing in the stable too long can result in fluid in the legs, bad circulation and boredom. If left for hours in the stable after being out all the time, the horse may become bored and develop bad habits such as weaving, crib-biting or bed eating.

The horse may develop bad habits through boredom

Concussive Damage

Injuries sustained from long or fast work over hard surfaces can occur, not just during the fittening process, but at any time when the horse is worked without care and attention.

When worked to excess on hard ground, the horse can develop various conditions windgalls (swellings in the fetlock region), splints, ringbone, navicular, pedal ostitis (inflammation of the pedal bone), bruised tendons or arthritis. Any of these conditions may cause degrees of lameness, from intermittent lameness to permanent unsoundness when the horse will never be able to work fully again.

Fast work in deep, muddy ground causes strained tendons, pulled muscles, torn ligaments, overreach wounds. The horse's shoes can be sucked off resulting in damage to the hoof.

Work on **hard ground** results in **concussive injuries**, work on **deep ground** results in **straining** injuries.

Preparation, care and attention are essential for all fittening programmes and the time allotted should be carefully planned so that the horse becomes fit without undue strain to his joints, muscles, tendons and ligaments.

Roughing Off

All horses and ponies need a rest at some time to relax and rest both mentally and physically. Those horses who hunt during the winter often have a summer break after the hunting season, polo ponies go out during the winter, show jumping, dressage horses and eventers need rest after a hard season. All horses deserve and need a holiday. Sometimes a period of rest is necessary to mend an injury or to allow the horse to recuperate.

The transition from being fully stabled to being turned out to grass must be gradual to allow the horse's physical processes time to adjust. This period is called 'roughing off'.

Depending on the time of the year and the fitness of the horse, it takes two to three weeks for a horse to be 'let down' from a hard condition to a soft condition.

◊ The physical state of the horse must be changed to cope with the outdoor conditions. For instance the horse being put out in winter needs to grow a coat and to build up grease and oils as an insulation barrier against the cold.

◊ The digestive tract needs adjusting to a grass diet.

To acclimatise the horse in preparation for him living out the following points are put into operation.

Ventilation
Create more ventilation without causing draughts by increasing the air flow through a slightly open window or opening the top door if this is normally closed.

Rugging
Decrease the amount of rugs so that the horse becomes used to the temperature and climate. Reduce by one rug every 7 days or put on a lighter rug.

Pasture time
Put the horse out to graze for a short period during the day and gradually increase this time.

Grooming
Stop thorough grooming. This will allow the coat to build up natural oils and grease for insulation against weather conditions. It will also stop toning up the muscles. All grooming, apart from a quick brush down and picking out the feet, must cease two to three days before turning out. Stop pulling and trimming the mane and tail.

Feed and exercise
During the roughing off period both food and exercise will need to be reduced gradually in relation to each other.

Feeding
The concentrates are reduced and roughage, hay or grass, increased. The food type itself can be altered, for instance from oats to barley, or from a high protein compound feed to a non-heating, high fibre Horse and Pony mix.

The amount of hard food is slowly reduced to a maintenance level whilst, at the same time, the amount of roughage is increased.

Exercise
The daily exercise is decreased in conjunction with the reduction of hard food. This will also allow the muscles to turn 'soft'.

General Health

There are other aspects of the horse's health that need attention before he is turned out.

Worming
The horse will need worming. If possible, the horse should remain in the stable or a paddock for 24-48 hours after worming, so that the pasture does not become contaminated. If this is not possible, all droppings in the field should be collected daily. Worming should continue every four to six weeks whilst the horse is out at grass.

Inoculations
The Vet may need to give the horse his normal yearly inoculations and check his general health before he goes out to grass.

Teeth
The equine dentist should inspect and possibly rasp the horse's teeth.

Shoeing
The Farrier will need to check and possibly trim the feet. The horse may be turned out unshod. He may have his front shoes left on or have grass tips fitted instead. The Farrier should visit every six weeks. The horse at grass will still need attention to his feet.

Mnemonic **WITS** (**W**orming, **I**noculations, **T**eeth, **S**hoeing)

Turning out

When the day comes to turn the horse out, choose a mild day not one bitterly cold or wet. During the winter the horse may need a New Zealand rug. In spring and summer apply a good insect repellent as some flies can be particularly irritating.

If the pasture is rich, a small feed can be given before turning out so that he does not gorge himself on the lush grass. If the grass or pasture is poor the horse can be turned out immediately.

During the roughing off period the horse can be put out into a field with a quiet companion or two. Turning an unfamiliar horse out into a herd leads to trouble. Fighting for dominance can result in injury. It is also better if the horse settles down straight away rather than becoming excited with the other horses and galloping madly round the field. The horse should not be put out on his own. Horses need the companionship of others and will fret if left alone.

The horse should be watched for the first few hours, monitored regularly over a couple of days and checked twice a day after that.

During the warmer months, 2 weeks is sufficient for roughing off horses in a moderate condition. If the horse is extra fit or the weather is extremely cold and wet, it is wiser to stretch this period up to 3 weeks to allow the horse more time to acclimatise.

Exam Tips

For the Stage II candidates will be questioned on the Fitness Programme and will need to know the different times it takes to reach fitness for different horses doing a variety of work. You will also need to know the pitfalls and problems that can arise and how these are avoided. Each candidate will need to know the causes of and injuries resulting from concussive damage.

CHAPTER 25
Boots and Bandages

The horse's legs are particularly vulnerable to injury and so various types of boots and bandages have been designed to provide **protection, support** and for **Veterinary or medical use.**

A horse should wear boots or bandages for,

- **Lungeing** - the horse working on a circle is more prone to brushing or over-reaching.

- **Ride and Lead exercise** - both horses, the one being ridden and the one being led, are vulnerable to injury.

- **Schooling** - it is wiser to protect horses (especially valuable ones) than risk injury.

- **Jumping** - protection against injury when show jumping or cross country. It is wiser to protect the horse's legs even when hacking.

- **Travelling** by trailer or horsebox.

- **Training** young horses who are vulnerable to leg injury because their paces are unbalanced.

- **Medical reasons** - to protect an injury.

Boots

Brushing boots

Description

This type of boot fits around the lower leg from below the knee or hock to the fetlock joint. The front boots are usually fastened by 2, 3 or 4 straps whilst the hind boots have 4 or 5.

Materials

Brushing boots are available in leather, felt, rubber or synthetic material.

♦ The **plain leather** boots are **durable** and **strong** offering **good protection and support**. They need to be kept clean otherwise they can rub.

♦ **Leather** boots **lined with sheepskin or felt** are also available. The lined boots are **comfortable**, but the **lining can become very heavy when wet**.

♦ **Synthetic boots** are very popular as they are **light** and, having **Velcro fastenings, are easy to put on** and **remove**. Types vary from the basic boots suitable for hacking and light schooling only, to sturdier types with a shell outer lining (plastic). Some boots have a double fastening and can be used for jumping or cross country competitions.

♦ **Felt** tends to **stretch** with use and becomes **heavy when wet**. This makes riding through water or in wet weather more difficult for the horse.

♦ **Rubber** is **not suitable** as it **causes the horse's leg to heat and sweat**.

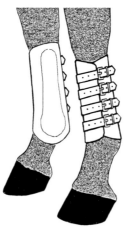

Leather boots with straps   Synthetic boots with Velcro

Function

Provide **protection** for the **lower fore and hind legs** against injuries caused by **brushing and strikes** (over-reach injuries on the tendons). They help to **minimise bruising** of the **cannon bone**.

Fitting

The boots should be fitted with the **straps facing backwards** on the **outside of the leg**. Wrap the boot around the leg and hold it in a slightly higher position than normal. Fasten the middle or second strap to the top and then the other straps working upwards and then down. Ease the boot down the leg into place. Adjust if necessary until all the straps are fastened with equal pressure.

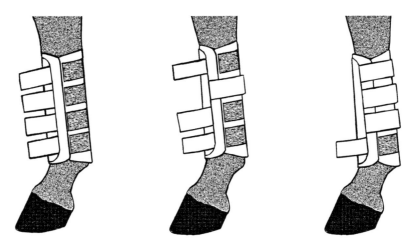

Some brushing boots feature a two strap fastening for security. The straps that fasten first have Velcro on both sides and the other straps fasten on top. The top straps should face backwards.

The boots must be fitted firmly enough to prevent slipping but not so tight as to damage the tendons. There should be just enough space to fit one finger in at the top between the boot and leg. To remove the boots, unfasten the bottom strap first and work upwards.

Competition or Hunter boots

Description

These are a type of brushing boot with a lining.

Materials

The outside is usually made of **plastic, the lining of sheepskin**. The fastenings are **elasticated straps** with buckles or hooks.

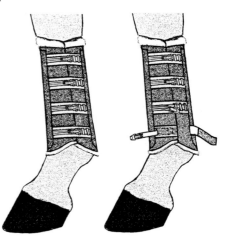

Function

They are **strong and secure** providing **protection when riding cross country**. The lining is warm and comfortable but can become heavy when wet.

Fitting

As with brushing boots.

Speedicut boots

Description

Similar to brushing boots but with a slightly **higher portion on the inside of the leg.**

Function

This boot extends over the **inside of the knee or hock** to **protect** against injuries resulting from **brushing higher up the leg** (**speedicutting**).

Tendon boots

Description

Similar to brushing boots except they have **open fronts**. The back of the boot is **padded and shaped to protect the tendons**. The straps, fastening to buckles or with Velcro, pass around the front of the leg. Sometimes referred to as Open-Fronted Competition Boots.

Function

Used particularly for **show jumping**. These boots are **lightweight, non-absorbent** in water and **provide protection for the tendons**.

Fitting

The boot is placed in position and the straps fastened on the outside of the leg. As with brushing boots, the tendon boot should not be too tight to bruise the cannon bone or damage the tendon.

Over-reach boots

Description

These are boots that fit around the **pastern covering the coronet** and part of the hoof. Sometimes referred to as 'Bell boots' because of their shape.

Materials

Made from **rubber or plastic**, with a variety of fastenings.

The rubber ones are shaped like an upturned cup with a hole in the middle. One type has no fastening; other designs include a strap and loop fastening or a strap with Velcro.

The plastic type is made up of separate overlapping plastic flaps looking rather like petals, hence the name petal boots. These are popular as they are easy to fit, strong, durable and remain in place during use. They can be a little noisy when the horse is moving and some people and horses find them distracting.

Figure 26: Rubber Over-reach Boot and Petal Boot

Function

These boots **protect the coronet and hoof** against injuries caused by over-reaching or low brushing. They can also be used to provide protection when travelling.

Fitting

The rubber type with no fastening is fitted by being squeezed over the hoof. The boot is turned inside out first, then pulled over the hoof until in place. This can be quite difficult.

The strap and loop type is wrapped around the foot. The loops fit through slits and then the strap is pulled through the loops. This, and the strap and Velcro type, are not as reliable as they have a tendency to come off especially in muddy conditions. Petal boots have a strap and buckle. They are much easier to put on and tend to stay in place.

Fetlock boots

Description

These boots cover the area of the fetlock. The straps fasten above the fetlock and an extended portion **covers the inside of the joint**.

The Yorkshire boot is a type of fetlock boot. Usually worn on the hind leg this boot provides light protection for the fetlock.

Materials

Fetlock boots can be made of **leather or plastic**, sometimes with a sheepskin lining.

Yorkshire boots are made from **woollen material** with a **wide fastening tape**. As the wool is porous these boots can become soggy and heavy in wet conditions.

Fitting

The fetlock boot is positioned over the joint with the protection on the inside. They must be sufficiently tight to stop them twisting around. All fastenings must be on the outside of the leg.

With Yorkshire boots the tape is attached just off-centre making one portion of material larger than the other. Fit with the larger portion uppermost. Fold the boot around the leg with the tapes lying flat and tie on the outside of the leg. Pull the top part down to partially cover the lower portion.

Sausage boot

Description

This is a **thick, rubber ring** with strap, worn around the pastern.

Function

Protects the coronet or pastern if the horse has a tendency to strike this area. Also used in the stable to prevent the horse from hitting and injuring himself when lying down.

Polo boots

Description

These are **protective boots with plenty of padding** covering the fetlock joint. They come in a variety of shapes but cover a greater area than the brushing boot.

Function

Used for polo ponies going at speed and turning quickly, they **protect against blows** from the ball or stick. Since they are bulky and absorbent these boots are **not** suitable for eventing.

Travelling boots

Description

These boots are designed to be **worn when travelling** in a trailer or a box. There are front and hind boots. Some types **cover and protect the whole lower leg** from above the knee and hock to below the coronet, whilst others are **shorter covering from below the knee and hock.**

Materials

Usually made of **cotton lined with sheepskin**, these boots are wrapped around the legs and then fastened with Velcro. There are different sizes to suit horses and ponies. The thicker and stronger the boot, the longer it will last. Thin travelling boots will soon lose their effectiveness.

Function

The great advantage with these boots is that they are **extremely easy and quick to put on.** The only disadvantage is that they **do not provide as much protection as bandages.**

Fitting

The front and hind boots can be similar in appearance; the hind ones are usually a little longer. Wrap the appropriate boot around the leg to cover all the vital areas, such as coronet and knee if the design of boot permits. Fasten the straps as firmly and as securely as possible with the straps on the outside of the leg pointing backwards.

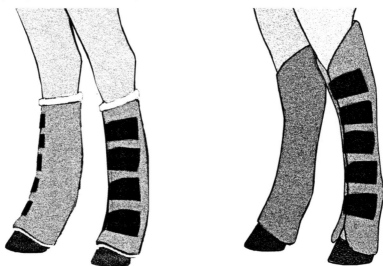

Knee caps or boots

Description

There are **two types**;

1. **Exercise or skeleton knee boot.**

   Consists of a padded portion at the front that covers the knee. It is fastened to the leg by a top and lower strap. This boot is fairly **small for flexibility**.

2. **Travelling knee boot.**

   This type is larger to **provide more protection**. Fastens with a top and a lower strap.

Materials

Usually made of **leather, or a mixture of leather with suede or wool.**

Skeleton or exercise knee boot

Travelling knee boot

Function

Exercise knee boots protect the knees from injury and bruising **during work** especially when the horse is being **ridden on the road**. Sometimes used to protect an **old knee injury** when **jumping**. **Travelling knee boots** protect the knees from injury and damage whilst **in the trailer or horsebox** and when loading or unloading.

Fitting

The boot is placed over the horse's knee with the pad to the front and the thick strap at the top. The **top strap is fastened quite firmly** so that the boot does not slip down over the knee. The **lower strap** should be **fastened very loosely** so that the horse can bend his leg. The **buckles should fasten on the outside of the leg** with the **strap ends facing forwards**. These are the only boots where the straps point forwards.

Hock boots

Description

A **boot shaped like the back of the hock** with an upper and lower strap.

Materials

They are usually made of **leather and hide, suede or canvas**. Some hock boots are fastened with two straps; some have a strap and Velcro.

Function

These **protect the hocks when travelling**.

Fitting

They are **fitted over the hock.** For boots with straps the **top strap is fastened firmly** and the **lower strap is left a little loose** to allow for movement in the joint. The **buckles of the straps** are **fastened** on the **outside of the leg**.

The boots with Velcro are manufactured from a material that allows movement and therefore the strap or straps can be fastened fairly firmly.

Care of Boots

As with all equipment, boots must be kept clean and supple. Boots should be cleaned every time after use. In certain conditions grit, sand, mud or dirt can work into the boot and cause friction sores on the horse's leg.

Leather boots are cleaned as leather tack. Synthetic boots can be washed either by hand or in the washing machine with a non-biological washing powder. (Some horses are allergic to biological powders.) Boots must be completely dry before being used again.

Straps and buckles are more secure as fastenings; Velcro tends to deteriorate and become unreliable. When cleaned in a washing machine, the Velcro fastenings will collect fluff. To prevent this, fasten the straps to each other to keep them clean. Check all boots regularly for wear and tear.

Treatment boots

The following boots are used in conjunction with medical treatment.

Overboot, Poultice boot or Equiboot

This is a large boot that fits over the entire foot. It can either be used as a protection if the horse cannot be shod but needs to work, or as a treatment boot to keep a poultice in place. Correct fitting of this boot is essential. If it is too tight it will bruise the heels; too loose and it will dislodge or come off completely. (See Chapter on Health.)

Treatment boot

Fitting from the foot to the knee, in appearance like a normal wellington boot. It is used to apply cold water to the leg for medical treatment.

There are occasions when boots should not be worn. During hunting or endurance riding, mud and grit can become trapped under the boot. Over a period of hours this causes friction sores that may become infected.

Leg Bandages

Leg bandages are used for **protection, medicinal purposes**, to **provide warmth** and for **drying off the legs**. There are two types of leg bandage; the stable or travel bandage and the exercise bandage. Bandages are used on the horse in the stable to protect an injury, keep it clean, for support or to provide warmth. Bandages used for travelling protect the horse's lower legs whilst he is in the trailer or horsebox. Exercise bandages are used in place of boots, for protection when the horse is working.

All bandages must be put on correctly. If wrongly applied, bandages can cause sores or pressure points, bumps, lumps and damaged tendons.

There are certain rules that need to be followed when applying bandages.

- A bandage should be put on over an inner lining, such as fibregee or gamgee. This will provide more comfort, warmth and greater protection against knocks and injury.

- Bandage in an anti-clockwise direction on the near side and clockwise on the off side.

- The same person must bandage all the legs. This will provide an even pressure.

- The bandage must be applied at the same pressure all the way down the leg. It must not be loose at the top and tight at the bottom or vice versa.

- To adjust the pressure of the bandage whilst it is being put on, it should be pulled against the front of the leg, the bone. The bandage must never be pulled against the back of the leg or tendon as this will cause damage.

- Fibregee is a felt-like material that can be quite difficult to fit especially when new. Washing it a few times will make it softer and more pliable. Gamgee, similar to cotton wool with a fine muslin or net covering, is very soft and pliable but not as strong or as durable as fibregee.

- Avoid wrinkles in the bandage as this will result in pressure points; areas of rubbing, sores, bruising or restricted circulation.

- The fastenings should lie on the outside of the leg. If fastened on the back of the leg they may damage the tendon; on the inside of the leg they may be kicked and undone; to the front they may bruise the bone. Tapes should be fastened firmly and then neatly tucked away. Any fastenings must be secure. In some cases this means stitching the tape to the bandage.

- Tapes must be tied at the same pressure as the bandage.

- Bandages should always be clean and dry. Wet bandages will tighten once they start to dry and can restrict the circulation within the leg.

- When using a leg bandage for medicinal purposes, always bandage the other leg for support, particularly in the case of the fore legs. The sound leg will carry more weight in an effort to compensate for the injured leg.

- After use bandages should be cleaned, dried and firmly rolled up correctly with the tapes on the inside of the roll.

Stable bandages

These are usually made of wool, flannel, acrylic or stockinette and are approximately 3 m (8 to 10 feet) long, and around 10 cm (4 to 4½ inches wide). Stable bandages are used mainly for protection of an injury. They can also be applied when the horse's legs are wet and need drying, to provide warmth in very cold weather or to prevent the horse's legs filling up with fluid if he is prone to this problem whilst standing in the stable.

Method

Make sure the leg is clean and dry. Take the fibregee or gamgee as a basis and wrap it around the leg. Check that it is long enough to fit from the knee or hock to just below the coronet.

Wrap the fibregee around the leg. Ideally the outside edge, facing to the rear, should lie in the hollow between the back of the cannon bone and the tendon.

Take the bandage, *with the roll on the outside*, and place the end by the knee. The bandage must be applied in the same direction as the fibregee. This helps to keep the fibregee in place.

Hold the end firmly against the leg until the tip can be folded over and secured by bandaging over it. Use an even pressure, pulling only against the bone. Bandage each turn so that it overlaps the previous roll by about half a width.

Wrap the bandage down the leg over the fetlock and pastern until it reaches the top of the foot. The last wrap can be slightly angled downwards across the front of the foot. Then start applying the bandage up the leg again. The first wrap can be slightly angled upwards to create an inverted 'V' centrally above the hoof.

Bandage up the leg, maintaining the even pressure until the tapes or Velcro strap is reached. The fastening should be on the outside of the leg. Tie the tapes into a bow firmly, but not too tightly, and tuck the ends neatly under the tape.

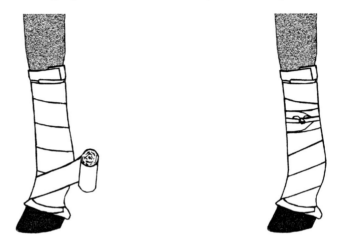

Test the firmness of the bandage by placing a finger down the top between the fibregee and the horse's leg. There should be room for at least one finger but never more than two. A bandage that is too tight will restrict the circulation, cause bruising and damage the tendon. A bandage applied too loosely will not offer support and could be a hazard. It may slip off and become caught around the horse's legs causing him to trip.

Stable bandages should be removed at least twice a day and the horse given half an hour to an hour without the bandages, allowing the circulation to return to normal. This can be further encouraged by massaging the legs upwards towards the heart.

Travel bandages

These are exactly the same as stable bandages, providing protection when the horse is travelling. This type of bandage may be fitted a little lower on the foot than the stable bandage, to protect the coronet.

Exercise bandages

These bandages are made of elasticated stockinette and are shorter in length, thinner and narrower than stable bandages. They are used for protecting the tendons against injury whilst exercising. They can also help reduce swellings and windgalls.

Removing the bandage

First undo the tape or Velcro strap. Then taking the bandage pass it from hand to hand, unwinding it from around the horse's leg. Remove the gamgee or fibregee. The bandage can now be washed and dried or, if being used again on the way home from a show, rolled up in preparation for use.

Bandage fastenings

Tapes should be wide and flat, if they are too narrow or curled up they could put pressure on the leg. After the bandage is washed, the tapes should be ironed.

Velcro is simple to use and efficient providing it is of a *sufficient length* to hold the bandage in place securely and is *kept clean*.

Sometimes fastenings need greater security. The tapes can be sewn to the bandage for safety. Alternatively self adhesive or insulating tape can be wrapped around the leg to cover the fastening. This should be applied at the same pressure as the bandage, certainly no tighter.

Use	Boots	Bandages
Travelling	Travelling boots (if these boots are not long enough to cover coronet or knee or hock, may have to use over-reach boots, travelling knee caps and hock boots).	Travel bandages with knee caps and hock boots.
Cross country	Brushing boots or competition boots. Over-reach boots.	Exercise bandages properly secured by stitching or insulating tape. Over-reach boots.
Dressage	No boots should be worn in competitions.	No bandages.
Show jumping	Brushing boots or tendon boots.	Exercise bandages properly secured.
Schooling	Brushing boots or tendon boots. Over-reach boots.	Exercise bandages. For flatwork these may cover the fetlock. Over-reach boots.
Road Work & Ride and Lead	Brushing or speedicut boots. Exercise knee caps, over-reach boots.	Exercise bandages. Exercise knee caps, over-reach boots.
At pasture	Leather or synthetic brushing boots can be worn by horses partially out at grass to protect their legs.	Do not use bandages.

Exam Tips

Candidates should have the ability to fit various types of boot; in particular brushing boots, tendon boots, competition boots, knee caps, hock boots, travel boots, fetlock boots, speedicut and over-reach boots. They should have a knowledge of when to use various boots; their advantages and disadvantages and the problems caused through ill-fitting.

In preparation visit your local tack shop and look at the variety of boots available, including the new designs currently on the market. Looking through horse magazines and catalogues will also help expand your knowledge. Observe what types of boot the show jumpers and cross country competitors use on their horses. Catalogues usually explain the materials used for the various boots as well as giving the prices.

Each candidate will be asked to put a **stable bandage** on a horse. The bandage and fibregee or gamgee will be provided. The art of good bandaging, beside being taught correctly, comes with practice. Bandaging can be quite difficult to begin with but, with constant repetition, it can become almost second nature. This is especially important in an Exam when the fingers refuse to respond to the brain, the bandage suddenly takes on a life of its own and the horse decides to dance an Irish jig. Those hours of practice seem little enough to deal with it all!

In addition, the fibregee used for Exams is often new, which makes it awkward to wrap around the horse's leg. It tends to be stiff and becomes crumpled under the bandage. In this case it would be quite in order to explain to the Examiner that the fibregee is new but that given a few washes it would soften and be easier to use.

You will need to practise putting a stable bandage on various horses. Horses with long cannons will need the bandage wrapped around with less overlap. Horses with short cannons, or smaller horses, will need a greater overlap. **Bandage all the horse's legs**; sometimes the offside and hind legs can prove more difficult.

Gain as much practical experience as you can about boots and bandages; this will increase your confidence in the Exam.

CHAPTER 26
Rugs

Rugs and blankets are used mainly during the colder months to keep a clipped horse warm in the stable and dry when out at grass. There are also rugs for specific circumstances such as the anti-sweat rug or cooler rug.

Rugs can be a fairly expensive item and so most owners begin by buying their new horse the essential rugs and add to these as and when required.

Revision

Rug fastenings, rollers and surcingles. Types of rug their advantages and disadvantages; Jute rug, blankets, stable rug, woollen day rug, anti-sweat rug, summer sheet, New Zealand rug. Rugs for the stabled horse. Measuring for a rug, putting on and fitting a rug. Removing a rug, basic care of rugs.

The New Zealand rug

Those horses and ponies who spend time at grass, especially those clipped during the winter, will need at least two New Zealand rugs. One can be worn whilst the other is drying. In really persistent rain or when the weather is windy, some wet does seep under the rug and this will need to be thoroughly dried before the rug is worn again.

Owners often find they need a third rug to act as a spare when one is drying and the other is being mended.

Materials

The New Zealand rug needs to be tough and waterproof to withstand rough usage and wet weather. Traditionally made of canvas, there are now various materials used for New Zealands; chemically proofed cotton, waxed cotton, proofed nylon and synthetics for the outer layer.

Linings are made from polypropylene thermal fabric, fleece, wool, acrylic fur or cotton. Some designs include a duvet type polyester filled layer for insulation. Others feature a nylon lining inside the chest area to prevent rubbing on the horse's shoulders.

It's the annual early winter competition of who can tear a hole in their New Zealand rug first !

Designs

There are various designs of New Zealand rug; different manufacturers have slightly different styles.

Some have darts at the front to give a better shape around the shoulder or around the hindquarters for a snug fit. Some have material insets around the front legs to give the horse freedom of movement.

Some New Zealands are designed with a tail flap, which helps to prevent rain blowing underneath the back of the rug.

Variations

New Zealands have different thickness for summer and winter use. Some are lighter and thinner. Others, for use in the worst weathers, are thicker with full linings for warmth. The lighter ones are most suitable for turn out use only, rather than on a horse or pony living out permanently.

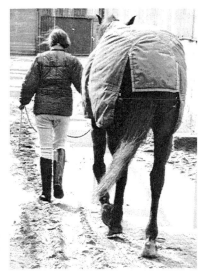

Figure 27:Harry off to the field with his tail flap rug.

A new design is the 2 in 1 rug, which includes a detachable quilt lining so that this New Zealand rug can be used in warm or cold weather. The quilt is fastened by Velcro to the outer rug.

There are neck covers and head covers to protect those areas on a clipped horse in the coldest weather. Some hoods and neck covers are separate, some are an 'all in one' and some include protective covering for the ears. These will also keep the horse clean if he rolls in the mud.

The Stable Rug

There are several types to choose from depending on the owner's preference, economy and the needs of the horse.

Figure 28:Bella in her Polywarm*

✳ The most popular is the stable rug usually known as the Polywarm . In really cold weather two of these can be worn provided they are properly secured. The synthetic material can be quite slippery though so an alternative is a Polywarm with a blanket underneath.

✳ The jute rug, the traditional rug before the development of synthetics, is made from natural fibres. Jute rugs can be worn with a blanket underneath for really cold conditions, though this combination can be quite heavy for a horse to wear. Special rot-proof Jute rugs are now available.

---

* Polywarm is a trade name.

✳ Duvet underblankets can keep a thin-skinned animal warm in winter. The duvet can be placed in the same position as the blanket, turned back over a stable rug and secured with a roller or surcingle. Alternatively the front of the duvet can be left up on the horse's neck to keep him warm.

Other rugs

There are other rugs that have their uses at specific times. The anti-sweat rug used when the horse is wet, keeps the horse from becoming chilled too quickly when drying. There are variations of this type of rug on the market now. 'Cooler' rugs are made with a much finer mesh which are designed to keep the horse warm and dry when cooling off. These also act as travel rugs during the warmer months.

- The woollen day rug is used for warmth on cooler days.
- The summer sheet can be used when travelling in the summer. It also keeps the horse clean.
- Exercise sheets are used on the horse when being exercised to keep his back dry.

All these rugs and sheets should have a fillet string at the back that fits under the horse's tail, to prevent the rug from blowing up in the wind. They all have a front fastening and can be further secured by a light, elastic surcingle.

Size

All types of rugs need to fit properly if they are to be effective. Sizes normally vary from the smallest around 3'9" to the largest at 7' and the range between increases at 3". A pony of 13 hands will need a rug size of 5'3" or 5'6" whilst a 16 hand medium hunter will need a rug size of 6'0" to 6'6". Though most rugs are sold by inch measurements, some manufacturers are now selling in metre lengths (1.98 m is 6'6").

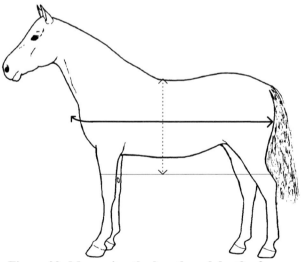

Figure 29: Measuring the length and depth of a rug

To discover the length of rug required, measure from the centre of the horse's chest around his body to the point on the hindquarters where the rug should finish.

To provide protection, particularly with the New Zealand and the Stable rug, the rug needs to reach down below the horse's belly. Ideally the rug should be a good hand's span below the elbow, a little longer if possible. It may be better to buy one that is a little larger in length for the horse but which gives him sufficient depth.

Fit

Once the basic length is known the actual fit around the body should be assessed. Many tack shops and mail order catalogues will allow a customer time to try a rug on the horse. This should be done on top of a summer sheet so that the rug can be exchanged if necessary.

- When the rug is fastened, run a hand under the rug from the withers round the horse's shoulders to the front fastening. Any tightness in this area, particularly around the point of shoulder, will definitely cause rubbing, bare patches and possibly sores.

- If the rug is too loose around the shoulders it will slip backwards.

- Watch the horse move in the rug. Any stretching of the rug around the shoulder (tight lines) will show that the rug is too small.

- New Zealand and Stable rugs should ideally slightly overlap at the front. If the front edges just meet or there is a gap the rug may be too small and will not protect the chest area. Some rugs are designed with an overlap.

- The fastenings also need to be tough, weatherproof and capable of securing the rug properly. Check the front straps and the leg straps at the back. These need to be thick and strong with robust buckles or clips.

Both the New Zealand and the Stable rug can be expensive items to purchase but it is wiser to buy better quality than cheaper, poor quality rugs. On the other hand buying the most expensive is not always the right choice. The ideal is to buy one that fits the horse and is tough enough to last.

There are several manufacturers who produce rugs. So if the rug is the correct length but does not fit around the shoulders or is too short in depth, the solution is to try another brand or design.

Care of Clothing

Rugs and blankets need care and attention if they are to last and do their job properly. Light rugs, Polywarms and blankets can all be washed either at home in the washing machine or more efficiently at the local launderette. Some launderettes will not permit the washing of rugs whilst others will take the rug, wash and dry it.

New Zealand rugs are different because of their waterproofing. They do need specialist cleaning. Some tack shops or saddlers will take in rugs for cleaning and repair. This rug does receive rough treatment and often has tears, rips, broken straps or fastenings, split seams and holes rendering the rug ineffective. A New Zealand rug that needs repairing should be taken to the tack shop in the summer. In the autumn everyone is having their New Zealands cleaned or repaired and sometimes owners must wait weeks before their rug is returned.

Jute rugs will shrink with washing; some tack shops refuse to clean these rugs for this reason. The rug can be washed in cold water by being laid on the ground and scrubbed with a brush.

All leather fittings should be cleaned with saddle soap and oiled. Metal clips can be cleaned with metal polish and have a light covering of Vaseline to prevent rusting.

When the spring arrives and brings the warmer weather, the stable rugs, blankets and New Zealand rugs will need to be stored. If they are cleaned and repaired first this will save time later in the year. It will also prevent stale dirt and dung from hardening or going mouldy. The rugs and blankets must be thoroughly dry before storing.

The storage area needs to be dry and airy to prevent mould. The rug should be folded neatly and wrapped in brown or greaseproof paper. Plastic bags are not suitable as these will make the rug sweat and cause condensation, resulting in mould. Moth balls can be placed in the folds, as these little insects love eating the natural fibres of the rug. If there are a number of horses and ponies, each rug should be named or labelled so that it is easily recognisable at the end of the summer.

New Zealand rugs may need waterproofing especially around the seams or any repair patches. This can either be done commercially by a cleaner or sprayed on with a can of waterproofing bought from the tack shop. Read the instructions carefully, lay the rug out on the floor somewhere convenient and spray all over the rug.

Exam Tips

Revise the information given for Stage I on different types of rugs and their uses. Look at some different designs of rugs. A visit to the local tack shop or looking at mail order catalogues and advertisements in the equestrian magazines will give information about the types of rugs on the market.

The care and storage of rugs is important, not only because rugs are expensive but also if they are damaged they will not protect the horse effectively and he may suffer. Rugs vary in price quite considerably but buying a cheaper rug to save money is not economical if the quality is poor.

CHAPTER 27
Travelling

Horses and ponies travel to various events, competitions or simply to hack in different surroundings. They may travel to a new home after being purchased by a new owner, or to the medical centre for veterinary care. Whatever the reason, when travelling the horse must be adequately protected and restrained to prevent injuries.

Protection

The most vulnerable areas are the hocks, knees and coronets. If the horse looses his balance he may step on the coronet with a shod hoof and the resulting damage will affect hoof growth for months. The horse may bump a knee or hock against the trailer or box and this may cause cuts and bruising.

The tail needs protecting against rubbing on the trailer's back door or the wall of the horsebox. The poll should also have protection, particularly for horses who raise their heads quickly and bang the poll on the roof.

Travel Clothing

Figure 30: Horse in travel bandages with knee and hock boots, tail guard and poll guard

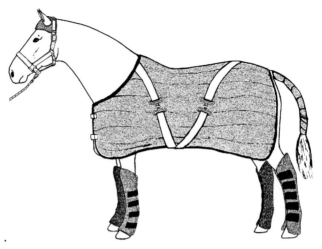

Figure 31: Horse in travel boots, tail bandage and poll guard

- **Protection for the legs**

  Travel boots, or travel bandages and fibregee or gamgee.

  Knee boots and hock boots if the travel boots do not cover this area; definitely needed with bandages.

- **Protection for the feet**

  Travel boots or bandages wrapped over the coronet or

  over-reach boots if the travel boots or bandages are not of a sufficient length.

- **Protection for the tail**

  Tail bandage.

  A tail guard can be put over a tail bandage for extra safety or used alone on long journeys.

- **Protection for the poll**

  Poll guard. (If a poll guard is not available, a long piece of sponge or thick cloth tied to the headcollar works effectively as a poll guard.)

Restraint

When travelling, the horse is restrained with a headcollar and lead-rope. The lead-rope is tied to a **piece of string attached to the securing ring.** The headcollar and lead-rope must be strong, in good condition and tied correctly otherwise the horse will free his head.

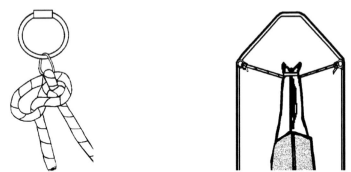

For single horses in a trailer without a central divider, two lead-ropes will be necessary. One rope is tied to the right side and one to the left side of the trailer. This will prevent the horse from moving around too much and keep his head steadier.

Rugs

On warm summer days, it is not essential for the horse to wear a rug when travelling. If transporting in the early morning or evening when the weather is likely to turn chilly, or there is a draught through the box, he may wear a light, cotton summer sheet. This has the advantage of keeping the horse clean when travelling to a show. If the horse sweats when travelling, an anti-sweat rug or cooler rug will keep him dry and cool.

During the late spring or early autumn a woollen day rug will prevent the horse becoming chilly. When the weather becomes a little cooler, a light Polywarm or stable rug can be used. During the late autumn and winter he should wear at least one stable rug and possibly a blanket depending on the temperature.

The horse should be kept warm but not too hot. If he arrives at his destination sweaty, he will need to be cooled down before being tacked up and ridden. On cold days, coming from a warm trailer, he may catch a chill with the change of atmosphere. He will also need grooming; dried sweat marks do not give a good impression in the show or competition ring.

All rugs worn when travelling must be sufficiently secured. Stable rugs will normally have crossover surcingles. Cotton or woollen day rugs should be fitted with a fillet string at the rear to go under the horse's tail. This will stop the rug from blowing up over the horse's quarters. An elasticated surcingle can be purchased separately and used as extra security. If the horse is to wear a tail guard this will usually need fastening around a surcingle anyway.

Though the horse should not travel in a New Zealand rug, it is advisable to take one when travelling. If it starts to rain on arrival at the show the horse can be kept as dry as possible before competing.

Putting on the Travel Clothes

There is no right or wrong order in which to prepare the horse for travel and some people find their own routine that suits them and their horse. The horse is suitably restrained first with a headcollar and lead-rope. The poll guard can be fitted onto the headcollar.

If the weather is warm and the horse is to wear a summer sheet or anti-sweat rug, it is easier to put the tail bandage on first. On cooler or cold days the horse should have the rug on first. The rug can then be folded back so that the top of the tail is uncovered when putting on the tail bandage.

If a tail guard is being used, the rug should be put on first, as the tapes on the tail guard will need to be fastened around the surcingle. A tail guard can either be fitted on its own or, for extra protection, on top of the tail bandage.

The leg bandages or travel boots should be fitted by one person so that the pressure is relatively equal on all legs.

If there are two people making the horse ready, one person can put the leg bandages or travel boots on the forelegs whilst the other person is putting the bandage on the tail. It is better to wait until the tail bandage is fitted before fitting the boots on the hind legs. Some horses lift their hind legs up at this point giving the person at the back quite a shock. Over-reach boots, knee boots and hock boots are then fitted if necessary.

Planning to Travel

The preparation for a journey begins a few days before so that there is no rush or panic on the day, very important if travelling to a competition.

- Prepare all the travel clothes for the horse. These should be clean, dry and in good condition. There will be time to repair or replace any equipment if necessary.

- Tack should be checked and cleaned if necessary. Prepare a grooming kit.

- Check the destination and route.

- Collect any paperwork (entry or acknowledgement forms, inoculation certificate if necessary).

- Prepare an equine medical kit. A human one too is a wise precaution.

The Horse

Monitor the horse's health. If he is ill or unsound, travelling should be avoided if at all possible, unless the trip is to the Vet. Check, in particular, his shoes. It is unwise to travel a horse with a loose shoe as he may easily remove it by treading on it in transit. If he is nearly due to be shod it should be possible to arrange a Farrier's visit a few days in advance.

For a horse who has never travelled before or for one whose reactions are unknown, he should be put in the trailer or box a few times first. It will also help to take him on short trips to accustom him to the movement of travel. This will also benefit a horse who has not been transported for some time.

If there is any doubt as to the horse's reactions or willingness to load, one or two experienced, strong assistants should help to persuade the horse to load quietly and minimise future problems.

The Trailer or Box

Make safety checks to the lights, front, rear, brake lights and indicators; brakes, tyre pressure, oil, water and towing bar. Fill the tank up the day before to avoid stopping at the garage with a trailer or horsebox full of excited horses on the way to a show.

If hiring a trailer or box for self-drive, make all the safety checks. Do not presume that the vehicle is safe or has been checked recently. With trailers the lights will need checking in any case, to test the connection between the towing vehicle and the trailer.

Preparing to Travel

Prepare the trailer or box first. The horse may become nervous or excited at the prospect of travelling if he is waiting around dressed for travel for any length of time.

Quickly repeat the safety checks, better to be safe than sorry. Check that there is string attached to the securing rings and that any loose objects, buckets or grooming kits, are removed so that these do not rattle when the horse steps on the ramp.

Park the trailer or box close to a wall or hedge. This blocks one way of escape. Park, if possible, with the interior of the trailer or box towards the light, so that the horse is not walking into a black hole.

Park on level ground, if possible, to prevent the ramp rocking when the horse enters. If on sloping ground, park downhill where the ramp will be a little less steep.

Collect together feed and water buckets; some water in a container; feed if necessary; spare hay and haynets; a skip and shovel to clean the trailer.

Tie the haynets to rings where the horses can reach the hay. Put some shavings or straw on the floor if necessary. Trailers with rubber matting, providing it is non-slip, may not need bedding.

Make sure the interior of the trailer or box looks inviting, light, airy, spacious. Some trailers have central partitions that can be moved to offer more space for the horse.

Loading

The person loading the horse should wear a riding hat, gloves and strong boots. Even if the horse is good to load and travel, there is always the possibility that he will tread on the person's foot, or swing his head around and catch the person's head. Some horses when stepping onto the ramp, or even when inside the trailer or box, will suddenly go backwards very quickly. Gloves will save the hands from friction burns. A short whip can also be useful to encourage the horse forward.

Ask two assistants to stand by the ramp, one on either side about half a metre away. One person can load one horse if necessary, but it is always safer to have assistance.

If the horse is unsure (or the handler is unsure of the horse) putting a bridle on over the headcollar is safer and gives more control. This should always be done if the handler has never loaded the horse previously. The bridle can be removed once the horse is in the trailer or box.

The handler leads the horse to the trailer in a straight line, walking up the ramp confidently and steadily without looking back.

The handler should hold the horse whilst the breech bar or strap (at the rear of the horse) is hooked into place first. Then the horse is tied to the string on the securing ring and the ramp put up slowly and as quietly as possible. If the central partition has been moved this will need replacing before the breech bar can be fastened.

The person putting the breech bar or strap in place should not stand directly behind the horse in case he kicks or rushes backwards. This also applies when putting the ramp up; if the horse rushes backwards the ramp could crush anyone standing directly underneath.

The horse should be tied fairly short so that he cannot swing his head around.

The handler can exit by the groom's door, which should then be locked.

When one horse only is travelling in a trailer with a partition, the horse must travel on the driver's side of the partition. Travelling on the crown of the road is smoother and keeps the trailer more balanced. In the case of two horses, the heavier horse should be on the driver's side. (In the UK this is the right hand side of the trailer.)

Loading problems

If the horse is unsure or hesitant about loading there are several ways of enticing him into the trailer or box.

- A carrot or handful of food will often persuade the horse to load.

- Another quiet horse already loaded can be used to quieten his fears.

- It may be the smell of a new trailer or box. Some bedding from the horse's stable can be placed on the floor.

- Moving the partition or opening the front ramp will make the interior look lighter and more inviting. In case the horse goes right through, the front breech bar must be in place.

- A couple of assistants standing a little distance from his hindquarters may prevent the horse from stepping back.

- The assistants could also hold a lunge line between them and slowly walk towards the horse's hindquarters. The line is held taut against the horse just above his hocks. For one assistant the lunge line can be fastened to one side of the trailer or box with the assistant holding the other end.

- A sharp quick tap with a whip on the hindquarters may persuade a stubborn horse to walk forwards.

- Sometimes horses are just afraid of the ramp and picking up each fore leg in turn and placing these on the ramp can help. Give the horse a little time to become accustomed to the feel of the ramp, then persuade him to walk forwards.

Dealing with difficult horses needs lots of patience combined with firmness. The handler should never become angry and hurt the horse; this may provoke a dangerous reaction from the horse and give him a bad memory of loading. Instead use bribery, deviousness and persistence.

Travelling

The trailer or box should be driven carefully particularly round bends or over bumpy roads. The maximum speed for vehicles towing trailers in built up areas is 30 mph, on single carriageways 50 mph, on dual carriageways and motorways 60 mph. However, when transporting a horse, it is safer to keep the speed below 50 mph even on good roads.

Stopping and starting at junctions should be **performed gradually** to prevent sudden braking, which can unbalance the horse. When approaching a point where the vehicle will have to slow down or stop, the driver needs to look ahead and prepare in plenty of time.

Unloading

Carefully choose the spot to unload, somewhere safe, quiet and level. Allow plenty of room for the horse to come down the ramp. Enter the trailer or box and untie the horse first.

Front unload

Enter by the groom's door and close it afterwards so that the horse does not try to leave by that route. Leave the front bar up until the ramp is down to prevent the horse rushing out and injuring himself or the handler.

Once the ramp is ready and the front bar unfastened lead the horse SLOWLY out of the door. Talk to him and reassure him. Watch that he does not bang his hips coming through the door.

Two horses will ideally need one handler each. Unload the horse nearest to the ramp first, then the partition can be swung over to allow the other horse room.

Rear unload

Once the ramp is down and the breech bar or strap unfastened gently encourage the horse backwards. Do not rush him; he should step down slowly. He may need to turn his head to look around; allow him to do this then ask him to step backwards again.

An assistant standing by the side of the ramp can help to guide the horse down the ramp as straight as possible. Keep talking to the horse to give him confidence.

Animal Transport Certificate

Those persons transporting horses or ponies for business or trade must now have a completed Animal Transport Certificate obtained from the MAFF. This includes professional riders or owners transporting horses to an event or those who frequently buy and sell horses as a trade when taking a horse or horses to a sale.

For the amateur owner or rider taking their horse or pony to a show, competition or gymkhana the Certificate is not necessary. It is not needed either for those taking their own horse to a sale. In these cases the horse or pony is classed as a pet and is not being transported as part of a business or trade. The European Directive based on the Welfare of Animals During Transport Order clearly states that 'this order shall not apply to the transport of pet animals, unless in the course of business or trade'.

However, there has been some confusion as to who should or should not hold an Animal Transport Certificate. Officials have stopped people who were transporting horses and insisted that they needed a certificate. The BHS are advising people to obtain a certificate when they transport their horse until this confusion is cleared.

New legislation for towing trailers

New legislation to comply with EC Directive on the Driving Licence will affect **new drivers only** after January 1st 1997. New drivers after this date, will have to take a further test to obtain a towing entitlement.

Existing drivers will not be affected except for those who wish to tow large trailers who hold a category C or D only on their licence. They will need to take a category E test.

A fact sheet will be issued by the Department of Transport explaining the Towing Trailers Entitlement.

At the present time there is no proposed change on the weight ratio, persons will still be able to tow their trailers with their existing cars. Towing vehicles however should have the manufacturer's recommended engine capacity for the trailer and horses that they wish to tow. Everyone transporting horses should also have adequate insurance cover.

Exam Tips

For the Stage II candidates will **not** be asked to actually load or unload a horse but will be questioned on the theory of travelling. You will need to know the safety checks necessary before travelling, the travel clothes the horse must wear and the reasons for these. You should be able to describe the methods of loading, unloading and dealing with difficult horses.

Gaining practical experience will be a tremendous help, either by assisting someone to transport their horse or by observing others loading horses into a trailer or box. Visit shows and competitions and make a point of observing the loading and unloading areas. It is very interesting watching the different methods people use; you will soon be able to discern between the correct and incorrect procedures. Ask a friend or someone at your yard or stable if you can 'groom' for them when they go to a show.

If you have the opportunity to load and unload, think through to yourself each action. This will help you to be logical and precise when describing the procedures to the Examiner. Remember always use a bridle, on top of the headcollar, for a horse who is unfamiliar or who has not been loaded before.

C H A P T E R   28
Clipping and Trimming

Clipping is basically cutting the horse's coat shorter. The part of the horse's body that is clipped varies depending on the reasons for clipping and other factors such as the horse's environment; whether he is fully stabled or out at grass.

Clippers are used, of which there are various designs, ranging from large clipping machines, electric hand clippers and the battery operated clippers used for small, delicate areas on the horse's body.

Reasons for clipping

1. To **remove part of the thick, winter coat** for horses in work to **prevent excessive sweating, stress and weight loss**.

2. To **prevent chills after sweating**. The working horse with a thick coat will sweat profusely and, consequently, take time to cool down and dry; he may become chilled and catch cold. The clipped horse dries more quickly.

3. **Cleanliness** - it is easier to groom and keep the clipped horse clean.

4. **Hygiene** - to prevent skin problems. Grooming the clipped horse is more effective, making it easier to remove scurf, dead skin and dirt.

5. **Appearance** - horses look neater and tidier when clipped.

6. **Medicinal purposes** - it is easier to treat wounds and injuries if the hair surrounding these is clipped.

Types of Clip

Though a horse or pony may be clipped on any area of the body, there are recognised styles which, having been developed over decades, provide the most efficient clip for the horse.

Full Clip

Total clip of whole body.

Used particularly for show horses and ponies, hunters with thick hair and for fully stabled horses permanently in hard work.   Horses with coarse hair may also be given a full clip because the saddle area becomes hot and sweaty, causing galls and sores.

In some cases, such as horses with finer hair, the saddle patch is left unclipped to protect this area.

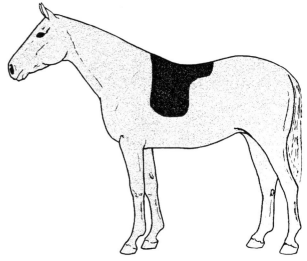

Figure 32: Full clip with saddle patch

Hunter Clip

Figure 33 Hunter clip

Total clip apart from the legs and saddle patch.

The hair is left on the legs to give some protection against thorns or injury whilst out hunting.   On the fore and hind legs, the clip slopes down slightly from front to back.   The saddle patch is left unclipped to prevent saddle sores and galls.

This clip, as the name implies, is given to hunters who are worked and go hunting all through the winter.   This clip is also given to horses in hard work such as riding school horses or show jumpers.

Blanket Clip

An area in the shape of a blanket or rug is left unclipped.

Clipped areas include the neck, chest, shoulders, part of the barrel, belly and the top portion of the hind legs. Sometimes a half-moon shape around the flank is clipped. Usually the legs remain unclipped as well.

Depending on the horse the head may remain unclipped, be clipped out partially around the cheeks and lower jaw (following the cheek piece of the bridle) or be clipped completely.

Figure 34: Blanket clip

This clip is given to horses and ponies in **medium or light work**, who may be **partially out at grass**. Also **young horses** or those who are cold-backed or prone to chills and Thoroughbred types with fine hair.

Chaser Clip

The whole head, neck from poll to middle of shoulder including chest, body to top of stifle is clipped.

This clip is used for **horses and ponies in medium work, young horses** and those **finer bred animals who may be prone to chills; generally finer coated Thoroughbreds.**

Figure 35: Chaser clip

Trace Clip

So named because the line of the clip follows the traces of the driving equipment.

From the throat, lower half of the neck, chest, half the shoulders, barrel, belly and from the stifle to halfway up the hindquarters. Half-moon shapes can be clipped around the flanks and dock.

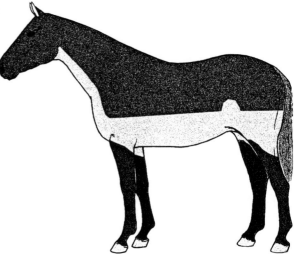

Figure 36: Low cut trace clip

Figure 37: Medium/high trace clip with clipped head

This clip can vary, depending on how high the hair is clipped. Sometimes the head is clipped.

For **horses and ponies** in **work** who are **partially out at grass,** when New Zealand rugs must be worn.

Neck and Belly Clip

The idea is to give a minimum clip removing the coat from those areas that are prone to sweating.

The lower part of the neck and belly. Sometimes the lower part of the jaw is clipped as is the area around the lower shoulders.   This clip is sometimes called a Sweat clip.

For **ponies** in **light or medium work** who are **out at grass** during the winter. The pony will need to wear a New Zealand rug when the weather is wet and cold.

Figure 38: Neck & Belly clip

These recognised types of clip **can be varied** to suit individual animals and their owners. The line of the blanket, trace or chaser clip may be cut higher or lower to suit the horse's appearance or his lifestyle.   The horse's head can either be clipped out completely, partially clipped or left unclipped if he objects to the clippers around his face.

When to Clip

The winter coat is normally clipped when it has grown through properly, from **late September** to **early or mid October.** The clip may need **repeating about every 6 to 8 weeks**, with the **last clip** being given around the **end of January**, **beginning of February**.   From February onwards clipping will spoil the summer coat coming through.

Most horses in full work will need about **two to three clips during the winter months**. This will vary though; some horses may need clipping more frequently whereas others may only need clipping **once or twice**. It really does depend on the rate of hair growth, the texture of the hair and the horse's lifestyle.

To reduce the number of clips during the winter and to delay the first clip, the horse may be 'rugged up' in August, providing the weather is not too hot. Putting rugs on a horse early in the year discourages the growth of his winter coat.

The first clip can then be given later, perhaps November. This is particularly useful if the horse objects to clipping and possibly has to be sedated. It also saves time by reducing the number of clips, and money if the owner has to pay someone to clip the horse.

Horses can be clipped at other times of the year. There are those with particularly thick coats who need clipping all year round. Show horses or ponies are often given a full clip before an early spring show if their winter coat is rough or their summer coat is not fully through. Event horses may be clipped during the summer.

When Not to clip

Horses and ponies living out at grass in the winter doing little or no work should be left unclipped. This will allow the coat to grow and provide protection against the weather. There are some horses with such a fine coat that clipping is never necessary.

Clippers

There are various types of clippers. The decision which type to purchase depends on the size of the horse to be clipped, his temperament, the number of horses to be clipped, personal preference and expense.

- **Heavy duty electric clippers or clipping machines** - for clipping large numbers of horses. These are mains operated and need a power supply, circuit breaker and probably an extension cable.

- **Battery clippers** - with battery pack for clipping a smaller number or a single horse. These are portable and can be used at shows or by professionals who travel to clip at different stables. Safe, easy to use, no electric cables or wires, can be used without a special clipping box.

  Batteries are rechargeable but this can prove more expensive. More than one power pack is needed if a number of horses are to be clipped. As the battery must be run down completely before recharging, the power is not consistent and the quality of the clip can decrease especially after 1-2 hours.

- **Manual clippers** are excellent for delicate areas such as round the horse's eyes, ears or belly. Useful for the horse who is 'clipper shy'. Can be very tiring and difficult to work by hand especially to clip a whole horse.

- **Lightweight clippers** are suitable for horses or ponies with fine hair.

- **Trimmers** are used for trimming around the chin, behind the elbows and other awkward places.

Clippers are produced by various manufacturers and vary in quality and price. Deciding which make to purchase, depends on the type of clipper needed for the job and the money available. Visit some tack shops first and ask for details of make and quality. Assess which type would be best suited for the horse or horses to be clipped.

There are different types of blades to choose from as well, coarse, medium or fine. A coarse blade will give a light clip and finer blades will give a much closer clip. A coarse blade will also clip a thick coated horse whilst finer blades will be used on a horse with finer hair.

For the person who owns one horse it will usually be more economical to pay someone to come and clip the horse. The fee varies depending on the type of clip, the size of horse and the time it takes if the horse is temperamental.

Care of Clippers

A pair of clippers is an expensive item and needs to be looked after with great care.

General care

♦ Always follow the **Manufacturer's instructions.**

♦ Store clippers in a **clean, dry and secure** place.

♦ Always **clean, oil and put away after use**.

♦ Check before every use that the **blades** are **sharp** and **unbroken.**

♦ Keep a **spare** pair of **blades** available.

♦ *Electric clippers should always be used with a **circuit breaker** for safety.*

♦ All **cables** should be well **insulated.**

Method of Clipping

Preparation

Good preparation is essential if the clipping is to proceed smoothly and efficiently.

The Clippers

Check the clippers a couple of weeks before clipping day, particularly if the clippers have not been used for some time.

For electric clippers, check the cables and the circuit breaker. For battery powered clippers, check that the batteries are working.

The Day

Choose a mild, dry day and clip mid-morning, if possible. If the day is cold, which often happens in winter, cover the horse with a blanket. Fold the blanket over to expose the areas to be clipped, then cover again once clipped to keep the horse warm.

Make sure there is plenty of time for clipping in case the horse becomes restless and must be given time to settle. Some horses are clipped over several days, being given partial clips every two or three days.

If the horse is frightened or difficult to clip, he may need sedating. In this case an appointment will have to be made with a Vet two or three days before the clipping day.

Decide first what type of clip is required so that time is not wasted with the horse standing around. This point is particularly important when someone else is doing the clip. There have been cases where the person clipping was half way through a full clip only to be told that it should have been a trace clip!

Clipping Area

Check the clipping area. This must be clean and dry with plenty of room, clear of all obstructions or obstacles. The area should be light; daylight is best but if not, a good strong electric light should be available.

The floor must not be slippery; a rubber matting floor is best. Alternatively put down a thin layer of straw or shavings. This will also help when clearing away the clipped hair afterwards.

Check the electric point is accessible and that the clipper cable is long enough to reach it or an extension lead is available. Check also that the cable will be out of the horse's way so that he cannot tread on, trip over or bite it. If the cable has sufficient length it can be suspended from a hook placed high on the wall or on the ceiling of the clipping room. Make sure there is a circuit breaker available.

The Horse

Groom the horse thoroughly so that he is clean. Dust and grease will damage the blades. The horse should be kept in the stable before he is clipped. A horse who has just come in from work or the field and is wet with sweat or rain should not be clipped.

Plait the mane to keep it out of the way or, if the mane is short, divide it into bunches and secure with elastic bands so that it sticks up in tufts.

Secure the tail with a tail bandage. The tail can be doubled up first to give further clearance for the clippers around the hindquarters.

Clothes

The person performing the clip should wear overalls to prevent the horse's hair from sticking to the clothes; a cap or head scarf is also useful for the same reason. Long hair should be tied back in case it becomes caught up in the clippers. When using electricity, rubber soled boots should be worn for safety.

The Assistant

It is always wiser to have an assistant to help when necessary, and to hold the horse if he is young or nervous. The assistant should stand on the same side of the horse as the person clipping, so that he or she can then be prepared for the horse's reaction if the clippers touch a sensitive spot.

The assistant should also be wearing overalls; rubber soled boots and have any long hair tied back.

Clipping

Check the tension of the blades. The method for doing this will be described in the Manufacturer's instructions. Normally this is done by turning the screw until the motor noise changes. The screw is then **turned back** a half turn. If the tension is too tight it will ruin the engine; too loose and it will tear at the horse's hair. The tension may need a further slight adjustment when the clipping starts.

After all the preparations are complete, put a headcollar and lead-rope or a bridle on the horse and ask the assistant to bring the horse into position.

Trace the outline of the area to be clipped with some chalk, some saddle soap, with a finger against the lie of the hair or with some vegetable oil applied with a brush. Anything that will be visible but which will not ruin the clipper blades.

To avoid startling the horse, turn the clippers on for a short while first outside the box, so that he becomes accustomed to the noise.

To further test the horse's reactions, the clippers can be turned off and laid against the horse's neck or shoulder.

Then holding the clippers in one hand, lay the *other* hand on the horse's neck and turn the clippers on so that he feels the vibrations. If the horse is calm the clip can now begin.

Start on the shoulder and neck as these are the easiest spots to clip and this will give the horse time to become used to the feel of the clippers. Clip against the lie of hair in long, smooth strokes, flipping any cut hair off the clippers after each stroke. The lines should be straight and even to achieve a neat clip.

Check the clippers regularly for heat by turning them off and *gently* placing them against the back of the hand. If the blades become too hot they will cause a 'clipper burn' on the horse. The clippers will need switching off from time to time and the hair brushing from around the motor air vent to prevent overheating.

The clippers will need regular doses of clipper oil. This oil comes in a little plastic bottle with a nozzle, which is *inserted into a hole above the motor. Oil should never be used on the blades as this will increase the friction and make the blades hot.*

The clippers can at intervals be turned off and the blades only, avoiding the motor, dipped into a bowl of cooling liquid such as paraffin or surgical spirits.

The Difficult Bits

Deciding when to clip the difficult spots such as the head, the belly, between the forelegs and hind legs, depends on the horse. Some horses become 'twitchy' towards the end of the clip and in these cases those areas can be tackled halfway through the clip. Other horses start off being restless and then settle down, so the difficult areas can be left until the end of the clipping time.

If the horse objects to the clippers around his head or ticklish parts, a small pair of dog clippers can be used instead. These are much quieter and less frightening to the horse. Unfortunately they are not sturdy enough to clip a whole horse.

When clipping the head and poll area, place and refasten the headcollar around the neck. An assistant should hold the horse at this point. If the horse is very quiet and there is no-one around to help, the lead-rope should be undone and left hanging through the safety string.

Before clipping the area behind the elbows, an assistant should hold the foreleg out to the front. This will tighten the skin and make it easier to clip.

For whorls of hair or where the coat lies in a different direction, the clippers are stroked around against the lie of the hair.

For a horse with a thick or coarse coat, this can be clipped first in the direction of the hair to thin it. A normal clip can then be given afterwards against the lie of the hair.

The Mane

A small strip of the mane may be clipped where the headpiece of the bridle fits, behind the ears (a bridle path); this does make it easier to fit the headpiece. Some owners prefer to leave the mane uncut.

The rest of the mane should not be clipped unless being specifically hogged. Any parts of the mane accidentally clipped will grow out in thick tufts and become untidy. Often a narrow border of the coat is left at the base of the mane to prevent cutting it accidentally.

The Tail

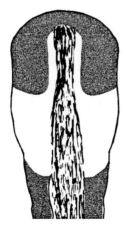

The tail is not cut at all and, to prevent any hairs being cut by accident, a small border of coat can be left around the top of the tail.

In a full clip a triangle is often left at the top of the tail.

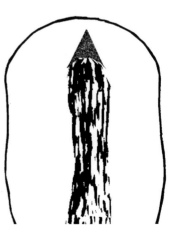

Finishing off

The time the clip takes will depend on the type of clip, the size of horse or pony, the efficiency of the clipper and the temperament of the horse. On average it takes approximately 50 minutes to 1 hour for a 16 hh middleweight horse having a full or hunter clip.

After the clip is finished, brush the horse down with a soft brush and wipe him over with a warm, damp cloth. Put his rug on and take him back to the stable for his reward. The area where the horse was clipped should be brushed out and cleaned.

Care of the Clippers After Use

After the horse is finished take the clippers apart, check the blades thoroughly, clean and oil. Put them away in the box and store them somewhere safe and dry. Looked after properly, clippers will last for years.

Dealing with Difficult Horses

Some horses object to being clipped. The horse may simply refuse to stand still or he can show total fear, quivering, rearing and pulling back.

If the horse has never been clipped before or, if he is new and there is no information as to how he is going to behave, test him first before clipping day to discover his reactions.

Walk him past another horse who is being clipped. Then try holding him closer so he can see and hear the clippers. If he seems docile, a pair of clippers, switched off, could be put next to his skin. If there is still no reaction, the clippers can be taken to a safe distance and turned on, being brought closer to him gradually.

Nervous Horses

If the horse shows nervousness or anxiety, standing him near to a quiet horse who is being clipped may alleviate his worry.

The horse could be given a trim first to accustom him to the feel of the clippers.

Music could help, having the radio or cassette player on may calm the horse and drown out most of the sound of the clippers. Some horses find music very calming.

For a really nervous horse it may take days before he becomes accustomed to the clipping procedure. If the fear or worry persists the horse may need some kind of diversion or restraint to keep him quiet.

- **A haynet** may divert the horse's attention for a while. This can make clipping the neck and head difficult though, with the horse constantly moving each time he pulls at some hay.

- Offering a **small feed** can help to quieten a horse for a while.

- Putting **a bridle** on the horse offers more control.

- **Twitching** the horse's upper lip can be effective.

- **Holding up a foreleg** offers some restraint. This is performed by an assistant, who should be competent to deal with the horse should he become awkward.

- In extreme cases the horse may have to be **sedated by the Vet**. This will need careful planning as the Vet's visit must be arranged to coincide with a convenient time and good conditions for clipping.

The Twitch

There are different designs of twitch, some of them quite ingenious, but they all have the same effect. They encourage the release of natural pain-killing chemicals, called endorphins, into the blood that dampen down the reaction to pain, rather like a mild sedative.

The twitch should **never** be applied **too tightly**, just firmly enough to stay on and quieten the horse. The length of time the twitch should be left on varies between individual horses. **Fine skinned Thoroughbreds, Arabs and certainly foals** should have the **twitch removed** after **5 minutes**. Twitching for longer may scar the skin and disfigure the horse for life. **Cobs, heavy horses and those with a thick skin** can have the twitch on for up to **20 minutes but no longer.** After removing the twitch, the muzzle will need massaging to encourage the circulation.

Twitching does restrict the blood circulation to the lip and if a twitch is left on too long or is applied too tightly, it will leave a permanent scar.

Pole Type

A small pole of wood with smooth ends and a loop of thick rope threaded through a hole. The rope of the twitch should be thick and smooth. A thin piece of string will cut into the skin and make it sore.

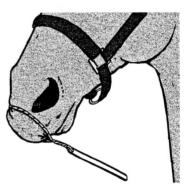

Place the loop of rope onto the hand and grip part of the horse's top lip. Slip the rope over the lip and twist the wood handle until the rope is tight. Hold the handle firmly and wait for the twitch to take effect, about 30 seconds.

Nutcracker Type

These are metal handles hinged at the top. They are put over the lip and held together by winding a cord around the handles.

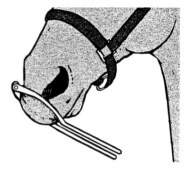

Hogging the Mane

On some horses and ponies the whole mane is clipped off completely. This is called a 'hogged' mane. Whilst this saves time with grooming, it is not usually the main reason for hogging.

Appearance A hogged mane usually suits cob types. Show cobs are often hogged for appearance. Also horses and ponies who have thick, bushy manes as it looks tidier hogged.

Medical reasons
Hogging the mane often helps with the treatment of various ailments or conditions.

Convenience Polo ponies are often hogged as the mane can obstruct the reins and stick.

Method

The preparations are made as for clipping. A clean area is prepared; clippers cleaned, oiled and ready. The horse is restrained with a headcollar and lead-rope or bridle. An assistant will definitely be required to hold the horse's head low and as still as possible whilst the mane is hogged.

The hogging starts at the withers and goes up the mane to the poll. Starting on the nearside, place the clippers at the base of the mane and move them smoothly up towards the ears on one side. Repeat on the offside. Stretch out any crinkled areas with the fingers and gently clip to give a clean, smooth, even cut.

A hogged mane may need clipping every 3 or 4 weeks. It can take up to two years for a mane to grow back and even then the hair will stick up in thick tufts. So, unless it is medically necessary, hogging should be carefully considered. This does not suit some horses at all.

Trimming

To give a neater appearance, certain areas of the horse can be trimmed with trimming clippers or with blunt, curved scissors.

Feathers   The long hairs around the back of the fetlock joints. When clipping move the clippers up against the hair very carefully. Alternatively trim with comb and scissors, working upwards against the hair direction.

Ears   The hair inside the ears should never be cut or trimmed as it keeps the ear warm and provides a natural protective barrier for the inner ear against dirt and infection. The only part that may be trimmed is the long hair that sticks out from the ear.

Hold the sides of the ear together and gently stroke the clippers downwards, from the tip to the base. Alternatively use blunt, curved scissors.

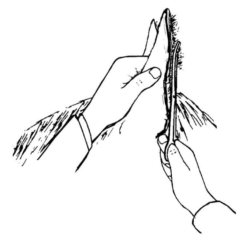

Whiskers   These are the long hairs that grow from the lower jaw. These may be trimmed with curved scissors to give a neater appearance, especially for show horses and ponies or those that grow thick 'beards'.

The long, stiff hairs around the nose and mouth should not be cut as they provide a sensory organ. The horse uses these to 'feel' for food. Any long hair around the eyes, the eyelashes and nostrils should be left untrimmed particularly for horses and ponies at grass.

Coronet and heels

    The hair above the coronet can be lightly trimmed in a neat line. Hair around the heels, unless it is very thick, is best left uncut.

Trimming the hair on a horse or pony is mainly done for appearance. Animals living out permanently at pasture can be lightly trimmed in the summer months around the fetlocks, back of the tendons and above the coronet. The hair of the ears should remain uncut but if these are thick and unsightly they can be given a light trim with scissors during the early summer.

In the autumn, winter and spring the grass kept animal will need all the protection his hair and coat can offer. The only exception would be in the case of a wound or injury when the area around the site needs to be trimmed so that treatment can be effective.

Exam Tips

Clipping may be covered in some depth at Stage II. You should learn the reasons for clipping, the different types of clip, when each clip is used and for which type of horse or pony. The Examiners may ask you to show the line of each clip on a horse. You should be able to describe or show how to clip, particularly around the awkward areas; behind the elbow and where the hair lies in a different direction.

The Examiner may ask questions about the different types of clippers, their care before, during and after use. You may even be requested to take a pair of clippers apart and put them back together. This will need practising before the Exam, if possible at the Exam Centre so that you become familiar with the clippers that will be used on the day.

In preparation, watch horses and ponies being clipped as often as possible. Offer your help in assistance, as this will give you valuable experience. You may even have the opportunity, under supervision, to try clipping parts of the horse yourself.

Find out as much as you can about the different kinds of clippers on the market, their advantages and disadvantages, prices and quality. The local tack shop will be able to help; ask to read through the manufacturers' instructions.

CHAPTER 29
Pulling & Plaiting

The horse's mane and tail grow constantly and need shortening to make them neat, easier to groom and plait. This is achieved by 'pulling' the hair from the mane and tail which, as well as reducing the length, also thins the hair making it more easy to manage.

Pulling

Pulling the hair from the mane and tail is not as painful as it sounds and though some horses do object, most horses will stand quietly, some even enjoy the process.

The mane

A stabled horse will have his mane pulled all year round. Horses and ponies permanently living out will have their mane pulled during the summer only. During the winter the mane is allowed to grow longer to help keep the neck and head warm.

Reasons for pulling the mane;

1. to shorten the mane.

2. to tidy the mane and make it neater.

3. to make a mane easier to groom.

4. to make a mane easier to plait. Long hair can be awkward to manage and makes large, untidy plaits.

5. to help a horse or pony stay cooler in summer. Particularly when grass kept horses and ponies grow thick, luxuriant hair, which can be very hot in warm weather.

6. to encourage the mane to lie flat.

7. to improve the visual effect of poor conformation.

8. to help the rider watch for muscle conformation and development on both sides of the neck.

9. to thin thick bushy manes.

10. to tidy up thin, straggly manes.

The best time to pull the mane is after exercise when the horse is warm. The pores at this time will be open making it easier to remove the hair. For horses or ponies with really thick or long hair, pulling the mane may have to be done over a period of a few days or even a couple of weeks to prevent soreness.

The mane should not be washed just before being pulled, as this makes the hair too slippery to pull properly. The horse should always be properly restrained when having his mane and tail pulled.

Before....

Method

The hair is pulled from *underneath the mane*. The top part of the mane should never be pulled as this will cause the hair to stick upright along the crest.

Brush and comb the mane out thoroughly with the body brush and mane comb. Choose a good strong comb for pulling.

A small metal mane comb is best; plastic combs are not strong enough. A box or crate may be needed to stand on to reach taller horses. Upturned buckets are not ideal as they tend to wobble. It is much safer to stand on a solid crate.

Start at the poll or the withers, whichever is most convenient and easiest. Some people prefer to begin with the poll as this is usually the most difficult. Many horses dislike their mane being pulled around this spot. Others prefer to start at the withers and work up, dealing with poll when the horse is settled.

i.   Take hold of a few strands of the longest hair from underneath the mane and, with the comb, gently backcomb the hair along this strand to the crest.

ii. Place the comb near the top of the hair at the crest.

iii. Wind the strands of hair around the comb and pull briskly. The lock of hair should come out easily. Some people prefer to wrap the hair around their finger and pull, but with experience this can result in a very sore finger.

Repeat this procedure for the whole mane until it is the length required. If a lock of hair does not come away after a couple of pulls, comb the hair out and try again. Do not keep tugging at the hair as this will make the area sore and the horse irritable.

The forelock can be pulled in the same way.

The mane should look as even as possible and, ideally, lie on the off-side (right) of the horse's neck. This can be encouraged by pulling the mane on the horse's right side. The mane can then be dampened.

Loose plaiting can help to encourage the lie of hair. The hair is plaited and the plaits are left hanging down the neck. With some horses it is impossible to make the mane lie on the off-side, they naturally have a left sided mane. This is not a problem providing the mane is neat and shows off the shape of the horse's neck to its best advantage.

.....and after

Depending on the rate of growth, the mane will need pulling every three to four weeks to keep the growth under control. Even with slow growing manes, longer hairs can be pulled out every few weeks to keep the edge tidy.

The tail

Reasons for pulling the tail;

1. For appearance.

2. To keep the tail tidy.

3. To make grooming easier.

4. So that the hindquarters can be clearly seen. This is especially important when showing the horse.

5. To keep the horse cool.

For horses and ponies living out, the tail should not be pulled during the winter and only slightly during the summer to make it tidy. A full tail offers protection and insulation against the weather.

The hairs are pulled from underneath down each side of the dock. This gives the tail a good shape. Though sometimes a few of the top hairs can be removed to thin the tail, if too much is taken from here the hair will stick out making the tail thin and uneven. Thick, overgrown tails may need to be pulled over a matter of days or weeks.

Method

   i.   Brush the tail thoroughly removing all knots, tangles and bits of bedding.

   ii.   Start at the top of the tail and take a thin strand of hair from behind the dock.

   iii.   Wind it around the comb and give a quick tug.

   iv.   Pull both sides equally as far down as the point of buttock.

Do not pull too much hair out at one time, especially if the dock area begins to look sore. Limit the amount pulled and complete after a few days. If the tail is pulled too drastically, the effect will be a bald, untidy appearance.

Most horses are very quiet and well behaved when having their tail pulled but as this is a potentially dangerous area in which to work, care should be taken. It is wiser to have an assistant to hold the horse and to offer help if necessary. If the horse does start to fidget the assistant can hold up a fore leg. For awkward horses or those who may not have had their tails pulled previously, the horse can be positioned in a stable with his hindquarters against the door. The tail can then be pulled from over the door.

After the tail has been pulled, the top can be dampened with a wet water brush and a tail bandage put on to preserve the shape.

Shaping the lower edge

There are two designs for the lower edge of the tail - the banged tail or the switch tail.

The Banged tail

The lower edge is cut straight across removing all the long and straggly hairs.

A 'correct' length of tail is just about 10 cm (4 inches or one hand span) below the hock. This can vary up to a hand's width below the chestnut depending on personal preference. Some people prefer a horse's tail short whilst others prefer it long and flowing. It can also depend on the tail, its thickness and appearance.

Method

Brush the tail thoroughly making sure it is completely free of knots. To calculate the correct length, place an arm under the top part of the tail and raise it slightly. The tail should be in the position that the horse would naturally carry it when working. With the other hand hold the tail at the top and slide the hand down the tail until it reaches the desired length.

Cut the tail straight across as level as possible. Now with both hands, hold the top of the tail and stroke down to the lower edge; trim any long hairs level. This may need repeating several times.

The Switch Tail

The tail is pulled the whole length to give the appearance of a natural point. The amount of hair pulled will need careful consideration. If too much is removed the tail will look thin.

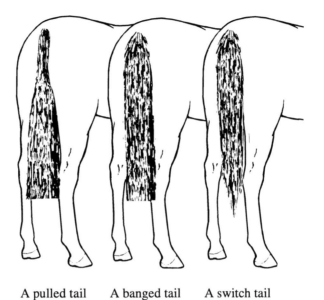

A pulled tail   A banged tail   A switch tail

Plaiting

The mane

The mane is arranged into small plaits along the crest and poll.

Plaiting a horse's mane not only helps to lay the hair correctly, it is also a requirement of many competitions and shows. Plaiting, used for cosmetic reasons, gives the horse a smart appearance, showing off the neck and crest. The mane should be pulled so that it is about 4 - 6 inches (10 - 15 cm) in length. Any longer makes it very difficult for normal plaiting.

The groom will need a mane comb, rubber plaiting bands or needle and thread, a pair of curved ended scissors, a water brush and a bucket of water. If using thread, the shade should correspond to the colour of the mane.

When sewing the plaits with needle and thread, take the horse out of the box. Do not use a needle in a box with bedding, especially straw. If the needle is dropped it is almost impossible to find.

Method

i. Dampen down the mane and, starting at the poll, divide it into equal sections securing each section with a rubber band. The number of plaits is not drastically important; some grooms prefer a few whilst others prefer more. Traditionally there should be an odd number along the neck, usually seven; plus the one at the forelock making an even number. As a rough guide each section is roughly the size of a mane comb.

ii. Plait each section *making the plait as tight as possible*. This is particularly important at the base of each plait, near the crest to make the plait secure and tidy.

iii. Wrap a rubber band or the end of the thread around the tip of the plait several times.

iv. Double the plait under itself and, if using thread, push the needle through the base of the plait at the crest.

v. Fold the plait again once or twice as required and sew at each turn to keep the plait secure. Cut the thread with the scissors.

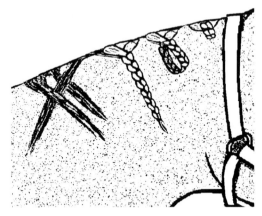

vi. When using plaiting bands, fold the plait under twice (once more if necessary) and secure with another band. The last couple of plaits at the withers are usually quite difficult as the hair can be thin and short. Keep the plaiting tight. The forelock is plaited last.

The number of plaits can be varied to enhance the shape and size of neck. A larger number of small plaits will make the neck look longer and more slender whilst a small number of thicker plaits will make a skinny neck look more developed.

When plaiting for a show, allow plenty of time, especially if nervous about competing and unused to plaiting.

On days when there is a really early start, the mane can be plaited the night before and left as 'loose' plaits, that is, the plaits are made tight but left unfolded. The plaits will need securing properly and it is possible that the horse will rub one or two and make them messy. Though ideally plaiting should be done the morning of the competition, preparing the plaits the night before certainly saves time the next day.

Sometimes a small amount of narrow insulating tape is wrapped around the base of the finished plait to give more security. If the tape is a contrasting colour to the horse (dark horse - white tape), the effect can be quite stunning.

The Tail

A tail plait is used for appearance, particularly grass-kept horses and ponies who do not have their tails pulled often. For show horses and ponies it allows the hindquarters to be shown.

If the horse's tail is to be plaited then it should not need pulling. A completely pulled tail will not have sufficient hair to plait properly. Plaiting should not be necessary in any case because the pulled tail should have a good shape and appearance.

Flat or ridge plait

The tail plait can be styled either as a flat or a ridged plait. The flat plait is easier. The hair is plaited from on top to underneath, so that the plait is flat with the hair.

The ridge plait, which takes more skill and practice, is where the hair is brought in underneath and plaited. The plait is then on top of the strands of hair.

Method

Once the tail has been brushed thoroughly, damp down the top part of the tail. On warm days, the tail can be washed and shampooed before plaiting and brushed when dry.

i.   Starting at the very top of the tail, take two sections of hair, one from either side of the dock.

ii. Bring these round to the front keeping them taut and pick some hair at the same level from the centre of the tail.

iii. The three sections are plaited together once.

Maintain the *tightness*, this is most important. Keeping the plait **close** to the tail can help to preserve the tension. If the plait is pulled out from the tail, it will not have the tautness and appear loose and untidy.

iv. Once the first sections have been plaited, two extra sections of hair, one from each side, are taken and combined into the plait.

v. Continue until about two thirds of the way down the dock bone. The centre of the plait should be straight and central on the tail.

vi. Plait the hair now without additions from the tail, until the end of the plait is reached.

vii. Secure with a plaiting band or needle and thread.

viii. Loop the plait under itself and slightly tuck it in between plait and tail.

ix. Secure it to the outside of the plait with another elastic band or with needle and thread.

Exam Tips

Pulling and plaiting the mane and tail can only be improved by practice. Expand your experience by pulling and plaiting the manes and tails of a variety of horses (taking care when pulling or plaiting a tail).

You will find that thick, unruly manes are almost impossible to plait; that hanging on grimly to that beautiful half finished tail plait whilst the horse insists on dancing around, does wonders for your fitness! Through frequent practice what seems a long laborious job in the beginning, will soon become a swift automatic action done whilst chatting to a friend.

In the Stage II you may be asked to describe the method of pulling a mane or tail. You may also be required to put in one or two mane plaits. Brush and comb the mane, dampen it down, if possible, and section the hair as if you were going to plait the whole mane. The Examiners do occasionally ask candidates to plait a tail.

Remember if using needle and thread, take the horse out of the box first. If you lose the needle in the bedding, the whole bed will either have to be taken out or a metal detector used. It has been done, in an Exam as well!

C H A P T E R   30
Stable Design

The purpose of the loosebox is to provide the horse with a safe, comfortable, durable place to live which is large enough for him and as fireproof as possible. Many horses and ponies remain in their box for most of the day so the stable needs to be a place where he will remain healthy and relaxed.

Situation of Looseboxes

Though the boxes should not be so close together as to allow horses to fight or bite each other, no box should be so isolated *that the horse cannot be regularly checked.* Even an isolation box kept for ill horses, should be within easy reach of the yard to allow regular attention.

Ideally, no large trees should overhang the box. The loosebox should be built away from any hazards.

There should be plenty of room for the horse to move around outside in front of the box with a good, firm access to the box itself. If the access flooring is prone to be wet, muddy and slippery, an area of concrete or loose chippings should be laid so that the horse does not slip.

The door and window should be facing away from prevailing winds. A north facing box will be cold and dark, but a box facing directly south (though better than one facing north) into the summer sunlight will become hot and oppressive during the day. Depending on the winds the box will be more comfortable facing south-east or south-west.

Stable Construction

The Floor

Drainage

One of the most important aspects of a loosebox or stable is drainage. Ideally the floor should be slightly sloped so that liquids, such as water or urine, flow to the back of the box and out into a drain.

The floor should have drainage channels; such as small indents in a herringbone design. If liquids are allowed to flow to the front of the box, this will form a pool at the door where the horse usually stands.

Flooring

There are many varieties of floor covering. The most basic flooring is made up of **packed down earth**. In some cases this is adequate, but not ideal as it can tend to become muddy, dirty and slippery.

Brick is possibly the best flooring being hard wearing, rot proof, strong, warm in winter, cool in summer, horse proof and fireproof. It is expensive though, takes time to construct and may chip.

Concrete is popular. It is quick to construct, hard wearing and, when roughened, non-slippery. It is hard on the horse's feet though unless there is a deep bed. In winter concrete can be very cold.

Rubber floorings are available on the market that can be laid on top of the floor. These are softer, non slippery and rot proof and can be used with or without bedding. When used without bedding they do not offer the horse much comfort to lie down.

There are different designs on the market; some are grooved and are laid down so that the grooves allow drainage to the rear of the box. If the rubber flooring is not fitted or cleaned properly, it can become very dirty and smelly.

The Walls

The criteria of any material used in box construction is that it is strong, weatherproof, fireproof, warm in winter and cool in summer.

Brick

This is an ideal material as it is fireproof, allows temperature regulation (not too hot in summer and not too cold in winter) and does not rot.

Modern looseboxes are rarely constructed from brick because of the expense and time needed in building.

Wood

Very popular being relatively cheap, easy to construct, lightweight, easily available and, if properly maintained, durable.

Wood does constitute a fire hazard especially in stable blocks. It rots easily, particularly in wet conditions, around the base and also harbours germs (ringworm lives in wood). Some horses will eat it or damage it by kicking, so it is not totally horse-proof.

Wood can tend to be hot in summer and cold in winter. This material is prone to weather damage and needs a lot of maintenance to keep it in good condition.

Concrete breeze blocks

These are frequently used being cheaper than brick and more sturdy than wood. They do not rot and need less maintenance, are fairly horse proof and fireproof.

They do need to be heavy; a wall of light breeze blocks can collapse. They are also time-consuming to put up and are not as warm as brick.

Brick and Wood

Looseboxes are often built with a compromise between brick and wood. A base is laid of three to four courses of brick, with the rest of the box being constructed from wood. This is cheaper and quicker to build than a complete brick stable and gives a rot-proof base.

Roofing

The roof must be sturdy and watertight to withstand weather conditions. It should slope to allow free drainage.

Plywood and felt

The felt is laid on top of the plywood. This type of roof is waterproof, easy to maintain and allows temperature regulation, keeping the stable cool in summer but warm in winter. It can however be a fire hazard.

Tiles or slating

Slates are not ideal as they can be dislodged in a high wind and let in rain. Tiles provide a good roofing material if they are properly maintained. A loose tile or slate falling off a roof can cause a hazard and possible injury.

Corrugated iron

Though in some cases this makes a good roofing material it is not ideal as it makes the stable hot in summer and cold in winter. It can also be extremely noisy in wind and rain. Corrugated plastic is not practical for the same reasons.

Guttering

Good guttering is essential at both the back and the front of the box. Down pipes should be positioned away from the window and door. An overhang of roof in front of the box is useful as this offers shelter from wind or rain both to horses and workers.

Size

The whole box must be spacious enough for the horse. Boxes are designed in many sizes, the minimum measurements necessary are:

- 3.5 m x 4.2 m (12 ft x 14 ft) for horses over 16 hands
- 3.5 m x 3.5 m (12 ft x 12 ft) for horses up to 16 hands
- 3 m x 3 m (10 ft x 10 ft) for horses up to 15 hands
- 2.5 m x 2.5 m (8 ft x 8 ft) for small ponies
- A foaling box needs to be 4.5 m x 4.5 m (15 ft by 15 ft)

Height

The ceiling or roof needs to be high enough so that the horse does not hit his head, about 3.5 m to 4.5 m (12 to 15 ft) high.

Stable Openings

Doors

Size

The door should be a minimum 1.2 m (4 ft) wide and, depending on the size of the horse, a height of approximately 3 m (10 ft). Doors for pony boxes are often smaller in size. Doors are made out of wood.

The door is split so that the top half can be left open whilst the bottom half is closed. This gives ventilation and allows the horse to look out whilst keeping him secure.

Fastenings

There should be a bolt at the top of the lower door for security. It is important to have a fastening at the bottom as well. Some horses kick the lower door and, without a fastening, the door will eventually warp or break from the hinge. Other horses are clever enough to open a top bolt and escape. A kick bolt is extremely useful; it offers security and is easier to open and shut. A normal bolt at the bottom of the door is often left undone, especially if going in and out of the box frequently. The top door should also have a bolt.

The box doors should NEVER be padlocked as this will make it difficult to free the horse in case of fire. Instead security padlocks can be fitted to the yard gate to prevent theft.

Position

The doors are fitted off-centre to prevent through draughts and away from the door of the next box to discourage bullying and biting.

The door should open outwards so that even if the horse becomes cast against it, the door can be opened. The lower edge should be flush with the ground to stop draughts and to prevent the horse trapping his feet underneath the door.

In many yards a chain is hung across the inside of the door, secured at one end and hooked at the other. This can be useful to stop a horse or pony from barging out and to allow the door to be left open during really hot weather for extra ventilation.

Horses or ponies do occasionally trap a leg over the chain. On occasions when the horse needs to be taken out of the box quickly, for example in a fire, unfastening the chain wastes time.

A bar, instead of a chain, inside the door is not a good idea. Horses often put their heads underneath and bang themselves if they pull back quickly. Ponies can creep underneath them.

Maintenance

Doors need regular maintenance. Any holes or broken pieces of wood should be repaired as quickly as possible.

Doors that have dropped on their hinges should be taken off and hung correctly. If the lower door has dropped and becomes stuck, the groom could become trapped between horse and door.

Some lower doors are fitted with a metal strip across the top to discourage the horse from crib biting on the wood. This can be quite effective if the metal is thick and strong. Thin, soft metal often forms sharp edges that stick out and cause injury to the horse.

Windows

Windows are situated 1.2 m - 1.5 m (4 ft to 5 ft) from the floor.

Glass windows should have a metal grille inside to prevent the horse coming into contact with, and possibly breaking, the glass. Perspex or wire mesh secured across the opening are also used and both are safer than glass.

To prevent draughts the window should be on the same side as the door and have a vent at the top that opens inwards.

Ventilation

It is important that the horse is allowed good ventilation without draughts. Windows, doors, roof vents and skylights properly designed and positioned can offer good ventilation. In stable blocks there is often a space between the walls and the roof allowing a free flow of air through the boxes.

Fixtures and fittings

The golden rule is to keep the number of fixtures and fittings inside the box to a minimum and what there is should be made as safe as possible. If there is anything that the horse can injure himself on, then he is sure to do so!

Kicking boards

These are often placed around the walls of the box up to a height of 1 m - 1.2 m (3 ft to 4 ft). Kicking boards are made of wood and help to prevent the horse injuring himself, or damaging the box when he kicks or becomes cast.

Feed containers

All feed containers need to be safe, secure and easily removed for regular cleaning.

Ordinary buckets are a hazard, they can be kicked around and the horse can become entangled in the handle.

Buckets hung from a hook are safer, easily removed and cleaned. The hook itself poses a danger though as the horse can injure himself on this fixture.

Permanent mangers cannot be cleaned easily and if the horse is out at feed time, the food remains in the manger vulnerable to vermin and birds.

Mangers, with a metal hoop fixture, can be removed for cleaning but again the metal hoop is a danger. Horses have put their heads through the hoop and become stuck. The hoop, too, can come loose from the wall of the box and hang down or fall off completely.

The above two fixtures are usually at the back of the box, which means the staff doing the feeding must walk to and fro past the horse. This is particularly dangerous if the horse is protective of his food.

A **rubber bucket** without a handle is safe, easily removed and cleaned but tends to break easily when the horse kicks it around the box. The bucket can be placed inside a rubber tyre to stop the horse from moving it.

A **feed bucket hung over the door** by two metal clasps is useful. It is convenient for the person feeding, easily removed and cleaned. Some horses do play with these buckets at the end of a feed however, and the bucket ends up on the ground either outside or inside the box.

Rubber feed skips are very useful and probably the most efficient, practical feed container. They are light to handle, easily removed and cleaned. They are also indestructible if kicked around the box.

With personal experience having tried all types of feed buckets and mangers the rubber feed skip is the best. With all the alternatives the feed container has to be removed after the horse has finished his food, because they pose a danger. Rubber skips are quite safe if left inside the box, even all night.

Metal hayracks used to be popular but have gone out of fashion now. Hayracks need to be positioned high enough to prevent the horse becoming caught in them. Yet this height allows dust and seeds to fall into the horse's eyes and nostrils when he pulls out the hay. The wide spacing of the bars allows the horse to pull out large lumps of hay and some of it is wasted. Old hay is often left in the rack and either eaten when stale or used as a nest by birds or vermin.

Rings

There should be two rings, one on each side wall at a height of approximately 1.5 m (5ft). These are used for hanging the haynet or tying up the horse. Both should have a small loop of string tied through.

Lighting

Interior lighting is essential; working around a horse in the dark is extremely dangerous.

- All electrical fixtures must be completely safe, secure and well away from the horse. Light bulbs must never be within reach; a naked bulb can explode if the horse bites it. All lights must be strongly protected with a thick glass covering and metal meshing.

- All electric cables must be properly fastened down, out of reach and correctly insulated. Any electric wiring, cables or fixtures of any kind should be regularly checked and maintained. Ideally there should be no socket within the box but, if there is, it must be safely covered and secure.

- Light switches should be outside the stable, out of reach of the horse and protected by a cover against the weather.

Some stables have a place to hang rugs, such as a wooden bar suspended on ropes or a strong piece of twine covered with a plastic tube. These do offer a place for the rug instead of being dumped on the floor or hung over the door (where the horse usually grabs them and dumps them on the floor)! Wet rugs should never be dried off in the box as this will give it a damp, unhealthy atmosphere. Rugs should be properly dried off in a rug room. The airing cupboard at home dries off rugs successfully though this often causes a lingering smell until the rug is completely dry (and some mothers do not like it)!

Special Purpose Boxes

Isolation Box

This is a special box for ill or invalid horses. It is used to minimise the spread of illness or disease and to offer the sick horse a quiet spot to recuperate. The box should be situated a little way from the main yard and downwind, though still convenient for staff keeping a watch over the sick animal. The size should be approximately 4.2 m x 4.2 m (14 ft x 14 ft). The doors and windows must be well fitted and draught proof; the walls and ceiling can be insulated if required. There may be a socket for a heat lamp. An adjoining room for the sick horse's clothing, grooming kit and feeding utensils is ideal.

Utility Box

This can be used for clipping, trimming, shoeing or veterinary attention. It should have a high ceiling of at least 4.2 m (14 ft). The floor needs to be non-slip with good drainage. The box should be well lit by natural light and electricity. There should be power points, rings and water available nearby.

Exam Tips

For this section of the Examination candidates need to be aware of the variety of materials available, their advantages and disadvantages, and to have an idea of their own personal preferences with reasons.

Learn to assess and be critical of planning, design and construction in looseboxes. Look at the advertisements in horse magazines for the latest materials on the market, types of flooring, lighting, loosebox design. This will give you a good idea of the practical side of constructing a box and its fittings.

To help with estimating box size, measure your own stride (usually around 1 metre or 3ft). You will then be able to stride out a box and give more accurate measurements than by guessing from appearance.

CHAPTER 31

Grassland Management

Good pasture land provides an environment where the horse and pony have the right quality and quantity of food to maintain good health. Good grassland management not only provides the right pasture, it also creates a safe habitat where horses and ponies can relax.

For any yard or establishment, well-maintained fields act as an advertisement. They increase the value of the property, reduce the feed bills by providing nutrition and can provide an extra facility, for instance a cross country course.

Revision

Inspections of fields, types of fencing, shelter, watering systems, unsuitable boundaries, field maintenance. Recognising the horse-sick field, maintaining good pasture. Turning the horse out and bringing him in. Problems catching a difficult horse. Safety in the field and paddock.

Good Pasture

The fields must first provide enough nourishing food for as long a period as possible throughout the year, especially for horses and ponies living out permanently. The pasture must also be an area where the animals can live in safety, free of illness and injury.

In order to fulfil these requirements the field must:

- be large enough for all the horses and ponies;
- provide a variety of quality grasses;
- have secure boundaries all round;
- provide a constant supply of clean water;
- provide shelter;
- have as few weeds as possible;
- have no poisonous plants;
- have no dangerous areas;
- be relatively free of worm infestation.

A field that has all these requirements is the ideal place for the horse whether partially out at grass or living out permanently. To achieve this depends upon selecting a good piece of land, discovering its quality for pasture and other uses, such as the possibility of growing hay. Then putting in the work to create and maintain a safe, secure and economic environment.

Suitable Land

When considering land as a potential for keeping horses, there are several aspects to consider.

The **size** needs to be **adequate for the number of horses and ponies** who will be living on it. When there are several horses or ponies living out permanently, each **horse** will need **1½ to 2 acres** and **ponies 1 acre each**.

Fields should **never be overstocked**. This will result in a lack of food and greater areas of 'bad' grasses where the horses do their droppings and contaminate the pasture.

Very large fields can be partitioned by fencing; an electric fence is effective for this purpose. Though this will be an added expense, a large acreage of rich pasture may cause over-eating and obesity, posing a problem for native ponies who may develop laminitis.

The best type of land is **gently undulating hills**, where the ground is **well drained**. This also gives the horses exercise whilst walking up and down the hills grazing. Flat land, especially in wet areas by a river or swamp, will be waterlogged. The right types of grasses will not grow in abundance and the wet conditions will cause problems with the horse's feet. Steep areas are fine for moorland ponies but horses may fall and injure themselves if the ground is too precipitous.

Access to the field should be relatively easy from the yard or a road. Fields situated by busy main roads though, can be noisy, suffer from polluted air and be vulnerable to thieves.

Soil Types

Soil is a mixture of substances; disintegrated rock particles, decaying organic matter and water. The name of any soil is determined by the predominance of one type of substance, for instance a sandy soil.

Determining what type of soil the pasture contains will indicate what sort of grasses will grow. For instance a sandy soil drains water easily, nutrients are washed away, particularly calcium, leaving this type of soil acidic. Clay soils hold water and, though nutrients remain, areas of clay tend to become waterlogged. A soil analysis will indicate when and what sort of fertiliser will be useful for present and future improvement.

Soil Analysis

The acidity or alkaline content of soil can be tested and measured by analysis. This is important because the soil type affects grass growth and quality. Too acid a soil will encourage the growth of the wrong types of plants. Too alkaline a soil restricts the grass from absorbing certain minerals.

Along with other nutrients, soil contains lime, phosphates, potash and nitrogen that are needed in varying amounts for the pasture to be suitable for horses.

When an analysis is done, the type and amount of fertilisers if needed can be calculated and the land dealt with accordingly.

Types of Fertiliser

There are basically **three types of fertiliser**;

- **organic** fertilisers made out of substances produced by living organisms, such as **manure or seaweed,**

- **inorganic**, generally **chemical** fertilisers,

- **semi-organic**, a **mixture** of both.

Soil can be analysed by ADAS (the Agricultural Development and Advisory Service of the Ministry of Agriculture, Fisheries and Food - results in one week) or by a fertilising company. The analyst must be aware that the land is for horses and not dairy cattle, as this does affect the fertiliser required.

Drainage

This is important for every pasture; particularly clay soils and low-lying, wet fields near rivers.

- Damp or wet conditions encourage the growth of undesirable grasses and a deficiency of the right grasses.

- The soil structure breaks down easily in wet areas, particularly if the field is overstocked, is used for other purposes or has heavy machinery driven over it.

- There is a risk of horses being hurt in the slippery, wet conditions.

- Horses can develop foot conditions, such as thrush (a disease of the frog) when stood in wet, muddy ground.

If the field does not have natural drainage, this is can be provided by ditches. These will need clearing out regularly, about twice a year. Where the ground is low lying or particularly wet, the ditches will be need clearing constantly to keep the field as dry as possible.

It may be necessary to employ a professional company or contractor to lay drainage either by inserting pipes or digging underground channels. This can be achieved without destroying the topsoil.

Grasses

Once the soil contains the required constituents, a variety of grasses suitable for horses will grow or can be sown. Grasses such as perennial rye grass, which should constitute about 50% of the sward, creeping red fescue about 25%, with meadow grass, sheep's fescue, cocksfoot and timothy together making 25%. Small quantities of white clover will offer the horse ideal grazing, though the pasture should not include an abundance of clover or it will be too rich, especially for small ponies. (Got to watch those small ponies!)

Hazards

These are areas that are potentially dangerous to horses and ponies and which must be dealt with before allowing animals onto the pasture. Hazards can either be removed from the fields or efficiently fenced off to keep them inaccessible.

Hazards include swamps or boggy areas, pits, holes made by rabbits or foxes, pot holes, deep ditches especially if they are difficult to see and large overhanging trees. Any muddy, slippery, poached areas (tracts of land usually near a water source churned up by animals) or steep dangerous approaches to rivers constitute danger. Rubbish dumps, places where people throw their grass cuttings or garden refuse, sharp stakes in the ground; any type of hazard must be dealt with to make the pasture is a safe place for horses. One particular hazard that must be removed or contained is that of poisonous plants.

Poisonous Plants

There are a number of plants, bushes and trees which, if eaten, by the horse can be fatal.

Plants such as ragwort, buttercup, foxglove, horsetail, St. John's wort, purple vetch, deadly nightshade, hemlock, yellow star thistle, spearwort, marsh marigold, cowbane, meadow saffron, autumn crocus, bracken and bryony.

Ragwort   Horsetail   Hemlock

Foxglove   Deadly Nightshade   St. Johns Wort

Bushes and trees include the laurel, yew, privet, laburnum, false acacia, box tree, rhododendron.

Laburnum   Rhododendron   Yew

Bushes and trees must either be fenced off or pulled up and removed. Plants must be pulled out by the roots and not left to wither in the field. Horses do not usually eat ragwort in its living state but will relish it when dry and withered. For large plots of land that are covered in poisonous plants, for example ragwort, this may require calling in a contractor to dig out and remove all the plants. Pulling thousands of plants out, a few at a time, will not reduce the problem.

Water

A constant supply of clean water with a safe approach is vital.

Shelter

Some form of shelter as protection against wind and rain in winter, strong sunlight and flies in summer is vital, particularly for animals living out all the time. Shelter can be provided naturally in the form of bushes, hedges, trees, walls, or in the valleys of undulating land. Artificial shelter in the form of a shed or wind break needs to be wide and high enough to protect a number of horses and ponies.

A shed should be light and spacious, facing away from the prevailing winds; sturdy enough to withstand all weathers and built on firm, flat ground. It should be open fronted so that no horse becomes trapped inside and bullied.

Access to all shelters should be firm and dry to prevent poaching. If necessary, a hard core or concrete base can be laid down outside.

Boundaries

To keep the horses and ponies absolutely secure, the boundaries all round the fields must be checked. Horses often lean over fences and break them, jump walls or creep through holes in bushes. Horrendous accidents are caused when horses stray onto roads. Owners may be liable for negligence or damage done by straying animals trespassing onto other people's land.

Post and rail, though expensive, is the best, providing a safe and secure boundary.

Post and wire is less expensive and safe providing the wire is taut and the lower strand is secured about 30 to 45 cm (12 to 18 inches) above the ground to prevent horses from squeezing through.

Electric fencing is efficient and safe as long as the horses are aware of it. There must be adequate warnings to prevent people from touching it.

Bushes or trees act well as a boundary and have the added advantage of providing shelter. All hedgerows must be checked first for any poisonous types of plant or for dangerous areas such as low hanging branches.

Walls must be strong and high enough to avoid being pushed over by the horses or of being jumped. All dry stone walling needs constant maintenance.

The boundaries need to be four to five feet (approximately 1½ m) in height, solid, strong and free of holes or gaps through which the horses or ponies can creep.

Unsuitable Boundaries

There are some types of fencing, which whilst being perfectly adequate for other animals, are not suitable for horses.

Barbed wire and horses do not mix. The sharp points can cut and injure a horse, even when he simply rubs his head against it.

Sheep or chicken fencing, where the wire is formed into squares, is often a source of injury when horses put their head or legs through and become trapped.

Sheep posts are made from sharp wooden stakes which can injure a horse quite severely.

Gates

Gates as part of the boundary must be high and strong enough to stop animals escaping. Gates also act as the access point and so must be wide enough to allow easy access into the field for both horses and vehicles such as tractors, trailers and horseboxes.

Gates must work efficiently. Trying to unfasten a monkey puzzle of a rickety gate whilst the horse is fretting to be let into the field, is a real headache. Gates must also be secure to deter thieves or vandals.

Beyond the boundary

One area that is often forgotten is that around the outside of the boundary. Often fields back onto private gardens where the owners, who are not necessarily knowledgeable about poisonous plants or bushes, may easily leave cuttings within reach of the horses, who then lean over and eat them. It is always a good idea to talk to any neighbours and inform them of the problems of poisonous plants, mentioning the dangers of grass cuttings, which are often thrown into fields. The horse can gorge himself on these. The problem is worsened if the cuttings are older and have started to ferment. This will cause serious colic. The grass itself may have been treated with a weed killer or some other chemical in which case it could be poisonous.

Maintenance of Pasture

Once the grassland has been prepared, regular attention is necessary to maintain its condition and value as a habitat for horses and to offer good quality grazing in a safe, healthy environment. Grassland is maintained on a daily, weekly, monthly and annual basis.

Daily Maintenance

- Check and, if necessary, mend any damaged boundaries.

- Watch for danger spots such as dumped rubbish, fallen trees or potholes.

- Clean the water trough if required. All artificial water containers must be kept spotlessly clean and constantly filled with clean water, especially during hot weather.

- Pick up droppings if this is practical.

- Look for and uproot any poisonous plants.

- Check the field shelter.

- Close inspection of all the horses and ponies at least once a day.

Weekly Maintenance

◊ Collect droppings once or twice a week (if not done daily and if practical).

◊ Harrow large fields (where the collection of dung is impracticable) on dry, hot days to kill off the worm larvae.

Monthly Maintenance

♦ Harrow fields if necessary to remove dead vegetation and allow new growth of grass.

♦ Long grass may need topping (cutting shorter) or mowing to encourage new grass growth.

Annual Maintenance

Drainage

Clear out the ditches or drain holes in late winter and early spring to reduce excess surface water and discourage the growth of poisonous plants and unpalatable herbage.

Harrowing

In late February before the grazing starts, harrowing aerates the grass roots, rids the ground of dead vegetation and allows the fertiliser to be absorbed. The ground must be sufficiently firm to take the weight of machinery without damaging the soil structure.

Re-seeding

If necessary to repair winter damage, new seeds are sown in late February or early March.

Rolling

After harrowing or seeding, the ground can be rolled. This flattens the ground, particularly useful for poached areas. Clay soils should not be rolled if possible; this can damage the soil structure, compressing it and reducing the drainage.

Fertilising

In early spring a dressing of fertiliser can be applied to the fields. If the horses cannot be taken off the land completely, the areas being fertilised can be sectioned off until they are safe for grazing again. The manufacturer should be able to give advice about the length of time needed before the horses are allowed back into the field.

Rotation

This is the method of dividing fields into smaller portions and alternating their use. One part is grazed by horses; one part can be grazed by other animals, whilst another part is left fallow. Resting a portion of the field allows the grass time to grow. These portions can then be 'rotated' that is the sequence of grazing and resting is alternated over periods of time.

Allowing other stock on the land such as cattle and sheep is beneficial to the pasture and the horse. Cattle and sheep graze on the unpalatable grass that the horse does not like. They also help to reduce the worm population. Some of the worm larvae passed by the horse die when ingested by cattle or sheep. Donkeys are not ideal as an alternative stock as they can pass lung worm onto horses.

Horses are quite destructive grazers. They crop portions of the land until nearly bare, sometimes pulling out the grass roots, whilst leaving other parts to grow rough vegetation. They create heavily poached areas and can break down fencing or boundaries. However, if the pasture is kept under constant supervision and the maintenance routines are dutifully followed there is no reason why pasture cannot offer horses a nourishing and secure environment for many years.

Exam Tips

Stage II students will not normally be practically involved in the overall maintenance of the field such as harrowing, re-seeding or fertilising. You will need to know about this maintenance in theory though and be able to describe the various procedures needed at different times of the year to keep the pasture at a high standard.

You will need to know the daily inspections necessary to keep the fields secure and safe for horses and ponies. You should be able to recognise when pasture is in a bad condition or is horse-sick and the improvements that will be needed to bring the field up to the required level.

C H A P T E R   32
Caring for Horses at Grass

Keeping a horse or pony at grass can, in many ways, be simpler and less time consuming than looking after a stabled horse. This is their natural habitat and native ponies, in particular, can stay healthier and more relaxed at grass. No horse or pony though, will fare well if turned out and forgotten. The grass kept animal still needs attention, a certain amount of exercise, supplementary feeding at certain times of the year and regular handling to maintain good health.

Daily Care

Routine

Early morning
The horse is checked in the field to make sure primarily that he is there, that he has not escaped or been stolen and that he is in good health.

In Autumn, Winter and early Spring hay is taken to the field and placed in hayracks or on the ground. The water supply is inspected and in Winter the ice is broken if possible. If the ice is too thick, buckets of water will have to be brought to the field. The horses and ponies can be given their concentrate feed if required.

Mid morning
A quick check is made of the field for poisonous plants, broken fencing and for hazards such as dumped rubbish or fallen trees. This can be done when catching a horse for exercise.

All the horses will be brought in at some time and given a close inspection, usually during grooming. In colder weather, when the horse is wearing a New Zealand rug, this will be checked every day for damage. If the rug is wet it will be replaced with a dry rug before the horse is returned to the field.

Evening
A last quick look at the horses and ponies to see that all is well. During the colder months more hay may be needed. The water is checked once more. The gate is locked and secured.

Inspections

When the horse is given his inspection he is checked for the following;

- **Parasites** - Bot fly eggs, lice, ticks, warble fly swellings on his back.

- **Injuries** - wounds from kicks or bites, cuts, swellings, puncture wounds.

- **Foot problems** - cast, worn or sprung shoes, split hooves, bruised soles, stones in the foot, thrush, over reach injuries, puncture wounds of the foot. Regular visits from the farrier are essential every four to six weeks.

- **Skin ailments** - mud fever, cracked heels, rashes or cracked skin, sores, scabs, lice, sweet itch, rain scald (a skin condition caused by damp conditions and bacterial invasion), sunburn, irritation from flies, grazes and galls.

Grooming

Grooming is necessary for the grass kept horse. It helps to keep him clean, improves the skin, tones the muscles, allows time to check for ill health and maintains the contact between the horse and handler. Some native ponies can revert to semi-wildness without regular handling. The degree of grooming differs with the seasons.

Spring - grooming helps to remove the Winter coat. Feet need checking for thrush and legs for mud fever.

Summer - a full grooming can be given. Check for fly bites and remove bot eggs from legs, belly and flanks. The horse or pony can be given a bath about once a month. Feet need checking for cracking due to dry weather. Hoof ointment or oil can be applied to hoof and sole.

Autumn - grooming is reduced now to allow the Winter coat to grow. Feet still need picking out daily and checking. Dried mud is removed from the coat to prevent skin problems such as mud fever.

Winter - grooming is limited to a quick brush down to remove dried mud. The feet are picked out. During the cold months, grooming should be minimal to prevent the removal of grease from the coat.

A horse or pony should never be groomed when wet; he must always be dried first. Grooming a wet horse will drive the mud into the skin and pores, causing skin irritations.

A handful of straw wiped in the direction of the hair (never against) will soak up much of the dampness. The ears and legs can be dried with towels.

To help the body dry off completely, a rug can be placed on the horse and thatched. The legs can be thatched, covered with stable bandages and the horse left quietly in a warm, dry area with a haynet and water for half an hour. When he is completely dry, the horse can be groomed.

Regular Care

Pulling and Trimming

The grass kept horse needs his mane, tail, forelock and feathers as protection against weather conditions and flies. During the Spring and Summer the mane can be pulled to make it tidier and easier to plait for shows. The tail can be banged to keep it out of the mud. Feathers may be trimmed during the Summer, but not in Autumn or Winter when the added protection is necessary. Some of the longer hairs under the jaw can be trimmed in Spring but the sensory feelers or whiskers round the chin and nostrils, as well as the hair inside the ears, should not be trimmed.

Worming

Horses and ponies at grass need to be wormed regularly every six weeks throughout the year. To make sure of this, a record can be kept of the dates the Wormer was given and the types of Wormers used.

Droppings should be frequently removed from the paddock, though this is not practical for large fields. Harrowing, rotating fields and an efficient worming programme for all the horses and ponies will diminish the risk of infestation.

Riding the horse at grass

Horses can be successfully worked from grass, even to quite a high standard. Hard feed will be necessary as a grass diet is incapable of maintaining a horse doing hard or fast work.

To work from grass

Bring the horse in from the field at least one hour before exercise, so that he is not worked with a full stomach. If the horse is reluctant to come in, a small feed given one hour before exercise should make him easier to catch in future. After his feed the horse can be groomed and inspected for injuries. It will also give him ample time to dry if wet. A horse or pony should not be ridden when wet; this will certainly cause chafing around the saddle and girth areas.

Although they can keep themselves relatively fit in a field, horses or ponies will be in a fairly 'soft' condition if not ridden regularly. The exercise, in this case, should be regulated. The horse should not be given long, hard or fast work; constant hard work may cause sprains and strains to muscles and tendons. He should be allowed frequent short rests to keep him fresh. The horse's back and girth area should be checked constantly for galls and sores.

After work, the horse or pony will need cooling down and completely drying off before he goes out or he may become chilled and catch a cold. Provided the weather is warm and the horse is not too sweaty, however, he can be turned out fairly quickly after work. He will probably have a roll and a walk or trot to ease his muscles.

Wintering out

Ponies

Most native ponies will Winter out quite naturally and maintain good health. The thick, winter coat, mane and tail will offer protection against adverse weather. Thorough daily checks are essential as it is difficult to assess condition at a glance through a thick, woolly coat. Any substantial weight loss and even wounds will not be apparent except under close scrutiny.

Work

Work will be limited as the pony will sweat up very quickly and will be difficult to dry in cold, wet weather. If the pony is doing more than very light work, he will need clipping to prevent excessive sweating. Once he is clipped he will need a New Zealand rug to keep him dry and warm.

Horses

Horses at grass tend to need more care during the Winter, though many will Winter out quite happily providing they are given enough food, have adequate shelter and are rugged up correctly. During bad weather the horse may need to be brought in and stabled at night. Snow, ice and cold periods do not affect horses and ponies as much as constant rain and wind.

Work

Generally horses will be worked more than ponies and so will need to be clipped. A New Zealand rug will be necessary to help him withstand the adverse weather conditions.

Rugging

When it is necessary to rug up there are a few points to consider.

- The horse or pony should be accustomed to wearing a New Zealand rug before it is left on day and night. Prepare him by putting the rug on for short periods during the late Summer and Autumn.

- The rug must fit well. A horse or pony wearing a rug that does not fit, will soon develop bare patches, sores, galls and wounds especially round the shoulders.

Some rugs seem to chafe no matter how good the fit. Sowing a lining of sheepskin or similar material onto the rug in the areas where chafing occurs can help to lessen this problem. Alternatively a 'vest' can be purchased which the horse can wear under his rug to protect his shoulders.

- The rug should be kept clean and dry, if possible. All straps should be kept clean and supple.

- Rugs should also be maintained in good condition; any holes, tears or inadequate waterproofing will allow the horse to get wet.

- Rugs should be removed daily so that the horse and rug can be properly inspected.

Safety at pasture

- No inexperienced person should turn a horse out or bring one in from the field alone. All those who are not trained, particularly children, should be supervised when dealing with horses and ponies at grass.

- The horse or pony should be restrained with a head collar and lead-rope (or bridle if led on the road) when going to and from the field.

- The gate should be opened wide enough for the horse then shut behind him.

- The handler should take the horse a little way into the field and turn him towards the gate before releasing him.

- Handlers and grooms should stand between the horse and the gate when turning out, not between the horse and field in case the horse rushes off, knocking the handler over.

- A horse or pony in the field should never be approached from behind.

- If food is taken into the field to try and catch a horse, this must be hidden. **Avoid** taking a bucket of food into a field where there are a number of horses and ponies; this will cause trouble; bullying, fighting and a stampede towards the handler.

- All gates must be secured and if possible padlocked.

Flies

These can be a real nuisance to horses and ponies at grass, causing sweet itch, tail rubbing, restlessness, unthriftiness, swollen eyes and infected wounds. Horses can quickly lose condition walking around constantly trying to escape from the flies; being unable to feed properly from the constant movement and irritation. Bot flies cause parasitic infestation.

The types of flies which attack horses are

- The house fly which causes eye irritation; excessive fluid and swelling around the eyes.

- The horn fly which bites the abdomen and causes crusts, ulcers and hair loss around the belly.

- The horse fly which bites and feeds on the horse.

- The black fly is not common in this country but will bite the horse and inject a toxin into the body.

- Midges which bite the horse during the early morning and late afternoon. The horse will be restless, swishing his tail and rubbing.

- Bot flies which lay their eggs on the horse in late Summer and Autumn. They are ingested when the horse bites himself. The larvae migrate to the horse's stomach. Large numbers in the digestive system may cause ulcers.

- Blowflies, also called screw or worm flies, invade wounds where they lay their eggs. These hatch out as maggots.

- Warble flies. These lay an egg under the skin in the horse. The larva hatches out and migrates to the horse's back. The grub causes a swelling before emerging through the skin. If the larva dies under the skin, this causes an abscess.

It is vital to protect horses and ponies against flies from very early Spring right through to late Autumn. A good fly repellent should be used regularly. If the flies are particularly numerous or the horse is bothered by midges and suffers from sweet itch, then bringing him into the stable early morning and evening will protect him during the worst periods. Other measures that help are fly fringes and garlic in the food.

There are always problems to watch out for and contend with when horses and ponies live out permanently at grass but with good Grassland Management, regular care and attention, most will stay healthy and even thrive within their natural environment.

Exam Tips

There are so many variations when looking after a horse or pony at grass and a great deal of the knowledge on this subject is gained from personal experience. Every horse and pony is an individual and will react differently within similar situations and conditions. The rules and considerations described are a basis on which to begin. These are then adapted to suit the animal concerned and the situations as they arise. One golden rule is to monitor the animal constantly and to react quickly to any change that may appear. In the Examination the candidate needs to know the basic rules and how to care for grass kept animals at different times of the year.

CHAPTER 33
Lungeing

Through good instruction and practice, lungeing a horse can develop into a fine art. Horses may be trained and fittened to a high standard on the lunge and it adds another dimension to training and exercise.

Reasons for Lungeing

Lungeing is used for a variety of reasons.

1. The horse is **able to work but cannot be ridden for some reason**.

    He may have an injury that prevents him from being ridden or wearing a saddle, in which case he would be lunged with a lunge roller.

2. The **rider is unable to ride.**

3. As **preparation for a competition or event**.

    To loosen up a stiff horse or to quieten down a high spirited horse.

4. To **tone up and develop the horse's muscles**.

    It also improves the paces by allowing freedom of movement and balance without the rider on the horse's back.

5. To **train the horse so that riders can be taught on the lunge.**

6. To **teach riders**.

    Being lunged is an excellent method of improving the seat and position.

7. To add **variety** to the **exercise** schedule.

8. When, in yards with no indoor school, **adverse weather conditions** make riding difficult.

9. To **save time** when more than one horse needs exercise.

10. As part of the **training** programme for a young or inexperienced horse to **teach acceptance of the bit** and **tack** and to **teach obedience** to the **voice aid.**

Where to Lunge

Horses should always be lunged in an enclosed area that is safe and preferably quiet. This could be an indoor school, an outdoor manege or even a fenced area within a field. If the horse is lunged in the middle of a vast meadow, he may take the opportunity of breaking away out of control.

The ground should be as flat as possible and the going good to firm. Horses should not be lunged in wet, sticky mud, on steep slopes, on slippery, very hard or stony ground.

Lungeing Equipment

The equipment is designed to make lungeing as safe as possible and comfortable for the horse.

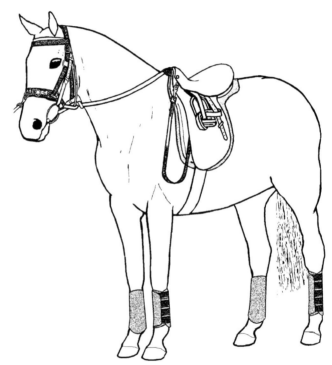

- **Lungeing cavesson**
  Similar to a headcollar, with headpiece, browband, cheekpieces or cheekstraps, noseband and throatlash strap. There are three rings on the noseband, a central swivel ring and two side rings.

  The noseband must be padded to prevent rubbing. Lunge cavessons are manufactured from a variety of products; leather, webbing, nylon web or synthetic material.

- **Lunge roller**
  Often used instead of a saddle. It fits on the horse over his back and round his girth. The roller is made of webbing or leather and has various ring attachments.

- **Breastplate**
  A breastplate is often used to keep the roller or saddle from slipping backwards. This is especially important when lungeing young horses.

- **Brushing boots/bandages**
  The horse should wear brushing boot or exercise bandages on all four legs. Overreach boots can also be fitted for protection.

- **Side Reins**
  Various materials are used in the manufacture of side reins, leather, nylon, cotton and synthetic webbing. Some side reins have an additional elasticated or rubber insert.

  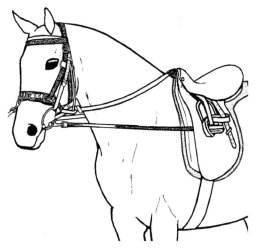

  Each side rein has a clip at one end that fits onto the bit. At the other end there is usually a buckle or thread-through fastening that allows the rein length to be altered.

  The side reins have various functions.

1. They teach **acceptance** of the **rein contact** on the bit.

   Side reins act in a similar fashion to normal reins and the rider's hands. They give a steady and even feel on the horse's mouth via the bit.

2. They keep a horse **'straight'**, important even when working on a circle.

3. Helps to **improve the horse's muscles** across his crest and back, by persuading the horse to work with his head in a more correct position.

4. They improve the horse's **balance** when working with a rein contact.

5. Gives more **control** of the horse and therefore **increases safety**.

6. To **teach a rider** on the lunge, by providing a horse in a better balance and outline. This teaches the rider the 'feel' of a horse who is going more correctly.

7. They **encourage a steadier head carriage**.

Side reins should never be used to force the horse's head into position or made too short to obtain a better head carriage. The side reins are there to encourage and show the horse the correct way. If the horse is forced into a position he will tense, become frightened and fight against the restraint.

- **Lunge Line**
Made of cotton or nylon webbing with a loop at one end and a clip at the other. Lunge lines vary in length from 25 feet (about 8 metres) to 30 feet (about 10 metres). New lunge lines can be a little stiff when first used and are better after being washed a few times.

  Another alternative is the thick rope type, which some people find easier to handle as it does not twist like the traditional types. The rope line, though, does have a tendency to become wrapped around the hand.

  There is a new lunge line on the market similar to an extending dog lead. This looks as though it could be quite interesting to use!

- **Lungeing whip**
The whip needs to be long enough to influence the horse.

Fitting the Equipment

For safety and comfort the lungeing equipment must be fitted correctly. Otherwise both horse and the person lungeing (the lunger) can be hurt severely if the tack fails at a crucial moment. The horse may suffer injury or sores, which will make him tack-shy.

Bridle

The bridle should have the noseband removed so that it does not chafe under, or interfere with, the lunge cavesson. The reins must be made safe. The best method is to loop them around each other and secure them through throatlash.

Lunge Cavesson

The cavesson noseband must be high enough to prevent it from interfering with the bit and putting pressure on the soft part of the nose. It is placed in the same position as the normal cavesson noseband, that is, two fingers' width below the projecting cheek bone and approximately four fingers' width above the corner of the horse's mouth.

Place the lunge cavesson headpiece on the horse's head behind the ears, on top of the bridle headpiece. Thread the cheekstraps and noseband *under* the bridle cheekpieces on both sides of the horse's head.

Fasten the noseband *firmly. It is important to secure the lungeing cavesson noseband and cheekpieces firmly. If the lunge cavesson is loose it will slip around the horse's head and possibly cause damage to the eye.*

Saddle and Side Reins

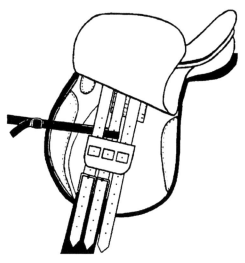

The saddle is put on and the girth fastened loosely. The side reins can now be attached to the saddle. This is easier before the girth is done up properly.

Pass the appropriate end of the side rein *under the first two* girth straps. The end of the side rein is looped around the second girth strap and passed *under* the first strap. If the girth is fastened to the first and third girth straps then the side rein is looped around the third girth strap.

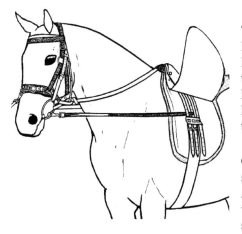

The height of the side reins should be about level with the horse's mouth when the horse's head is in a comfortable position. If the side reins are too low they will force the horse's head lower into a 'fixed' position and have a strong pull on the bit. Too high and there will be little or no effect.

Check the length of the side reins by stretching each one towards the horse's head. A useful estimate of length is that the clip will just reach the bit ring when the horse is standing with his head in a natural, relaxed position. Check also that the side reins are of equal length.

Fasten the clips of the side reins onto the saddle 'D' rings. The girth can now be done up correctly.

Secure the stirrups by looping the leathers through the iron so that they do not drop down whilst lungeing and hit the horse's side.

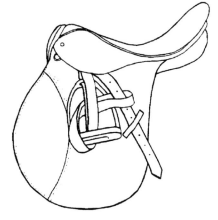

Brushing Boots

Fit the brushing boots or exercise bandages with an even pressure all round and low enough to protect the fetlock. Put the overreach boots on if using them.

Lunge line

When ready to lunge, attach the lunge line to the middle ring of the cavesson. Check that the metal portion, on which the rings are situated, is firmly secured to the cavesson noseband. Small straps, fastened either by stitching or with Velcro, hold the metal portion in place and these can sometimes work loose.

The line is coiled or folded up and held in the hand farthest away from the horse (usually the left hand as the horse is led on the nearside). The lunge whip is tucked under the same arm. The horse is then led by holding the line near to the horse's head in the right hand.

Clothes

The lunger should wear a riding hat, gloves and strong boots for safety. Any loose clothing should be fastened. Wearing clothes that provide protection, especially when lungeing a young horse, is vital.

Method of Lungeing

The horse or pony is normally lunged first on the left rein. Stand by the horse's head, on the nearside, hold the lunge whip securely under the left arm with the lash wrapped neatly around the handle and sort out the lunge line.

The Lunge Line

The lunge line can be held in one of two ways, loops or folds. Take time to practise both methods to see which one works the best. The loops can twist if not properly managed, particularly when changing the rein. The folds, though not prone to twisting, can feel quite thick in the hand.

To sort out the lunge line; hold all the line in the right hand. Starting with the loop end pass the line to the left hand and continue until most of the line lies in neat loops on the left palm. The loops should be large enough so that the line does not become wrapped tightly around the lunger's hand.

Lunge line held in loops   Lunge line held in folds

If the line is in a real mess or knotted, hold onto the line near to the horse's head with the right hand and throw the rest of the line onto the floor away from the horse. *This is the only time the lunge line should come into contact with the floor.* Sort out the line by first looping it into the right hand. Now loop or fold the line back into the left hand with the end of the line underneath.

Both methods are correct but, if it is at all possible, it is better to use the first method, and avoid throwing the line on the floor.

To Start

Keep the whip firmly secure underneath the left arm with the handle to the front and slightly raised so that it does not accidentally touch the horse. Hold the lunge line near to the horse's head with the right hand and the loops or folds in the left.

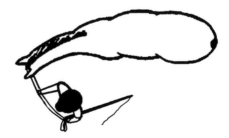

Walk a few paces with the horse and at the same time firmly ask him to walk on. After a few paces, let the horse walk forward on his own. Keep well away from the hindquarters.

Pass the whip into the right hand by stretching the right arm behind the back and taking the whip from under the left arm. Manoeuvre the whip so that the handle is held in the right hand with the lash end pointing towards the horse. Raise the whip towards the horse's hocks.

Allow or encourage the horse to increase the size of the circle until around 15 to 18 metres. The circle should be no larger as this places the horse out of control of the lunger.

To prevent straining the horse's muscles, tendons and ligaments, keep him on the large circle for the warm up period of five to ten minutes at least. Ponies can start on a 15 metre circle. Later, the circle may be decreased if required but should never be too small to cause difficulty to the horse or pony.

The Position of the Lunger

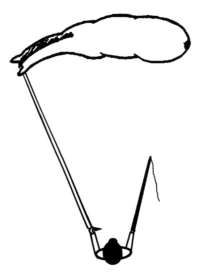

The body should be relaxed, straight, shoulders back and down, elbows bent, lower arms flexible, upper arms hanging in a natural position close to the body. The whip is held out at hip level; it should not drag on the floor.

The lunger's body should be facing and stay parallel with the horse's body, the lunger following the horse's movement around the circle. The shape made by the horse, lunger, lunge line and whip should be triangular or a pizza wedge shape. This should be maintained all the way through the lungeing if possible.

The lunger should avoid 'being in front' of the horse's movement. This will encourage the horse to stop and swing inwards with his forehand. The lunger should never come too close to the horse's hindquarters as this may encourage the horse to kick.

Ideally the lunger should not need to walk around but should be able to stay approximately in the centre of the circle following the horse's movement.

Lungeing Aids

The Voice

The voice is the main aid in lungeing and of utmost importance. The voice commands *must be firm and fairly loud*. A polite whisper will not have any influence on the horse. The horse must know the lunger is there and hear the authority within the voice. This does not necessitate shouting; the lunger needs to project the voice.

Make the commands simple and direct. A lunger who is constantly asking the horse to move forward with a quiet voice will be totally ignored. Whereas a voice that orders the horse to 'TROT ON' in a way that implies misbehaviour will not be tolerated, will immediately command the horse's attention.

For upward transitions the voice is raised slightly at the end of the command. For downwards transitions the voice is lowered at the end of the command, which is often drawn out - 'Wa-a-a-l-k.' The horse very quickly becomes accustomed to the tone of the voice as well as the actual words.

It will also help if the lunger precedes any command with the horse's name 'Harry.....and Wa-a-a-l-k.'

The Whip

The whip must be used with discretion. This does not imply that it should not be used at all; discretion means using the whip *when it is needed and in such a way as to obtain a response.*

The whip in the normal position is held pointing towards the horse's hocks. To encourage forward movement it can be moved backwards away from the horse, (kept parallel with the ground) and then swept towards the horse's hocks again. This can be combined with the voice command. Sweeping the whip in a firmer, quicker movement often encourages a lazy horse forwards.

If the horse is a real sluggard and ignores any commands, he can be taught respect by flicking the whip at his hindquarters so that the lash comes into contact with his rump for a split second. *Lungeing is training the horse to obey the voice aid. Though the whip must never be used in anger or to beat the horse, he must be taught to respect and obey commands.*

The whip's position can be altered to correct the horse. Pointing the whip towards the horse's girth encourages him to stay on the circle or to enlarge the circle; it prevents him from 'falling in'. When pointing towards the shoulder it prevents the horse from swinging his hindquarters outwards or his forehand in.

The Lunge Line

The lunge line is used in various ways, not just as a connection between horse and lunger. The line is often considered a replacement of the reins (as the whip, a replacement of the legs) and can be squeezed with the hand and released in a similar way.

Working on the Lunge

Once the horse has walked a couple of circuits he can be instructed to 'Trot on'. The trot should be active and forwards. A stiff horse may begin with a stilted trot, but after a couple of circles he must be made to trot more actively.

When ready, the lunger brings the horse to walk with a calming command - 'walk' or 'steady' depending on how the horse has been taught. For walk to halt the command is either 'Whoa', 'Halt' or 'Stand'.

Change of Rein

Ask the horse to halt and when he is still, reverse the whip so that the handle is towards the horse. If the horse has been worked on the left rein, tuck the whip firmly under the right arm.

Pass the end of the lunge line into the right hand and, whilst moving towards the horse's head, slide the left hand down the line looping it onto the right hand. This should ensure that the line does not become twisted on the new rein.

Move towards the horse's neck and shoulder and, when a few feet away, walk in front of the horse to the offside, keeping the whip away from the horse.

With the line looped in the right hand, lead the horse with the left hand on the line near his head. Walk him in an arc to the centre of the circle. Ask him to walk on the new rein as previously and change the whip by stretching the left hand behind the back. Proceed to work the horse onto a large circle.

Side Reins

When not in use, the side reins should be clipped to the 'D' rings on the saddle by the pommel. The side reins can be fitted once the horse has worked on both reins.

When putting the side reins on, remember to keep the whip under the arm away from the horse. If fitting the reins on the nearside of the horse, keep the whip under the left arm. When working on the offside of the horse, secure the whip under the right arm.

Fitting the Side Reins

When in use, the side reins are clipped to the bit rings **BELOW the normal reins**. They should be equal in length.

* Check the length of rein by encouraging the horse to bring his head into a correct position and measuring one side rein to this length. Alter accordingly. Repeat on the other side.

* The length should be comfortable for the horse, allowing a slight contact on the bit. Horses who find bending the head and neck difficult should not be forced into a position. Over a period of time, weeks maybe months, the horse will develop a more advanced outline, his head carriage will alter and the side reins can then be shortened.

* To check that the reins are equal stand in front of the horse and straighten his head. If one rein appears loose, then tighten it. Once the side reins are fitted, work the horse on a large circle as normal.

* When changing the rein, the side reins can remain attached to the bit. The horse should be walked in a large arc to the centre of the circle, not bent too sharply when the outside side rein will pull at the horse's mouth.

*Side reins should **never** be left fastened to the bit rings when leading the horse in and out of the lunge area.*

Body Language

The movements and position of the lunger's body can be very influential when lungeing and can persuade the horse to obey the voice commands. If the horse is lazy and refusing to work actively, stepping towards the horse may make him think and act. (The slack of the lunge line must be taken up with the whip hand and the loop passed to the hand holding the line, *so that the line does not drop onto the floor.*) The lunger may then have to walk a small circle to keep the horse going forwards. When the horse is obedient, the lunger can regain the central position.

Time

The length of time a horse is lunged depends on his fitness. As part of a fittening programme for a horse or pony, 5 to 10 minutes will be sufficient. For a fit horse, the lungeing period can last up to 30/35 minutes maximum. For a horse that becomes lively, lunge until he is calm, then allow 15 minutes more to loosen him up.

Assessing the Horse

The aim of lungeing is to exercise the horse, to improve his physique and paces.

The Walk

The horse should walk freely forward with his hindquarters swinging and pushing his body with impulsion. He needs to stretch his frame and use shoulders and hindquarters. Ideally he should be **tracking up**, that means the imprint of his hind legs oversteps those left by his forelegs. *A fast walk is not necessarily a good walk*. It is better for the horse to take long, stretching strides than short, quick, pottery ones.

The Trot

The trot should be active, swinging and free. Again ideally the horse should be tracking up but, if this is not possible, at least the trot should feel as though 'it is going somewhere'. Sometimes it is more beneficial to ask for a fast trot and then to steady it rather than allowing the horse to drag, stumble or jog around the circle.

Transitions

The horse should obey the commands to change pace promptly. The command should be repeated and enforced when necessary so that the horse learns to obey. After the command the new pace should be active and forwards.

Finishing Off

The horse is usually allowed a couple of minutes free trot and walk without the side reins to finish. He can then stretch his head and neck down. If he is very sweaty, he should be allowed to cool down at walk for three to five minutes.

When the lunge is finished, ask the horse to halt, change the position of the whip so it is tucked underneath the arm holding the lunge line, with the handle to the front. Walk towards the horse's neck, taking up the lunge line and looping it over the hand at each step.

Exam Tips

The two important factors for the Stage II lungeing are **practice and confidence**. You must show that you are competent at handling the equipment. Sorting out and correctly using the lunge line and whip must be almost automatic, so that in the Exam you do not appear to be fumbling. Take lessons in lungeing techniques and practise as much as you can on a variety of horses.

Timing

The other important aspect of the lungeing session is timing. A period of 15 minutes goes very quickly. It does not allow much time for checking and altering tack, sorting out the lunge line, whip and side reins, as well as lungeing the horse on both reins.

When practising, at first you may naturally be very slow but as you grow in competence you will become more adept at sorting out the equipment. As a trial one day, give yourself a fifteen minute session to lunge. This will emphasise just how swiftly those minutes pass.

The Exam

The lungeing session for the Stage II takes place in an enclosed area an indoor or outdoor school. The school may be divided into two with one candidate in each half. The Examiners may allocate the horses or you may be asked to choose one. There will be two possibly three Examiners assessing the lungeing. Each candidate should be wearing a riding hat and gloves.

♦ Though the horse is brought in fully tacked, or has been lunged previously, **check the equipment thoroughly**. There is no guarantee that the equipment is correct, for instance the stirrups may not be secure, the girth may be loose or the side reins, even though used before, not the correct length.

♦ Side reins are not compulsory in Stage II, but it is advantageous to use them. If the side reins, whilst appearing the correct length with the horse in the centre of the circle, are too loose once the horse is being lunged, calmly adjust them during the next change of rein.

♦ In the Exam the horse is worked at **walk and trot only**. These paces should be **active**. A common fault at Stage II is not having the horse going forwards with sufficient activity.

♦ If the horse chugs along at his own pace completely ignoring you, authority is needed. Use the voice and MEAN IT! It is much better to speak in a loud voice than continuously whisper without any reaction. Do not be afraid to use the voice. Asking the horse for frequent transitions can also encourage activity and obedience.

♦ If the horse still refuses to go forward, take up some of the lunge line and walk a few paces towards the horse. You may need to walk a larger circle nearer to the horse for a circuit or two before regaining your central position when the horse is moving actively.

♦ If the horse does go forward and breaks into canter from trot, it is not a problem. Ask the horse to 'STEADY' and quietly bring him forwards to trot again.

♦ The lunge line should never touch the floor whilst lungeing is in progress. The line should be as free of twists as possible and should never become wrapped tightly around the hand.

♦ The lunge whip should **never** be dropped on the floor or allowed to drag along the ground.

♦ You should avoid stepping back whilst in the centre of the circle. This usually happens if the horse falls in. Use the whip towards his shoulder to make him go out again. You should never come too close to the horse's hindquarters.

After the session the Examiners usually ask the candidates how they felt about the lungeing. If you felt you could improve on certain aspects, then say so. This shows that you know what is wrong and are willing to learn. Do not, though, proceed to detail a great list of your wrong doings, be concise, positive and constructive. As long as you handle the equipment with confidence, persuade the horse to go forwards actively and show that you can lunge safely you will succeed.

CHAPTER 34
Safety

Safety is a very important part of the British Horse Society's training programme. The BHS place great emphasis on the prevention of accidents and, in cases where accidents do occur, the procedures to follow to minimise the effects.

Working with, riding and handling horses and ponies can be a dangerous occupation to both humans and animals. Though incidents do happen, despite all precautions, many accidents are caused through negligence, carelessness and ignorance. One of the aims of the BHS is to reduce the number of accidents through education and training.

Revision

Safety precautions; in the yard, in the stable, when hacking, for children. Fire precautions and regulations. Safety on the public highway; the Country Code. Accident procedures, assessment of situations, prevention, assessing the casualty, sending for help. Accidents whilst hacking, on the highway. Injuries, assessing the casualty, stemming bleeding, dealing with a conscious casualty, an unconscious casualty, opening the airway. The recovery position. How to deal with fire. Sending for help, details to give. Accident report book.

Safety and accident procedures are such essential part of the BHS exams that all Stage II students are strongly advised to study the safety section covered in the Stage I.

General rules of safety

Students working towards their Stage II will have handled and cared for horses for some time. Through experience, they should know of the dangers and the basic precautions necessary to prevent accidents.

♦ Wear the correct clothing, when working around horses or riding. Do not wear jewellery, except for a wedding ring.

♦ All tack should be properly fitted and maintained.

♦ Approach and handle the horse correctly in the yard or stable. Do not walk directly around the back of a horse or kneel, sit or lie on the ground close to a horse. Keep the horse properly restrained when working or handling him.

♦ All yard or stable equipment should be kept clean and stored correctly.

♦ Always keep quiet around the yard and the horses. Keep to a walk; do not run around horses.

♦ Fire precautions - do not smoke on the yard. There should be frequent fire drills and all the staff should know how to use the fire fighting equipment and the procedures in case of a fire.

♦ When taking out hacks, always inform someone of your route. Keep the pace down to that of the least experienced rider. Check all tack before going out and take spare lead-ropes and a hoof pick. A portable phone is also a useful safety precaution.

The country code

The rules of the country code are there to protect all those who live in the country as much as those who use the countryside for recreation. With consideration and courtesy from horse riders, local authorities may be encouraged to maintain and hopefully expand the bridleways.

Gates should be left as riders found them, so if the gate was shut then it must be closed again after the riders have passed through. **Litter should never be dropped** in the country and anything that may start **a fire should be avoided**. **Livestock** in fields **should not be disturbed** and **boundaries of fields should not be damaged**. **Riders should keep to the designated bridleways** and **round the edge of fields** if the farmer permits riding on his land.

Most safety precautions are common sense and for anyone working around horses these become second nature. Occasionally however accidents do happen and, for those involved, knowing what to do, will greatly reduce the risk of further injuries or damage.

Accident Procedures

All personnel on the yard should be instructed in safety precautions and be capable of calling the emergency services. The telephone numbers for local hospitals, doctors and the Vet should be easily accessible and visible. For all equestrian establishments, there should be someone on the yard who has their First Aid Certificate. There should also be a well-provisioned first aid kit.

For each accident (an event resulting in injury) or incident (a minor event that may have serious consequences) there is a set of procedures which, if followed, will minimise injury and panic.

1. **Assess the situation**

2. **Prevent any further accidents**

3. **Assess the casualty**

4. **Send for Help**

In any situation think about these four points. Acting on these in progression will help to calm everybody and keep the problem under control. In most accidents the injuries are made worse when people panic, and they do so because they are often thrown into confusion.

Having a plan of action immediately gives people confidence, and once panic has been averted, the situation can be dealt with safely and quickly.

Mnemonic

Assess - **P**revent - **A**ssess **C**asualty - **He**lp = **APACHe**

Assess the situation
No matter how serious or minor the accident, take a few seconds to assess the situation either by **observation** or by **asking people for information.** This will help in preventing other accidents, assessing the injuries and in the decision to send for help.

> *Example* - girl enters the office with a cut across the palm of her hand. When asked how it happened, she states that she accidentally broke a bottle in the yard and, whilst trying to clear it up, she sustained the injury. Is there still glass in the yard? Yes, she answers. Was there anyone else involved? No, she replies. Where is the glass now? Still on the floor just outside the door to the indoor school where the horses and riders will be exiting and entering. From the information gathered, a responsible person can be sent to the scene; to warn everyone, clear the area and remove the glass whilst the girl has her wound treated.

Prevent any further accidents
Make the area safe first. Taking a few vital seconds to collect information from the scene can prevent further casualties.

Never put yourself or others in danger;

> *Example*; a group cantering quietly along a forest track. Suddenly one horse bolts, *taking off at speed with the rider gamely holding on. Assess the situation; if the* whole ride gallops after the bolting horse this could turn into the flat race of the year and result in carnage. *Prevent further accidents.* Bring the whole ride to walk quietly; talk to the riders; keep everyone calm. Leaving the assistant escort or another competent rider in charge, to keep the group at walk, slowly trot off to find the horse and rider. It may be that the bolting horse, discovering he is alone, will slow down and hopefully stop.

Assess the Casualty
Once the situation is safe and under control, the casualty can be assessed.

Thankfully in most cases the casualty will be perfectly all right and may, after a minute or two, return to their work or remount and continue riding. The casualty, though, should be monitored for a while after the incident for mild or delayed shock. Even bruising could indicate internal injury, for instance someone kicked by a horse in the stomach. Minor wounds should be attended to by the First Aider on the yard.

If the casualty is obviously hurt or is unable to move, gather every bit of information possible from the casualty by **asking questions** and by **observation**.

Ask if they feel pain in any part of their body or if they feel faint or sick. Observe their response; listen for a slurring of their speech, confusion in their answers. Watch for the colour of their skin, is it flushed or unusually pale, watch their eyes for dilation of the pupils. Observe their movements. This may indicate any physical injuries such as a damaged bone or muscle. Keep observing, it may be that there is one obvious injury such as a broken leg, but there may also be a secondary injury that may not be so visible, for instance a head injury. Observe and collect ALL the information possible about the casualty.

Then **if in any doubt as to the casualty's state of health, keep them still, warm and calm. Send for professional help.**

In an accident involving several casualties the priority should be to attend to those that are quiet. A casualty who is injured but conscious will be moaning, groaning or even screaming and it is tempting to deal with these first. The unconscious casualty however, will be lying quietly, possibly with an obstructed airway, which could mean death within minutes.

The Unconscious Casualty

There are various states of unconsciousness from a faint, which may last only seconds, to a coma. In the case of fainting, the casualty will revive quite quickly. The decision must then be made to send for help depending on any injuries sustained. For an unconscious casualty there are procedures to follow which will ensure the safety and care of all those concerned.

If the casualty remains unconscious

- Remember to assess the situation first - *the casualty may have been rendered unconscious by an electric shock from a cable.*

- Prevent further accidents - *if the casualty is still holding onto the cable this could result in the rescuer receiving a shock as well.*

- Keep calm and **SEND FOR MEDICAL HELP IMMEDIATELY**. If someone else is sent to call for help, ask them to return and confirm that help is on its way.

- Once it is safe to do so, check the casualty's RESPONSE by calling out his name and gently shaking his shoulders. If the casualty revives quickly, cover him with a coat to keep him warm.

- Do not remove the riding hat unless it is absolutely necessary.

Check the airway

Any person who suffers unconsciousness is in danger of a blockage of the airway. Obstacles in the mouth can block the windpipe. The control over the muscles of the tongue and around the airway is lost and the tongue itself can fall into the back of throat and restrict the air supply. Clearing and opening the airway will help the casualty to breathe.

To check and open the airway

1. Put one hand on the casualty's forehead and two fingers of the other hand under the chin. Tilt the head back very gently. This opens the air passage.

2. Look inside the mouth for obstructions. Remove any obstacles (bits of food, false teeth) gently with your fingers.

The safety harness has been unfastened so that the mouth can be opened. The hat should not be removed unless absolutely necessary.

Check the breathing

Lean over close to the casualty's mouth and listen for breathing. At the same time watch the ribcage for a gentle rise and fall.

Check the circulation

This is achieved by feeling the pulse of the carotid artery in the neck. Gently place two fingers on the casualty's neck on the nearest side of the windpipe. Check for 5 seconds.

The above is the **ABC** of assessing the unconscious person. **A**irway, **B**reathing and **C**irculation.

✚ If the casualty is **not breathing** and has **no pulse**, send for **HELP immediately** - **dial 999**. If there are other people around ask for medical assistance from anyone who is qualified.

✚ If the casualty is **not breathing** but there **is a pulse**, opening and clearing the airway will often encourage breathing. Send for **HELP** immediately.

✚ If the casualty **is breathing** and **has a pulse** but remains unconscious (also applies if the casualty starts breathing when the airway is opened) send for **Help** immediately and;

✚ Look for any other **life-threatening** injuries such as arterial or venal bleeding. Deal with the injury. (A broken bone on its own will usually not be a life-threatening injury but if the bone has severed an artery, the bleeding must be stemmed.)

Bleeding

Types of bleeding

arterial - from artery bright red spurts of blood

venal - from vein darker red gushes

capillaries - ooze

With arterial or venal ruptures the bleeding must be treated to prevent heavy fluid loss to the body.

The bleeding is arrested by applying **direct** pressure onto the wound. Lay a clean cloth, handkerchief or scarf onto the wound and press. If the casualty is conscious he may be able to maintain this pressure with his own hand. Elevate the wounded limb if possible, by raising it higher than the rest of the body; this slows down the rate of blood supply to that area.

NEVER APPLY A TOURNIQUET! If incorrectly applied, this can result in worse damage to the area.

Once the ABC has been checked, and any potentially fatal condition or injury treated, the casualty should be checked for spinal damage before being put into the recovery position.

Body check

Check by feeling gently down the spine. If the casualty is flat on his back, do not move him to check his spine; instead feel underneath the casualty's neck and lumbar region. Persons lying down have natural hollows in these areas and the back can be checked here without movement to the body. Feel for any unnatural lumps, bumps or abnormal angles of the body.

If the casualty has spinal damage they should not be moved.

Keep monitoring **the casualty until help arrives**; keep the airway open.

If there are no spinal problems, the casualty is breathing, has a pulse and once any serious injuries have been treated, the casualty can be put into the recovery position. This is vital if the unconscious person has to be left, for instance to send for help if there is no-one else around.

Recovery position

- Kneeling by the side of the casualty, clear and open the airway first.

- If the casualty is wearing glasses remove them and any bulky objects in the pockets.

- Straighten out the injured person's legs.

- Take hold of the casualty's nearest arm and place it on the ground, palm uppermost. The arm should be almost straight out from the shoulder with the elbow bent at right angles to the body.

- Bring the other arm over the casualty's chest and lay the back of the hand against the casualty's nearest cheek.

- Take hold of the leg on the far side and bend it gently at the knee.

- Holding onto the casualty's bent leg and the hand lying against her cheek, gently and slowly roll the casualty over towards you onto her side.

- Cover the injured person with a coat or blanket.

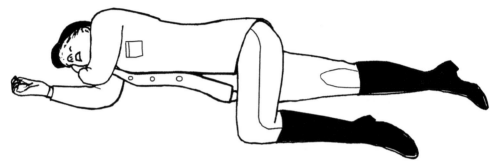

This is the procedure for someone lying flat on the back. If the casualty is lying in another position, for instance on her side, then the procedure can be modified to exclude the unnecessary actions.

The Conscious Casualty

A conscious casualty will still need observing and monitoring to minimise any effects of an accident. The four priorities are:

Breathing
Can the casualty breathe properly? Though this normally applies to an unconscious person any casualty may have difficulty breathing. Perhaps there is an obstruction in the air passage (choke) or the casualty may suffer from asthma; this too can cause breathing problems especially during times of stress.

Bleeding
Is there blood coming from a wound and if so what type of blood vessel is ruptured?

Bones
Are any bones broken?

Shock
Is the casualty suffering from shock? This can be just as life-threatening as any injury.

If there are injuries that need medical attention it must be stressed that *unless you are a qualified medical practitioner or First Aider you should not give medical treatment of any kind.* However, if the injuries or conditions are life-threatening and there is no-one qualified in the vicinity you will have to take basic life saving actions.

Keep the casualty calm by talking to him; reassure him. Observe the casualty and look for signs of bleeding or broken bones. Gather as much information as possible from him about the accident and any pain he may be feeling.

- Check for movement in fingers and toes, could be indicative of spinal damage.
- Stem any obvious, serious bleeding by applying direct pressure.
- Cover the casualty with a coat or blanket.
- **Send for help.**

Shock

In any situation one condition that should be watched out for is shock. This is a serious condition that, if not treated quickly, can affect the vital organs and *result in death.*

Causes

Shock is a failure of the circulatory system to provide oxygen and nutrients to parts of the body. This can result from a **heavy loss of body fluids** such as **external or internal bleeding, severe vomiting or diarrhoea**. It can also be a result of a **heart attack** when the heart fails to pump the blood around the body. If the **vital organs** are affected, particularly the brain, these **will fail** with possible **fatal** results.

Symptoms

The casualty's **skin** will turn **pale** and will feel **cold** and **clammy**. The **breathing** will be **rapid** and **shallow**; the casualty may **yawn or gasp for air**. The casualty may become **restless** or even **aggressive** and may suffer from **nausea or vomiting**. There will be a **rapid pulse**. Eventually the casualty will feel **drowsy** and slip into **unconsciousness**.

Treatment

1. **Send for medical help**.

2. Treat the injury first to alleviate the cause of shock.

3. Keep the casualty warm. Lay the casualty on a blanket or coat and, if the weather is cool, put a cover over on top. Raise and support the legs to improve the blood supply to the vital organs and brain.

4. Loosen any tight clothing.

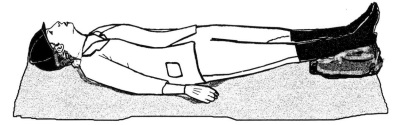

A rolled up coat or jacket will suffice to raise the legs.

5. Reassure them. This is vitally important. Keep talking calmly to the casualty until help arrives.

In any sort of accident always observe the casualty or those involved and watch out for shock.

Minor injuries

Many injuries sustained are of a minor nature and can be dealt with by the First Aider. If there is no-one qualified around, there are basic first aid procedures that will help to minimise the seriousness of these injuries.

Wounds

In the case of minor wounds where the capillaries under the skin are ruptured, the ooze of blood will help to clean the wound itself. This type of bleeding usually stops within about 20-30 minutes.

The wounds sustained are grazes, bruises, lacerations, incised and puncture wounds. If wounds are deep or wide, they may require stitching by a medical practitioner. Bruises can hide internal injuries and, if in any doubt, the casualty should be sent or advised to visit hospital or their own doctor.

With minor wounds first aid can be given:

1. **Arrest the bleeding** by direct pressure and by elevating the injury site.

2. **Clean** either by rinsing under a cold water tap or by using a sterile pad and mild, antiseptic solution. Cold water will also help bruising by reducing the swelling.

3. **Dress** the wound by applying some antiseptic dressing. For closed bruises apply cold, either with an ice pack or cold towels.

4. **Protect** the wound by covering with a plaster or sterile pad and bandage.

   If there are particles in the wound, grit, sand or bedding, clean out under a running tap.

   If there is a large particle stuck in a wound, for example a piece of glass, metal or wood **do not try and remove it**. Send for medical help immediately.

With minor cuts and bruises, basic first aid will normally be sufficient to treat the injury. For more complicated injuries the casualty should always be advised to see a doctor. For any wound where there is excessive bleeding or if the bleeding refuses to stop and there is a risk of infection, send for **medical help**.

Important note:
All those who come into contact with horses should have a tetanus inoculation and keep this up to date.

Bones

Broken bones are more correctly referred to as fractured bones. A fracture occurs where a bone is either broken or cracked. Muscles and tissues around the fracture can be affected as well as blood vessels, nerves and other organs in the body, for instance a broken rib may affect the lung.

Recognising that a bone has been fractured is usually not difficult. The casualty if conscious will normally show indications of pain, loss of movement, tenderness, swelling and bruising around the fracture site. There may be distortion of the limb.

The casualty may have suffered from a fall, a kick, a violent blow or unusually heavy pressure, for example when a horse treads on a person's foot and breaks a bone.

Treatment

Fractured bones must be treated by a professional medical practitioner; send for help immediately. The casualty will, in most cases, need to go to hospital and may have an X-ray before the fracture is treated. There are a few important points to consider before the casualty is treated professionally.

1. **No food or drink**. It may be tempting to offer the injured person a strong cup of tea with plenty of sugar, but medical treatment or surgery may be necessary. The casualty should have ***nothing to eat or drink***.

2. **Keep the fractured bone as still as possible.** For fractures of minor bones the casualty may move to a safe area whilst keeping the injured part of the body still. An injured hand can be held against the chest or tucked into the jacket.

In the case of a fractured bone in the ribcage, upper or lower arm or collarbone, the fracture site or limb should be immobilised. The casualty may naturally protect the injured part by holding it still to avoid pain. A tie or scarf can be made into a sling.

*If there is excessive pain with even the slightest movement the casualty should remain as still as possible. In the case of fractured bones in the elbow, leg or around the hip, and most certainly with damage to the spine or head, **the casualty should not be moved**, unless in a life threatening situation.*

Here the arm is inserted into the jacket.

Here a tie has been made into a sling.

3. **Keep the casualty warm and calm.** Use a jacket or blanket as a cover and stay with the casualty, reassure him by talking quietly. Watch for shock.

4. **For open fractures** where there is also an open wound, any flow of blood should be restricted by direct pressure. Cover the wound with a clean or sterile pad and, taking care not to move the limb, apply pressure carefully.

Strains or sprains

The muscles, tendons and ligaments around a fracture can be damaged, but just as easily these tissues can suffer injury without a fractured bone.

A **strain** is a **partial tearing of a muscle or tendon.**

A **sprain** is when a **ligament is damaged** at or near a joint.

When the **muscle or tendon** is **torn completely,** this results in a **rupture.**

Again medical help should be sent for immediately. Often small strains or sprains, though painful, tend to be ignored, but this can cause permanent damage unless treated medically straight away.

Before medical help arrives;

*   Elevate the injured limb and support it in a position most comfortable for the casualty. This will reduce the blood flow to the area and decrease bruising.

*   Apply cold to the injured part, either with an ice pack covered with cloth or with damp cold towels.

The casualty must be advised to seek medical advice, either by going to hospital or by seeing the doctor as soon as possible.

Dealing with accidents

It is very easy to read about dealing with accidents. In practice being faced with a fallen rider who is obviously out cold, bleeding from an injured leg, with the rest of the ride about to panic is not simple. Almost everyone will experience a second or two of panic. For those who have an idea of the procedures, the brain will click into gear and the person will be able to control the situation.

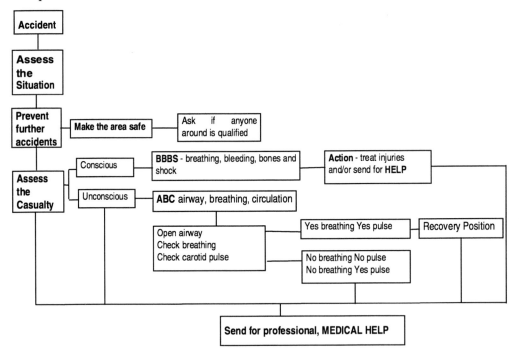

Sending for help

Having assessed the situation and the casualty; the decision can now be made to send for professional help if necessary and the type of professional aid required. *Under no circumstances should anyone who is **not** medically trained give medical treatment of any kind.*

When making an emergency call state:

1. Telephone number
2. Exact location of accident
3. Type and seriousness of accident
4. Number
5. Gender, possible age of casualty or casualties and any further information such as medical conditions like asthma
6. Details of any dangers or hazards in area.

Call the Vet if a horse is injured.

Call the police if a horse is loose on the road or the accident involves a vehicle.

Accident Report Book

After every incident, no matter how trivial, there is one very important procedure to complete.

REPORT IN THE ACCIDENT BOOK.

All equestrian establishments must have an Accident Report Book and BHS Accident Report Form for incidents occurring on the Road.

The report must include **all relevant details; facts only** not opinions or suggestions.

The **date, time** and **situation** of the accident.

The **names and addresses** of the **injured party**, any **witnesses** involved and the **person in charge**. The **names** of the **horses** involved.

The **type of injuries** sustained and any first aid that was given.

A **factual account** of the accident.

Results; whether the casualty was taken to hospital.

This report should be **signed** by the **person in charge** and any **witnesses** if possible.

The report can be completed later with information regarding the casualty, their stay in hospital if any and the outcome of the accident.

Learning First Aid

Most safety rules and regulations are common sense and if done as a routine will become a habit not a chore. Occasionally though, people become careless either through laziness, bad instruction or by following a bad example and there will, of course, always be the accident that just cannot be avoided.

If there is at least one person who can control the situation, the results will be less serious. Knowing what to do, when and how, will help to keep everyone calm.

It is an excellent idea to learn first aid, in whatever walk of life. First aid courses are available from the Red Cross, St. John's Ambulance or St. Andrews Ambulance Association. Taking one of these courses will not only give the person confidence to deal with incidents but can result in a life being saved.

Exam Tips

At Stage II level you will need to be familiar with the safety precautions necessary when working with and around horses, in the yard and the stable. You should know the safety rules of riding on the public highway and in the countryside.

You now need to take a personal view and think how you would instruct a new client coming to the stable, children starting to ride, a new working pupil, anyone who needs to be taught the correct and safe methods of dealing with horses and ponies. You would need to inform people about the correct clothing, the standard of hat, what type of boots are suitable. You need the basic knowledge about safety but you should also practise communicating this to other people.

The First Aid section covers quite a variety of injuries and wounds. This is not only relevant to the Stage II Examination but will also give any person who has to deal with accidents and injuries the confidence to keep calm within a difficult situation. Remembering a set of procedures focuses the mind and stops panic.

CHAPTER 35
Exam Information

The BHS Stage II Examination, as a progression from the Stage I, not only introduces new subjects but also expands on topics already covered at the Stage I level. The Examination lasts all day even for those taking the Care Section only. The riding section is normally completed by lunch time but some centres do organise the jumping after lunch.

Whilst no single Examination will cover the whole syllabus, candidates should have a knowledge of all the topics required.

Training Preparation

As well as the theoretical subjects included in the Stage II, there are a number of practical topics that will need some first hand experience. The Examiners do not expect candidates to be perfect in every subject, but they will be looking for candidates who clearly have given some time to study and who have practical knowledge of handling horses.

Working pupils (WPs) will have an advantage over candidates who are not in the industry professionally, but even WPs will not have the practical experience in all the subjects required. Indeed it is often difficult for those who are performing the same tasks every day to gain experience in other areas such as clipping, tacking horses up for a dressage or a jumping competition. So all students should make their experience as comprehensive as possible. Be observant around the yard, watch the Farrier at work, offer to help whenever the Vet visits and hold the horse when someone is clipping; this will increase and improve your practical experience.

Assessment

All students should have an assessment of their riding and stable management skills from a BHS qualified instructor; preferably one who is knowledgeable about the standard required, before the Exam. A good instructor will point out any weak areas, which can then be improved before the Exam day.

Applying for the Exam

The British Horse Society will supply information on request about the Examination, application forms, addresses of Exam centres with dates and the current fees. All students will need to be members of the British Horse Society when they apply for and take the Stage II.

The address is:

> Training and Education Department,
> British Horse Society,
> British Equestrian Centre,
> Stoneleigh Park,
> Kenilworth,
> Warwickshire, CV8 2LR
>
> Telephone Number: 01203 696697

Prospective candidates can telephone the BHS before applying for their chosen Examination Centre, to check that the venue and the date required are available.

On acceptance of the application the BHS will send a confirmation letter to the candidate with accompanying notes. These should be read carefully.

Prior to the Exam

The Riding and Road Safety Test has to be taken before the Stage II. During the winter months there are very few, if any, of these Tests taking place. It is frustrating to enter for the Stage II only to find there is not a Riding and Road Safety Test available beforehand and then have to cancel the Stage II Exam.

Exam Preparation

Once the Exam Centre and date have been confirmed, check the location and the route to the Centre if this is unfamiliar. Travelling there at least once before Exam day will at least alleviate the anxiety of trying to find the Centre on the day.

Clothing

Check that all clothing and equipment necessary are correct. A hacking jacket, a short or long whip can be bought or borrowed for the day. If buying new leather boots remember that to be comfortable, these need at least six weeks for breaking in.

Candidates will need to wear a shirt with long sleeves, a tie or stock, a hacking jacket, beige jodhpurs or breeches, long riding boots and gloves. A BSI hat with the correct harness is essential. A body protector for the jumping is not compulsory at present but candidates are advised to check before the Examination in case of any change in policy.

Candidates should also take a sweatshirt and a water proof jacket. These can often be worn in the care section. If it is very hot the Examiners will often allow candidates to ride and perform the care section without their jackets. For this reason the shirt must have long sleeves.

A whip no longer than 30 inches will be required in the flatwork and a short whip in the jumping.

Long hair must be tied back. Apart from a wedding ring no jewellery should be worn; earrings and studs should be removed for the Examination.

The Examination Day

Candidates need to arrive at the Test centre 30 to 45 minutes before the Examination. This will give candidates the opportunity to walk around the jumping course before the Exam begins. Candidates who arrive late may not have sufficient time to check the course thoroughly and, if very late, may even be prohibited from taking the Exam altogether. At the very least, this will cause problems for the Examiners and increase the nervousness of the candidate.

For those of us who need loosening up or become nervous and tense, a short lunge lesson before the commencement of the Exam is a definite benefit. Many Examination Centres offer a private lunge lesson an hour or so before the Exam starts and it is worth enquiring in advance.

Format

All the candidates should go to the Reception or Office area about ten minutes before the Exam commences, usually at 8.30 or 9.00 a.m. The Chief Examiner will introduce himself or herself and the other Examiners (normally three) to the whole group.

The candidates will then be given name tags and numbers to wear for identification. Any documentation necessary, for example the Riding and Road Safety Certificate, can be presented now.

The candidates will be divided into groups and each Examiner will take one group to their respective area for testing.

The whole Examination is split into sections; Riding - flatwork and jumping, Practical, Practical Oral, Theoretical testing and lungeing.

The lunch break is usually taken around 1.00 p.m., for 45 minutes. The Exam continues after lunch. A timetable will detail the times and sessions for each group.

The whole Examination finishes about 4 - 5.00 p.m. It can, therefore, be quite an exhausting day. If required, the riding and care sections may be split so that each can be taken on separate days. This is, however, more expensive.

Example of Stage II Timetable.

British Horse Society Stage II Examination						
Timetable Candidates 1-5 Group A / 6-10 Group B / 11-16 Group C						
Times	Flatwork	Theory	Practical/ Oral	Practical	Lungeing	Jumping
09.00	Group A	Group B	Group C			
09.55	Group B	Group C	Group A			
10.50	Group C	Group A	Group B			
11.45						Candidates 1-8
12.30						Candidates 9-16
1.15	L	U	N	C	H	
2.15				Candidates 1-8	Candidates 9-16	
3.00				Candidates 9-16	Candidates 1-8	
3.45	Exam	Ends				

The results will be given as soon as possible after the Exam finishes. There will then be time to confer and obtain advice from the Examiners.

The British Horse Society

The main purpose of the BHS is to improve the quality of life of every horse and pony. To fulfil this purpose the Society organises and promotes the training of all those who are interested in the art of equestrianism. It also encourages the use and protection of horses and ponies, providing a valuable information source for all the disciplines involved with horsemanship.

The BHS was formed in 1947 and is a registered animal welfare charity. It has been the governing body to the various divisions of Dressage, Horse Trials, Driving and Vaulting. However, this is now changing; many of the disciplines are setting up on their own to manage their own finances.

The Society is governed by a Council through the General Purposes and Finance Committee.   All the sub-committees that look after the various disciplines are responsible to the Council.

The Society is also there to help and give recommendations on any aspect of horse management.

Aims of the Society

The BHS pursues its policy of improving the life of horses and ponies by;

- providing systematic training and qualifications in all aspects of horse management and care.

- encouraging the safe use and protection of all horses and ponies.

- giving help, advice and information throughout a horse's or pony's life including breeding and training.

BHS Training

The British Horse Society encourages training to a very high standard of proficiency providing recognised qualifications for the industry within this country and abroad. Many countries send their students to Britain to be trained at BHS approved establishments and indeed most countries consider a BHS qualification a very desirable commodity.

BHS approved establishments are inspected regularly and, consequently, maintain a high standard.

Members

Membership of the Society is by annual subscription. Members have special privileges such as competing in BHS shows, entrance to facilities and enclosures at events around the country, free Personal Liability and Accident Insurance and a free legal and tax helpline.

Full members are automatically entitled to free equestrian related Personal Liability Insurance up to £2,000,000 and for free equestrian related Personal Accident Insurance up to £10,000. (Special conditions apply to the Republic of Ireland.)

Members can also receive advice on legal matters through a free 24 hour helpline, even for non-equestrian related matters, and expert advice from a tax helpline.

Members receive a free yearbook and three issues annually of the magazine 'British Horse'. A full range of BHS goods, including books and videos, is available from the Bookshop. These are detailed on a list which is periodically sent to members or can be obtained by ringing the BHS.

Exam Tips

Prepare as thoroughly as possible for the examination; this will give you confidence. Learn the theoretical subjects and try to relate these to the practical, every day working routine with horses.

Prepare all the clothing and equipment the day before. If you do not normally ride in a shirt, tie and hacking jacket, it helps to ride for a few sessions before the 'Big Day' in your Exam clothes. You will then become accustomed to riding in these clothes and it will not feel so strange.

During the theory, practical and practical/oral sessions give clear, concise answers to questions and draw on your own experiences and observations. Think, too, of your body language. A person who stands straight, shoulders back and has an eye contact with the Examiner is going to give a better impression than someone slumped, head bent, mumbling inaudible sentences to the floor.

The Examiners are not specifically looking for candidates who are word perfect, nor are they expecting you to be an expert on every subject. They are looking for a person who is quietly confident (though not over-confident) and competent enough to deal with situations as they arise.

Above all, believe in yourself; you *are* sufficiently competent to pass. Think of your motivation for entering the Exam, to learn and gain knowledge of the subject you care about - horses.

Good Luck

A P P E N D I X

Recommended Lectures and Practical Sessions

At the Stage II level, candidates are expected to have a deeper theoretical knowledge and a wider practical experience than at Stage I. The theory can be covered by home study from this book and from lectures which will reinforce this information. The practical experience is gained both from working with and handling horses on a regular basis and from practical lectures to cover areas outside the student's scope.

For those who do not work with horses, the practical lectures are vital. Candidates will need to show that they are accustomed to handling and working with horses and have an understanding of their daily needs and routines.

1 Psychology and Anatomy

- Discuss different breeds and identify some in the yard. Talk about equine perception.

    ⇒ Practical - observe the reactions of horses in the stable and the field.

- Discuss the skeleton and bones.

    ⇒ Practical - indicate on a horse the position of the main organs and the bones.

2 Digestive System, Worming and Teeth

- Discuss the digestive system and learn the different sections of the gut thoroughly.
- Talk about the problems of worm infestation and how these parasites can be reduced by worming procedures and good stable management.

    ⇒ Practical - look at some different types of Wormers.

- Briefly discuss teeth. Look at health records. Discuss calling the Vet, when and what information to give.

3 Health

- Discuss temperature, pulse and respiration. Talk about minor illnesses, wounds and treatment of wounds. Discuss wound dressings, poultices, fomentations.

    ⇒ Practical - treat a minor wound.

4   Watering and Feeding

- Briefly discuss water, watering systems and dehydration.
  - ⇒ Practical - look at alternative watering systems in the stable and field. Discuss their advantages and disadvantages.
- Feeding. Revise the rules for feeding.
- Discuss the nutrient values of different foods.

5   Food Values

- Discuss the advantages and disadvantages of traditional and compound foods.
  - ⇒ Practical - look at and discuss samples of different food.
- Discuss amounts and types of feed to give specific horses and ponies; in light work, invalid, young and old. Discuss feeding horses and ponies at grass.
  - ⇒ Practical - weigh different foods from a scoop. Look at feed charts and design one. Make up some cooked foods and discuss when to feed these.

6   Hay

- Discuss hay, types and differences and when to feed these.
- Discuss quality, prices and availability of different types of hay. Look at samples of seed hay, meadow hay and HorseHage. Talk about the reasons for feeding damp hay.

7   Shoeing

- Talk about the foot, internal structure.
- Look at some different types of shoe - concave, fullered; hunter; grass tips, and talk about uses.
  - ⇒ Practical - watch the farrier and observe the use of farrier's tools. On a quiet horse practise removing a shoe.

8   Saddlery

- Look at different types of bits and discuss their action and uses. Look at bit attachments, rubber rings, a brush pricker, grass reins and an Australian Cheeker.
  - ⇒ Practical demonstration on how to measure a horse's mouth and fit various bits.
- Look at different types of saddles, martingales and breastplates.
  - ⇒ Practical demonstration on checking the fit of various saddles. Fit different martingales and breastplates.
- Look at girths, surcingle girths and cruppers. Talk about numnahs and saddlecloths, their advantages and disadvantages.

9 Boots and Bandages

- Discuss various types of boots, advantages and disadvantages.

  ⇒ Practical demonstration on how to fit various types of boots.

- Discuss bandages, materials and uses. Discuss the stable bandage, uses and correct fitting.

  ⇒ Practical - put on a stable bandage to fore and hind legs.

10 Roughing Off and Fittening

- Discuss Roughing off.

- Discuss all aspects of fittening.

- Learn about the timetable for fittening horses for different activities.

- Talk about the problems and illnesses caused by incorrect fittening and concussive damage.

11 Clothing and Grooming

- Revise rugs; uses, fitting, care of, storage, cleaning, advantages and disadvantages of different types.

- Revise grooming, strapping and quartering, kit, use and cleaning; times it takes to groom.

12 Pulling and Plaiting

- Discuss mane and tail pulling and plaiting.

  ⇒ Practical - pull a section of a mane and tail. Put two plaits in a mane and plait a tail.

13 Travelling

- Discuss protective clothing for a horse travelling.

  ⇒ Practical - prepare a horse for travelling. Take off travelling clothes and tack up horse ready for eventing or dressage competition.

14 Clippers

- Discuss various clipping machines, their advantages and disadvantages.

- Talk about care of clippers, before, during and after clipping.

  ⇒ Practical - take apart a pair of clippers and reassemble them.

15   Clipping

- Discuss types of clip, when to clip and trim and when not. Talk about clipping awkward areas and methods of restraint for difficult horses.

  ⇒ Practical - mark out on a horse the different clips and discuss when to use these. Practise, under supervision, clipping a quiet horse or pony.

16   Stable Construction

- Discuss the construction of boxes, materials used, advantages and disadvantages.

  ⇒ Look at boxes and stable yards and discuss amenities, fixtures and fittings. Observe problem areas and possible difficulties with fixtures in loose boxes.

17   Grassland Management

- Discuss all aspects of grassland management, types of pasture, possible problems with horses and ponies at grass. What to look for in a field. How to care for the pony at grass, grooming, exercise and feeding.

  ⇒ Practical - walk around a field, observe and detail good and bad points. On visits to the countryside try and identify some poisonous plants.

18   Lungeing

- Discuss rules of lungeing, when and where to lunge.

  ⇒ Practical - put on lungeing gear and check the fitting. Practise lungeing as frequently as possible.

19   Safety

- Revise safety regulations and procedures, in yard, out on a hack and when riding on the Public Highway.

- Discuss accident procedures and learn how to make a report in the Accident book.

20   General

- Revise any sections necessary. Revise the aims of the British Horse Society.

- Discuss the Examination, techniques, format, application.

  ⇒ Practical - mock exam or time spent answering questions on topics in the syllabus.

Index

Index

A

accident procedures 310
accident report book 321
aims of the Test 1
airway
    opening the 313
alimentary canal 103
anatomy 85
    skeleton 86
animal transport certificate 245
australian cheeker 187

B

bandages
    fastenings 229
    reasons for 217
    removing 229
barley 145
BHS Examination Structure xiv
    table of BHS qualifications xiv
bit
    action of 181
    bit guards 186
    materials 180
    size of 185
    types of 179
bit rings
    types of 183
bitting
    principles of 180
blanket clip 249
bleeding 314
bone
    fractured 318
    joints 95
    structure 94
boots

care of 225
reasons for 217
types 217
bran 146
    phosphorus/calcium ratio 146
breastgirth
    aintree 201
breastplates
    hunting 200
breeds 80
    hot, cold and warmbloods 82
    native 80
    stud books 82
    table of native breeds 81
    types 82
bridle
    fitting 178
    points of 177
British Horse Society
    address 324
    aims 326, 327
    membership 327
    telephone number 324
    training 327
brush pricker 186
brushing boots 217
buffer 167

C

caecum 106
cardiac sphincter 105
care
    after exercise 204
cast horse 119
characteristics 77
chaser clip 249
clip
    types of 247
    when not to 252